1234

D1138147

HELENS COMMUNITY LIBRARIES

Jue for return on or before the last date shown. Fines are
due books. Renewal may be made by personal application
e, quoting date, author, title and book number.

WITHDRAWN FROM
ST HELENS COLLEGE LIBRARY

10.

ST. HELENS COMMUNITY LIBRARIES

3 8055 00795 5974

WITHDRAWN FROM
ST HELENS COLLEGE LIBRARY

Beginning
AutoCAD 2000

Other titles from Bob McFarlane

Beginning AutoCAD   ISBN 0 340 58571 4

Progressing with AutoCAD   ISBN 0 340 60173 6

Introducing 3D AutoCAD   ISBN 0 340 61456 0

Solid Modelling with AutoCAD   ISBN 0 340 63204 6

Assignments in AutoCAD   ISBN 0 340 69181 6

Starting with AutoCAD LT   ISBN 0 340 62543 0

Advancing with AutoCAD LT   ISBN 0 340 64579 2

3D Draughting using AutoCAD   ISBN 0 340 67782 1

Beginning AutoCAD R13 for Windows   ISBN 0 340 64572 5

Advancing with AutoCAD R13 for Windows   ISBN 0 340 69187 5

Modelling with AutoCAD R13 for Windows   ISBN 0 340 69251 0

Using AutoLISP with AutoCAD   ISBN 0 340 72016 6

Beginning AutoCAD R14 for Windows NT and Windows 95   ISBN 0 340 72017 4

Advancing with AutoCAD R14 for Windows NT and Windows 95   ISBN 0 340 75053 1

Modelling with AutoCAD R14 for Windows NT and Windows 95   ISBN 0 340 73161 3

An Introudction to AEC 5.1 with AutoCAD R14   ISBN 0 340 74185 6

Beginning AutoCAD 2000

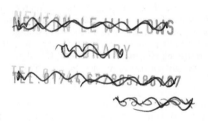

Bob McFarlane
MSc, BSc, ARCST, CEng, FIED, RCADDes
MIMechE, MIEE, MIMgt, MCSD, MILog, MBCS

*CADD Course Leader, Motherwell College,
Autodesk (UK) Educational Developer*

ARNOLD

A member of the Hodder Headline Group
LONDON

Co-published in North, Central and South America
by John Wiley & Sons Inc., New York • Toronto

ST. HELENS
COLLEGE

629.895 MAC

OCT 2000

123461

LIBRARY

First published in Great Britain 2000 by Arnold,
a member of the Hodder Headline Group,
338 Euston Road, London NW1 3BH

Co-published in North, Central and South America by
John Wiley & Sons Inc., 605 Third Avenue,
New York, NY 10158–0012

http://www.arnoldpublishers.com

© 2000 R. McFarlane

All rights reserved. No part of this publication may be reproduced or
transmitted in any form or by any means, electronically or mechanically,
including photocopying, recording or any information storage or retrieval
system, without either prior permission in writing from the publisher or a
licence permitting restricted copying. In the United Kingdom such licences
are issued by the Copyright Licensing Agency: 90 Tottenham Court Road,
London W1P 0LP.

Whilst the advice and information in this book is believed to be true
and accurate at the date of going to press, neither the author nor the publisher
can accept any responsibility or liability for any errors or omissions
that may be made.

British Library Cataloguing in Publication Data
A catalogue record for this book is available from the British Library

Library of Congress Cataloging-in-Publication Data
A catalog record for this book is available from the Library of Congress

ISBN 0 340 76097 4
ISBN 0 470 39488 9 in North, Central and South America only

1 2 3 4 5 6 7 8 9 10

Commissioning Editor: Sian Jones
Production Editor: Julie Delf
Production Controller: Iain McWilliams
Cover design: Stefan Brazzo

Produced by Gray Publishing, Tunbridge Wells, Kent
Printed and bound in Great Britain by The Bath Press, Bath
and The Edinburgh Press Ltd, Edinburgh

What do you think about this book? Or any other Arnold title?
Please send your comments to feedback.arnold@hodder.co.uk

Contents

Preface

AutoCAD 2000 is the latest release of (probably) the most used CADD draughting package in the world. This new release has several new features compared to R14, allowing the user to improve his or her draughting skills and hence increase productivity.

This book is intended for:

- new users to AutoCAD who have access to Release 2000
- experienced AutoCAD users wanting to upgrade their skills from a previous release to R2000.

The objective of this book is to introduce the reader to the essential basic 2D draughting skills required by every AutoCAD user, whether at the introductory, intermediate or advanced level. Once these basic skills have been mastered, the user can progress to the more demanding topics such as 3D modelling, customization and AutoLISP programming.

The book will prove invaluable to any casual AutoCAD user, as well as the student studying any of the City and Guild, BTEC or SQA CADD courses. It will also be useful to undergraduates and postgraduates at higher institutions who require AutoCAD draughting skills as part of their studies. Industrial CAD users will be able to use the book, as both a textbook and a reference source.

As with all my AutoCAD books, the reader will learn by completing worked examples, and further draughting experience will be obtained by completing the additional activities which complement many of the chapters. All the drawing material has been completed using R2000.

I hope you enjoy learning with Release 2000 as it is (to me) the best release yet.

Your comments and suggestions for work to be included in any future publications would be greatly appreciated.

Bob McFarlane

Acknowledgement

The following are reproduced and adapted with permission from *Engineering Drawing from First Principles*, by Dennis Maguire: Activity 11, Activity 14, Activity 16, Activity 25, Activity 29, Fig. 40.5.

Chapter 1

What's new in AutoCAD Release 2000?

AutoCAD Release 2000 has several new features including:

Head-up design environment

- Multiple document capability
- AutoCAD Design Centre
- Quick dimensioning
- New object snaps
- New tracking ability
- Partial opening of drawings
- Real-time 3D rotation
- Multiple active work planes
- New UCS manager
- New view dialogue box
- New toolbar appearance compatible with Windows 98.

Improved access and usability

- New properties window
- New object properties
- Quick select of objects
- New shortcut menus
- New drawing information storage facility
- New text control capabilities
- Layer properties manager
- New dimension styles manager
- New quick leader command
- Revised boundary hatching
- New save drawing dialogue box.

Streamlined output

- Quicker preparation for plotting
- New irregular shaped viewports
- New lineweight ability

Many (but not all) of these new features will be discussed in this book.

Chapter 2

System requirements and installation

The requirements for using Release 2000 are:

1 RAM and hard disk space:
   - 32 MB of RAM (recommended)
   - 50 MB of hard disk space (minimum)
   - 64 MB of disk swap space (minimum)
   - 10 MB of additional RAM for each concurrent AutoCAD session
   - 3.6 MB of free disk space during installation only.

2 Software – one of the following operating systems is required:
   - Windows NT version 4.0 (or later)
   - Windows 95
   - Windows 98.

3 Hardware:
   - Pentium 133 (minimum) or a compatible processor
   - 800 × 600 VGA monitor with 256 colours (1024 × 768 recommended)
   - CD-ROM drive for installation
   - Windows-supported display adapter
   - Mouse or other pointing device
   - Printer or plotter.

4 Installation – Release 2000 can be installed for:
   - an individual user
   - on a network.

The installation procedure should follow the instructions given in the installation guide, supplied with the AutoCAD Release 2000 package.

Chapter 3

Using the book

The book aims to help the reader on how to use AutoCAD Release 2000 by a series of interactive exercises. These exercises will be backed up with tutorials, thus allowing the reader to 'practice the new skills' being demonstrated. While no previous CAD knowledge is required, it would be useful if the reader knew how to use:

- the mouse to select items from the screen
- Windows packages, e.g. maximize/minimize windows.

Concepts for using the book

There are several simple concepts with which the reader should become familiar, and these are:

1 Menu selection will be in bold type, e.g. **Draw**.

2 A menu sequence will be in bold type and be either:

   a) **Draw**   or *b*) **Draw–Circle–3 Points**
   Circle
   3 Points

3 User keyboard entry will also be highlighted in bold type, e.g.

   a) coordinate entry – **125,36**; **@100,50**; **:@200<45**
   b) command entry – **LINE**; **MOVE**; **ERASE**
   c) response to a prompt – **15**.

4 Icon selection will be displayed as a small drawing of the icon where appropriate – usually the first time the icon is used.

5 The AutoCAD R2000 prompts will be in typewriter face, e.g.

   a) *prompt*   `from point`
   b) *prompt*   `second point of displacement.`

6 The symbol **<R>** or **<RETURN>** will be used to signify pressing the RETURN or ENTER key. Pressing the mouse right-button will also give the <RETURN> effect – called right-click.

7 The term **pick** is continually used with AutoCAD, and refers to the selection of a line, circle, text item, dimension, etc. The mouse left button is used to **pick an object** – called left-click.

8 Keyboard entry can be **LINE** or **line**. Both are acceptable.

Saving drawings

All drawing work should be saved for recall at some later time. Drawings can be saved:

- on a formatted floppy disk
- in a named folder on the hard drive

It is the user's preference as to which method of saving drawings is used, but for the sake of convenience, I will assume that a floppy disk is used. Thus, when a drawing is being saved or opened, the symbol **A:** will be used, e.g.

a) save drawing as A:WORKDRG
b) open drawing A:EXER_1.

Chapter 4

The Release 2000 graphics screen and terminology

Starting AutoCAD Release 2000

AutoCAD R2000 is started:

a) from the Windows 'Start screen' with a double left-click on the AutoCAD 2000 icon
b) by selecting the windows taskbar sequence:

Start–Programs–AutoCAD 2000–AutoCAD 2000

Both methods briefly display the AutoCAD 2000 logo and then the startup dialogue box as shown in Fig. 4.1. This dialogue box has four options:

1 Open a Drawing.

2 Start from Scratch with English and Metric settings.

3 Use a Template.

4 Use a Wizard.

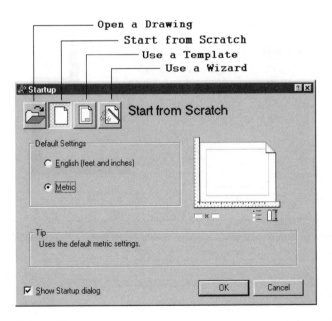

Figure 4.1 Startup dialogue box.

At this elementary stage:

a) pick (i.e. left-click with the mouse) Start from Scratch
b) pick Metric (black dot denotes active)
c) pick OK.

The AutoCAD 2000 graphics screen will be displayed, and will now be discussed in some detail.

The graphics screen

The AutoCAD 2000 graphics screen (Fig. 4.2) displays the following:

1 The title bar.

2 The 'windows buttons'.

3 The menu bar.

4 The Standard toolbar.

5 The Object Properties toolbar.

6 The Windows taskbar.

7 The Status bar.

8 The Command prompt window area.

9 The coordinate system icon.

10 The drawing area.

11 The on-screen cursor.

12 The grips box at the cross-hair intersection.

13 Scroll bars at the right and bottom of the drawing area.

14 The Layout tabs.

15 The Modify toolbar.

16 The Draw toolbar.

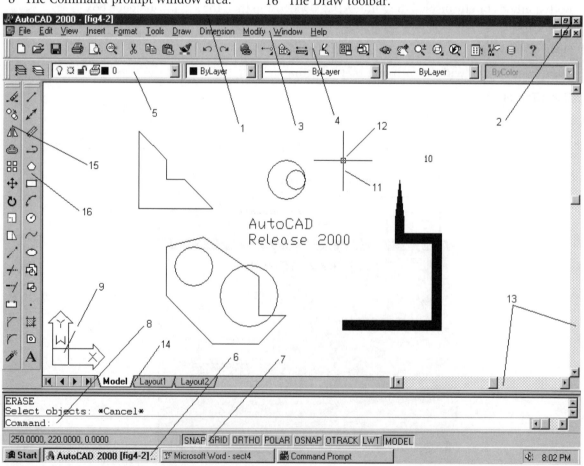

Figure 4.2 The R2000 graphics screen.

Title bar

The title bar is positioned at the top of the screen and displays the 2000 icon, the AutoCAD release version and the current drawing name.

The Windows buttons

The Windows buttons are positioned to the right of the title bar, and are:
- left: minimize screen
- centre: maximize screen
- right: quit current application.

The menu bar

The menu bar displays the default AutoCAD menu headings. By moving the mouse into the menu bar area, the cursor cross-hairs change to a **pick arrow** and with a left-click on any heading, the relevant 'pull-down' menu will be displayed.

The full menu bar headings are:

File Edit View Insert Format Tools Draw Dimension Modify Windows Help

Figure 4.3 displays the full menu pull-down selections for four of the menu bar headings, i.e. File, Format, Draw and Modify.

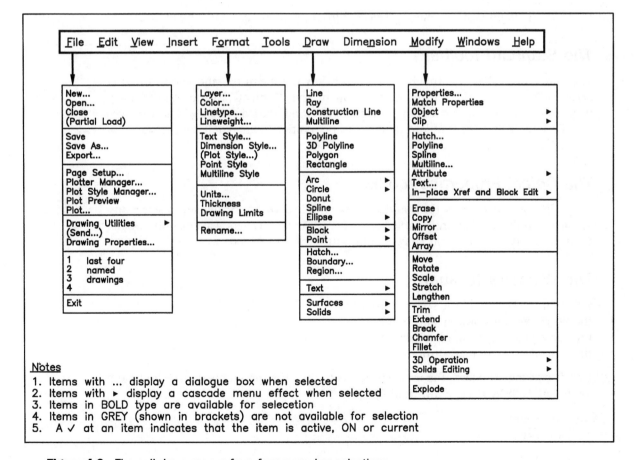

Figure 4.3   The pull-down menus from four menu bar selections.

Menu bar notes

1 Pull-down menu items which display '...' result in a screen dialogue box when the item is selected.

2 Pull-down menu items which display ▶ result in a further menu (termed **cascade**) when selected.

3 Menu items in **bold** type are available for selection.

4 Menu items in **grey** type are not available for selection.

5 Menu items which display a ✔ are active, i.e. ON.

6 Menu bar and pull-down menu items can be selected (picked) with the mouse or by using the **Alt** key with the letter which is underlined, e.g.

   a) Alt with M, activates the Modify pull-down menu
   b) then Alt with y, activates the Copy command.

7 Certain items can be activated using the control (**Ctrl**) key with a letter/number. The most common items are:

   a) Ctrl with N – New drawing
   b) Ctrl with O – open drawing
   c) Ctrl with S – Save drawing
   d) Ctrl with P – Plot drawing
   e) Ctrl with 1 – Properties dialogue box.

8 In this book, items will be generally selected from the menu bar with the mouse.

The Standard toolbar

The Standard toolbar is normally positioned below the menu bar and allows the user access to 28 icon selections including New, Open, Save, Print, etc. By moving the cursor pick arrow onto an icon and leaving it for about a second, the icon name will be displayed in yellow (default). The standard toolbar can be positioned anywhere on the screen or 'turned off' if required by the user.

The Object Properties toolbar

Normally positioned below the Standard toolbar, this allows a further seven selections. The icons in this toolbar are Make Object's Layer Current, Layers, Layer Control, Color Control, Linetype control and Lineweight Control (new to R2000).

The Windows taskbar

This is at the bottom of the screen and displays:
- the Windows 'Start button' and icon
- the name of any application which has been opened, e.g. AutoCAD
- the time and the sound control icon.

By left-clicking on 'Start', the user has access to the other programs which can be run 'on top of AutoCAD', i.e. multi-tasking.

The Status bar

Positioned above the Windows taskbar it gives useful information to the user:

a) on-screen cursor X,Y and Z coordinates at the left
b) drawing aid buttons, e.g. SNAP,GRID,ORTHO,POLAR,OSNAP,OTRACK,LWT (note: these drawing aids will be discussed in detail later)
c) MODEL/PAPER space toggle.

Command prompt window area

The command prompt area is where the user 'communicates' with R2000 to enter:

a) a command, e.g. LINE, COPY, ARRAY
b) coordinate data, e.g. 120,150, @15–<30
c) a specific value, e.g. a radius of 25.

The command prompt area is also used by AutoCAD to supply the user with information, which could be:

a) a prompt, e.g. from point
b) a message, e.g. object does not intersect an edge.

The command area can be increased in size by 'dragging' the bottom edge of the drawing area upwards. I generally have a two- or three-line command area.

The coordinate system icon

This is the X–Y–W icon at the lower-left corner of the drawing area. This icon gives information about the coordinate system in use. The default setting is the traditional Cartesian system with the origin (0,0) at the lower-left corner of the drawing area. The icon (and origin) can be positioned anywhere in the drawing area, and can also be 'turned-off' by selecting the menu bar sequence **View–Display–UCS Icon–On** which removes the ON tick. The same procedure is used to toggle the icon ON. It is user's preference as to whether the icon is on or off. I generally leave it on.

The drawing area

This is the user's drawing sheet and can be any size required. In general we will use A3-sized paper, but will also investigate very large and very small drawing paper sizes.

The cursor cross-hairs

Used to indicate the on-screen position, and movement of the pointing device will result in the coordinates in the status bar changing. The cursor is also used to 'pick' items for editing. The 'size' of the on-screen cursor can be increased or decreased to suit user preference with the menu bar sequence **Tools–Options** and:

a) select the 'Display tab' from the Options dialogue box
b) adjust the cross-hair size to suit. 100 gives a full-screen cursor.

The Grips box

This is the small box which is normally 'attached' to the cursor cross-hairs. It is used to select objects for modifying and will be discussed in detail in a later chapter. As the grips box can cause confusion to new AutoCAD users, I would recommend that the box be 'turned off'. This can be achieved with the following keyboard entries:

Enter	*Prompt*	*Enter*
GRIPS<R>	Enter new value for GRIPS<1>	0<R>
PICKFIRST<R>	Enter new value for PICKFIRST<1>	0<R>

Scroll bars

Positioned at the right and bottom of the drawing area and are used to scroll the drawing area. They are very useful for larger sized drawings and can be 'turned-off' if they are not required with the **Tools–Options–Display Tab** menu bar selection.

Layout tabs

Allows the user to 'toggle' between model and paper space for drawing layouts. This is new to R2000.

Modify and Draw toolbars

By default, AutoCAD R2000 displays these two toolbars at the left of the screen. Toolbars will be discussed later in this chapter.

Adapting the graphics screen

The graphics screen can be 'customized' to user requirements, i.e. screen colour, scroll bar, screen menu, etc. This is obtained with the menu bar sequence **Tools–Options** and the resultant Options dialogue box has nine selection tabs including:

a) Display, allowing:
   – scroll bars on or off
   – screen menu on or off
   – layout elements
   – display resolution

b) Open and Save, giving information on:
   – drawing formats which can be saved
   – time for automatic save (default 120 minutes)
   – temporary file extension

c) Drafting aids allowing the user to set:
   – object snap priorities
   – tracking method

d) User Preferences with details of the Windows behaviour, object sort method and coordinate entry method.

I generally leave the options as they are installed, although I prefer to work with:

- a white drawing area background
- no screen menu
- scroll bars
- a three-line command prompt window.

Terminology

Release 2000 terminology is basically the same as previous releases, although there are a few new features. The following gives a brief description of the items commonly encountered by new users to AutoCAD.

Menu

A menu is a list of options from which the user selects (picks) the one required for a particular task. Picking a menu item is achieved by moving the mouse over the required item and left-clicking. There are different types of menus, e.g. pull-down, cascade, screen, icon.

Command

A command is an AutoCAD function used to perform some task. This may be to draw a line, rotate a shape or modify an item of text. Commands can be activated by:

a) selection from a menu
b) selecting the appropriate icon from a toolbar
c) entering the command from the keyboard at the command line
d) entering the command abbreviation
e) using the Alt key as described previously.

Only the first three options will be used in this book.

Objects

Everything drawn in R2000 is termed an **object** or **entity**, e.g. lines, circles, text, dimensions, hatching, etc. The user 'picks' the appropriate entity/object with a mouse left-click when prompted.

Default setting

AutoCAD R2000 has certain values and settings which have been 'preset' by AutoDESK and are essential for certain operations. These default settings are displayed with **< >** brackets, but can be altered by the user as and when required. For example:

1 From the menu bar select **Draw–Polygon** and:
   prompt   `_polygon Enter number of sides<4>`
   respond **press the ESC key** to cancel the command

   Note: *a*) <4> is the default value for the number of sides
           b) _polygon is the active command.

2 At the command line enter **LTSCALE <R>** and:
   prompt   `Enter new linetype scale factor<1.0000>`
   enter   **0.5 <R>**

   Note: *a*) <1.0000> is the LTSCALE default value
           b) we have altered the LTSCALE value to 0.5.

The escape (Esc) key

This is used to cancel any command at any time. It is very useful, especially when the user is 'lost in a command'. Pressing the Esc key will cancel any command and return the command prompt line.

Icon

An icon is a menu item in the form of a picture contained within a named toolbar. Icons will be used extensively throughout the book, particularly when a command is being used for the first time.

Cascade menu

A cascade menu is obtained when an item in a pull-down menu with ▶ after its name is selected, e.g. by selecting the menu bar sequence **Draw–Circle**, the cascade effect shown in Fig. 4.4 will be displayed. Cascade menus can be cancelled by:

1 Moving the pick arrow to any part of the screen and left-clicking.

2 Pressing the Esc key – cancels the 'last' cascade menu.

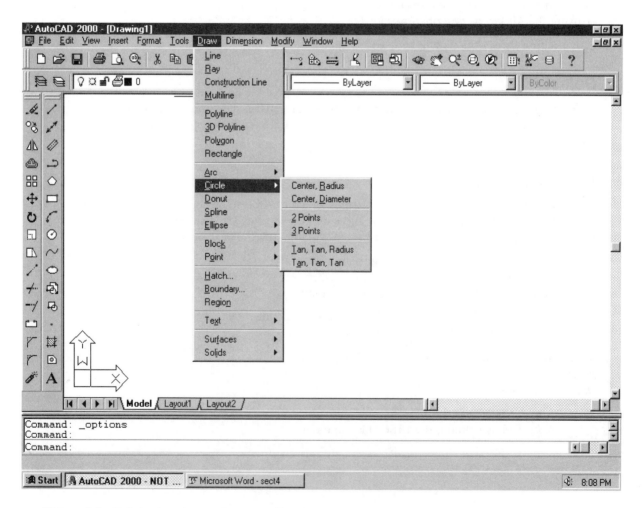

Figure 4.4 Pull-down and cascade menu effect.

Dialogue boxes

A dialogue box is always displayed when an item with '...' after its name is selected. When the menu bar sequence **Format–Units** is selected, the Drawing Units dialogue box (Fig. 4.5) will be displayed. Dialogue boxes allow the user to alter parameter values or toggle an aid ON/OFF. Aids are toggled using the small box adjacent to their name and:

a) a tick in the box means that the aid is ON
b) a blank box means that the aid is OFF.

Most dialogue boxes display the options On, Cancel and Help that are used as follows:

OK: accept the values in the current dialogue box
Cancel: cancel the dialogue box without any alterations
Help: gives further information in Windows format. The Windows can be cancelled with File–Exit or using the Windows Close button – right-most in the title bar.

Figure 4.5   The Drawing Units dialogue box.

Toolbars

Toolbars are aids for the user. They allow the R2000 commands to be displayed on the screen in icon form. The required command is activated by picking (left-click) the appropriate icon. The icon command is displayed in yellow (default colour) by moving the pick arrow onto an icon and leaving it for a second. There are 24 toolbars available for selection, and four are displayed by default when R2000 is started, these being the Standard, Object Properties, Modify and Draw toolbars.

Toolbars can be:

a) displayed and positioned anywhere in the drawing area
b) customized to the user preference.

To activate a toolbar, select from the menu bar **View–Toolbars** and the Toolbars dialogue box will be displayed. To display a toolbar, pick the box by the required name. Figure 4.6 displays the Toolbar dialogue box with the Dimension, Draw toolbars toggled on (there are other toolbars also toggled on). When toolbars are positioned in the drawing area as the Object Snap and Dimension toolbars in Fig. 4.6 they are called **floating** toolbars.

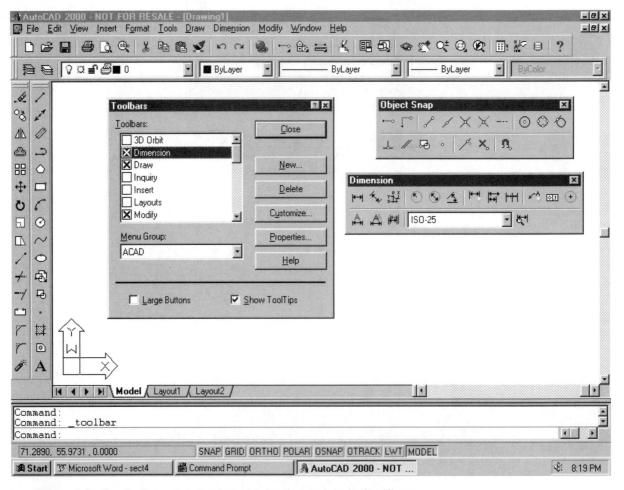

Figure 4.6 The Toolbars dialogue box with floating and docked toolbars.

Toolbars can be:

1 Moved to a suitable position on the screen by the user. This is achieved by moving the pick arrow into the blue title area of the toolbar and holding down the mouse left button. Move the toolbar to the required position on the screen and release the left button.

2 Altered in shape by 'dragging' the toolbar edges sideways or upwards/downwards.

3 Cancelled at any time by picking the 'Cancel box' at the right of the toolbar title bar.

It is the user's preference as to what toolbars are displayed at any one time. In general, I always display the Draw, Modify, Dimension and Object Snap toolbars and activate others as and when required.

Toolbars can be **docked** at the edges of the drawing area by moving them to the required screen edge. The toolbar will be automatically docked when the edge is reached. Figure 4.6 displays two floating and four docked toolbars:

a) Docked: Standard and Object Properties at the top of the screen; Draw and Modify at the left of the screen. These four toolbars 'were set' by default

b) Floating: Object Snap and Dimension. These two toolbars were 'activated' by me.

Toolbars **do not have to be used** – they are an aid to the user. All commands are available from the menu bar, but it is recommended that toolbars are used, as they greatly increase draughting productivity.

When used, it is the user's preference if they are floating or docked.

Fly-out menu

When an icon is selected an AutoCAD command is activated. If the icon has a ◢ at the lower right corner of the icon box, and the left button of the mouse is held down, a **fly-out** menu is obtained, allowing the user access to other icons. The following fly-out menus are available from the Standard toolbar:

• Temporary Tracking Point: object snap icons
• UCS: UCS options in icon form
• Distance: properties icons
• Named view: the viewpoint preset icons
• Zoom: the various zoom options in icon form.

Wizard

Wizard allows the user access to various parameters necessary to start a drawing session, e.g. units, paper size, etc. It has two options – **Quick** and **Advanced**. We will investigate how to use the Wizard in other chapters.

Template

A template allows the user access to different drawing standards with different-sized paper. The following are supported in R2000:
• Standards: ansi, din, iso, jis.
• Sizes: A0, A1, A2, A3, A4 and A, B, C, D, E.

The use of templates will be investigated later in the book.

Toggle

This is the term used when a drawing aid is turned ON/OFF and usually refers to:
a) pressing a key
b) activating a function in a dialogue box, i.e. a tick signifies ON, no tick signifies OFF.

Function keys

Several of the keyboard function keys can be used as aids while drawing, these keys being:

F1	accesses the AutoCAD Help menu
F2	flips between the graphics screen and the Text window
F3	activates the Drafting Settings dialogue box
F4	toggles the tablet on/off (if attached)
F5	toggles the isoplane top/right/left
F6	coordinate on/off toggle
F7	grid on/off toggle
F8	ortho on/off toggle
F9	snap on/off toggle
F10	polar on/off toggle
F11	toggles object snap tracking off
F12	not used.

Help Menu

AutoCAD R2000 has an 'on-line' help menu which can be activated at any time by selecting from the menu bar **Help–AutoCAD Help** (or pressing the F1 function key). The Help Topics dialogue box will be displayed allowing the user to:

1 Select the Index tab.

2 Enter a word/phrase, e.g. COORD.

3 Coordinate data entry priority options will be highlighted.

4 Pick Display.

The screen will display information about the topic which has been entered. The user can cancel the display with the top right windows button, or select Help Topics to return to the Index.

File types

When a drawing has been completed it should be saved for future recall and all drawings are called *files*. Release 2000 has three main file types with the extensions:

.dwg: drawing file

.dwt: drawing template file

.dwf: drawing web format.

Drawing names should be as simple as possible. While operating systems support file names which contain spaces and periods (.), I would not recommend this practice. The following are typical drawing file names that I would recommend:

- EX1
- EXER-1
- EXERC_1
- MYEX-1
- DRG1, etc.

When drawings have to be saved during the exercises in the book, I will give the actual named to be used.

This completes this rather long chapter. Now let's draw!

Chapter 5

Drawing, erasing and the selection set

In this chapter we will investigate how lines and circles can be drawn and then erased. When some line and circle objects have been created by different methods, we will investigate the selection set – a powerful aid when modifying a drawing.

Starting a new drawing with Wizard

1 Start AutoCAD with:

    a) a double left-click on the R2000 icon
    b) select from the Windows taskbar the sequence:

    Start–Programs–AutoCAD 2000–AutoCAD2000

2 When either of the above options is selected, the R2000 logo will be displayed for a short time and then:

    prompt   `Startup dialogue box`

    respond   *a*) pick Use a Wizard icon (right-most)
                  b) pick Quick Setup – Fig. 5.1
                  c) pick OK

Figure 5.1 The Use a Wizard Startup dialogue box.

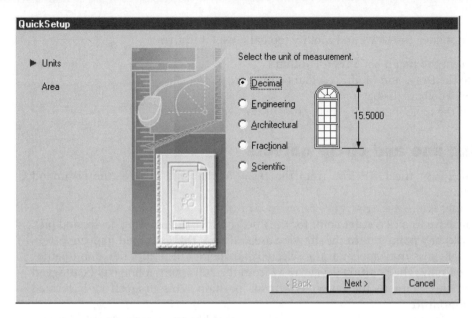

Figure 5.2 The Quick Setup (Units) dialogue box.

prompt   Quick Setup (Units) dialogue box
respond   *a*) Select Decimal Units – Fig. 5.2
            b) pick Next>
prompt   Quick Setup (Area) dialogue box
respond   *a*) enter Width: 420
            b) enter Length: 297 – Fig. 5.3
            c) pick Finish.

3   The AutoCAD 2000 drawing screen will be displayed and should display the Standard
    and Object Properties toolbars at the top of the screen, and the Modify and Draw toolbars
    docked at the left of the screen.

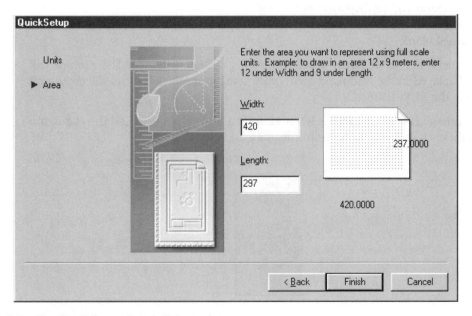

Figure 5.3 The Quick Setup (Area) dialogue box.

4 *Note.* The toolbars which are displayed will depend on how the last user 'left the system'. If you do not have the Draw and Modify toolbars displayed then:

  a) select from the menu bar **View–Toolbars**
  b) activate the Draw and Modify toolbars with a cross
  c) close the Toolbars dialogue box
  d) position the toolbars to suit, i.e. floating or docked

Drawing line and circle objects

1 *a*) Activate (pick) the LINE icon from the Draw toolbar and observe the command prompt area
   b) the prompt is `_line Specify first point`
   c) you now have to pick a **start** point for the line, so move the pointing device and pick (left-click) any point within the drawing area. Several things should happen:
      i) a small cross **may** appear at the selected start point – if it does not, don't panic
      ii) as you move the pointing device away from the start point a line will be dragged from this point to the on-screen cursor position. This drag effect is termed **rubberband**
      iii) as the pointing device is moved, a small coloured box **may** be displayed with text similar to *Polar: 80.00<0.* If it does, don't panic and if it does not don't worry. We will discuss this in the next chapter
      iv) the prompt becomes: `Specify next point or [Undo]`

2 Move the pointing device to any other point on the screen and left-click. Another cross may appear at the selected point and a line will be drawn between the two 'picked points'. **This is your first R2000 object**.

3 The line command is still active with the rubberband effect and the prompt line is still asking you to specify the next point.

4 Continue moving the mouse about the screen and pick points to give a series of 'joined lines'.

5 Finish the LINE command with a right-click on the mouse and:
   a) a pop-up menu will be displayed as Fig. 5.4
   b) pick Enter from this dialogue to end the LINE command and the command line will be returned blank.

6 From the menu bar select **Draw–Line** and the `Specify first point` prompt will again be displayed in the command area. Draw some more lines the end the command by pressing the RETURN/ENTER key.

7 At the command line enter **LINE <R>** and draw a few more lines. End the command with a right-click and pick Enter from the dialogue box.

Figure 5.4 Command right-click pop-up menu.

8   Right-click on the mouse to display a pop-up menu as Fig. 5.5 and pick **Repeat LINE**. Draw some more lines then end with by pressing the RETURN/ENTER key.

9   *Note:*
   a) the different ways of activating the LINE command:
      – with the LINE icon from the Draw toolbar
      – from the menu bar with Draw–Line
      – by entering LINE and the command line
      – with a right-click of the mouse (if LINE command has already been used)
   b) the two ways to 'exit' a command:
      – with a right click of the mouse
      – by pressing the RETURN/ENTER key
   c) cancelling a command with a mouse right-click, **may** display the dialogue box similar to Fig. 5.4
   d) a right-click on the mouse will display a dialogue box as Fig. 5.5 with the **last command** available for selection, e.g. Repeat LINE.

10 From the Draw toolbar activate the CIRCLE icon and:
   prompt   _circle Specify center point for circle...
   respond   **pick any point on the screen as the circle centre**
   prompt   Specify radius of circle or [Diameter]
   respond   **drag out the circle and pick any point for radius**.

11 From the menu bar select **Draw–Circle–Center,Radius** and pick a centre point and drag out a radius.

12 At the command prompt enter **CIRCLE <R>** and create another circle anywhere on the screen.

13 Using the icons, menu bar or keyboard entry, draw some more lines and circles until you are satisfied that you can activate and end the two commands.

14 Figure 5.6(a) displays some line and circle objects.

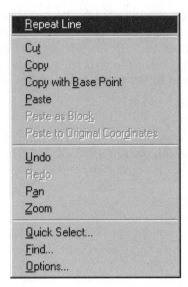

Figure 5.5   Right button pop-up menu.

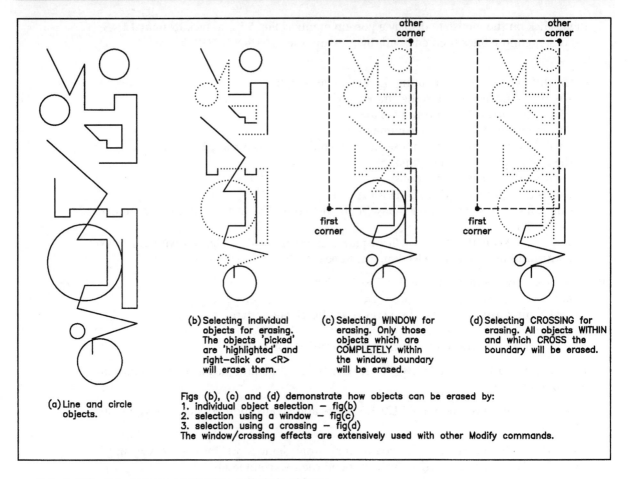

Figure 5.6 Drawing and erasing line and circle objects.

Blips

Several users may have small crosses at the end of the lines drawn on the screen and at the circle center points. These crosses are called **blips** and are used to identify the start and end point of lines, circle centres, etc. The are *not objects/entities* and will not be plotted out on the final drawing. Personally I find then a nuisance and always turn them off. This can be achieved by entering **BLIPMODE <R>** at the command line and:

prompt   Enter mode [ON/OFF]

enter   **OFF <R>**

If you do not want to turn the blips off, then by selecting the Redraw All icon from the Standard toolbar, the drawing screen is regenerated and the blips are removed.

Erasing objects

Now that we have drawn some lines and circles, we will investigate how they can be erased – seems daft? The erase command will be used to demonstrate different options available to us when it is required to modify a drawing. The actual command can be activated by one of three methods:

a) picking the ERASE icon from the Modify toolbar
b) with the menu bar sequence **Modify–Erase**
c) entering **ERASE <R>** at the command line.

Before continuing with the exercise, select from the menu bar the sequence **Tools–Drafting Settings** and:

prompt   Drafting Settings dialogue box
respond   pick Options
prompt   Options dialogue box
respond   pick the Selection tab and ensure:
    a) noun/verb selection not active, i.e. no tick in box
    b) use shift to add to selection not active
    c) press and drag not active
    d) implied windowing active, i.e. tick in box
    e) Object Grouping active
    f) Pickbox size: set to suit (about 1/3 distance from left)
    g) pick OK when complete
       prompt   Drafting Settings dialogue box
       respond pick OK.

Now continue with the erase exercise.

1 Ensure you still have several lines and circles on the screen. Figure 5.6(a) is meant as a guide only.

2 From the menu bar select **Modify–Erase** and:
  prompt   Select objects
  and   cursor cross-hairs replaced by a 'pickbox' which moves as you move the mouse
  respond   **position the pickbox over any line and left-click**
  and   the following will happen:
    a) the selected line will 'change appearance', i.e. be 'highlighted'
    b) the prompt displays Select objects: 1 found and then: Select objects.

3 Continue picking lines and circles to be erased (about six) and each object will be highlighted.

4 When enough objects have been selected, right-click the mouse.

5 The selected objects will be erased, and the Command prompt will be returned.

6 Figure 5.6(b) demonstrates the individual object selection erase effect.

Oops

Suppose that you had erased the wrong objects. Before you **do anything else**, enter **OOPS <R>** at the command line.

The erased objects will be returned to the screen. Consider this in comparison to a traditional draughtsman who has rubbed out several lines/circles – they would have to redraw each one.

OOPS must be used **immediately** after the last erase command and must be entered from the keyboard.

Erasing with a Window/Crossing effect

Individual selection of objects is satisfactory if only a few lines/circles have to be modified (we used erase). When a large number of objects require to be modified, the individual selection method is very tedious, and AutoCAD overcomes this by allowing the user to position a 'window' over an area of the screen which will select several objects 'at the one pick'.

To demonstrate the window effect, ensure you have several objects (about 20) on the screen and refer to Fig. 5.6(c).

1 Select the ERASE icon from the Modify toolbar and:

prompt	`Select objects`
enter	**W <R>** (at the command line) – the window option
prompt	`Specify first corner`
respond	**position the cursor at a suitable point and left-click**
prompt	`Specify opposite corner`
respond	**move the cursor to drag out a window (rectangle) and left-click**
prompt	`??? found and certain objects highlighted`
then	`Select objects`, i.e. any more to be erased?
respond	**right-click or <R>**

2 The highlighted objects will be erased.

3 At the command line enter **OOPS <R>** to restore the erased objects.

4 From the menu bar select **Modify–Erase** and:

prompt	`Select objects`
enter	**C <R>** (at command line) – the crossing option
prompt	`Specify first corner`
respond	**pick any point on the screen**
prompt	`Specify opposite corner`
respond	**drag out a window and pick the other corner**
prompt	`??? found and highlighted objects`
respond	**right-click**.

5 The objects highlighted will be erased – Fig. 5.6(d).

Note on window/crossing

1 The window/crossing concept of selecting a large number of objects will be used extensively with the modify commands, e.g. erase, copy, move, rotate, etc. The objects which are selected when **W or C** is entered at the command line are as follows:

window: all objects *completely within* the window boundary are selected
crossing: all objects *completely within and also which cross* the window boundary are
        selected.

2 The window/crossing options **is entered from the keyboard,** i.e. W or C.

3 Figure 5.6 demonstrates the single object selection method as well as the window and crossing methods for erasing objects.

The selection set

Window and crossing are only two options contained within the selection set, the most common selection options being:

Crossing, Crossing Polygon, Fence, Last, Previous, Window and Window Polygon.

During the various exercises in the book, we will use all of these options but will only consider three at present.

1 Erase all objects from the screen – individual or window?

2 Refer to Fig. 5.7(a) and draw some new lines and circles – the layout is not important

3 Refer to Fig. 5.7(b), select the ERASE icon from the Modify toolbar and:

prompt	Select objects
enter	**F <R>** – the fence option
prompt	First fence point
respond	**pick a point (pt 1)**
prompt	Specify endpoint of line or [Undo]
respond	**pick a suitable point (pt 2)**
prompt	Specify endpoint of line or [Undo]
respond	**pick points 3, then 4, then 5, then right-click**
prompt	Dialogue box with options
respond	**pick Enter**
prompt	??? found and certain objects highlighted
respond	**right-click or <R>.**

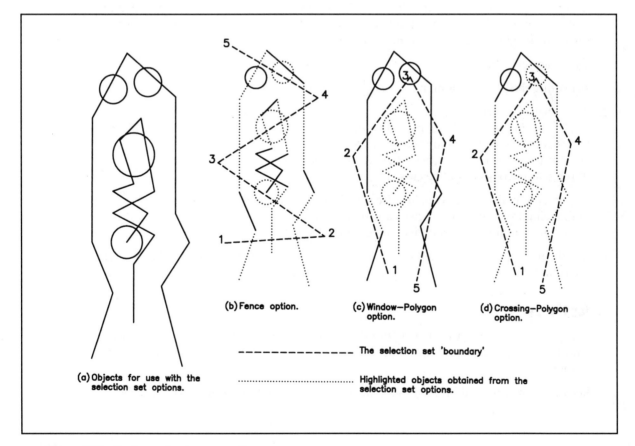

(b) Fence option.

(c) Window—Polygon option.

(d) Crossing—Polygon option.

– – – – – – – – – – – – – The selection set 'boundary'

.... Highlighted objects obtained from the selection set options.

(a) Objects for use with the selection set options.

Figure 5.7 Further selection set options.

4 The highlighted objects will be erased.

5 OOPS to restore these erased objects.

6 Menu bar with **Modify–Erase** and referring to Fig. 5.7(c):

   prompt   Select objects
   enter   **WP <R>** – the window-polygon option
   prompt   First polygon point
   respond   **pick a point (pt 1)**
   prompt   Specify endpoint of line or [Undo]
   respond   **pick points 2,3,4,5 then right-click and Enter**
   prompt   ??? found and objects highlighted
   respond   **right-click** to erase the highlighted objects.

7 OOPS to restore the erased objects.

8 *a*) Activate the ERASE command
   b) enter **CP <R>** at command line – crossing polygon option
   c) pick points in order as Fig. 5.7(d) then right-click and Enter
   d) right-click to erase objects.

9 The fence/window polygon/crossing polygon options of the selection set are very useful when the 'shape' to be modified does not permit the use of the normal rectangular window. The user can 'make their own shape' for modifying.

Automatic windowing

In the exercise to erase objects using the window and crossing options, we enter W and C at the command line. While this method is satisfactory, AutoCAD allows to user to select the window boundary without entering the W or C.

This is achieved by:

1 Activating the ERASE command.

2 At the Select objects prompt:
   a) pick a point with a left-click of the mouse
   b) drag out the window and then left-click
   c) right-click the mouse or press RETURN/ENTER
   d) the selected objects will be erased.

3 The order in which window points are specified are important:
   a) dragging from left to right gives a window selection
   b) dragging from right to left gives a crossing selection.

4 It is the user's preference whether to use the automatic window option, or enter W/C at the command line.

Activity

Spend some time using the LINE, CIRCLE and ERASE commands and become proficient with the various selection set options for erasing – this will greatly assist you in later chapters.

Read the summary and proceed to the next chapter. Do not exit AutoCAD if possible.

Summary

1 The LINE and CIRCLE draw commands can be activated:
   a) by selecting the icon from the Draw toolbar
   b) with a menu bar sequence, e.g. Draw–Line
   c) by entering the command at the prompt line, e.g. LINE <R>.

2 The ERASE command can be activated:
   a) with the ERASE icon from the Modify toolbar
   b) from the menu bar with Modify–Erase
   c) by entering ERASE <R> at the command line.

3 All modify commands (e.g. ERASE) allow access to the Selection Set.

4 The selection set has several options including Window, Crossing, Fence, Window-Polygon and Crossing-Polygon.

5 The appropriate selection set option can be activated from the command line by entering the letters W,C,F,WP,CP.

6 The term WINDOW refers to all objects completely contained within the window boundary.

7 CROSSING includes all objects which cross the window boundary and are also completely within the window.

8 OOPS is a very useful command with 'restores' the previous command.

9 Blips are small crosses used to display the start and endpoints of lines. They are **not objects** and should be turned off.

10 Redraw All is a command which will 'refresh' the drawing screen and remove both blips and any 'ghost image' from the screen. The command is best used from the icon in the Standard toolbar.

Chapter 6

The 2D drawing aids

Now that we know how to draw and erase lines and circles, we will investigate the aids which are available to the user. R2000 has several drawing aids which include:

Grid   allows the user to place a series of imaginary dots over the drawing area. The grid spacing can be altered by the user at any time while the drawing is being constructed. As the grid is imaginary, it does **not** appear on the final plot.

Snap   allows the user to set the on-screen cursor to a pre-determined point on the screen, this usually being one of the grid points. The snap spacing can also be altered at any time by the user. When the snap and grid are set to the same value, the term **grid lock** is often used.

Ortho   an aid which allows only horizontal and vertical movement.

Polar tracking   allows objects to be drawn at specific angles along an alignment path. The user can alter the polar angle at any time.

Object Snap   the user can set a snap relative to a pre-determined geometry. This will be covered in detail in a later chapter.

Getting ready

1   Still have objects from Chapter 5 on the screen?

2   Begin a new drawing with the menu bar sequence **File–New** and:
     prompt   Create New Drawing dialogue box
     respond   *a*) pick Use a Wizard
                  b) pick Quick Setup
                  c) pick OK
     prompt   Quick Setup (Units) dialogue box
     respond   pick Decimal then Next>
     prompt   Quick Setup (Area) dialogue box
     respond   *a*) set Width:420 and Length: 297
                  b) pick Finish.

3   A blank drawing screen will be displayed.

Grid and snap spacing – keyboard entry

1 At the command line enter **GRID <R>** and:
prompt   Specify grid spacing (X)...
enter   **20 <R>**.

2 At the command line enter **SNAP <R>** and:
prompt   Specify snap spacing or ...
enter   **20 <R>**.

3 Refer to Fig. 6.1 and use the LINE command to draw the letter H using the grid and snap settings of 20.

4 Using the keyboard, change the grid and snap spacing to 15.

5 Use the LINE command and draw the letter E.

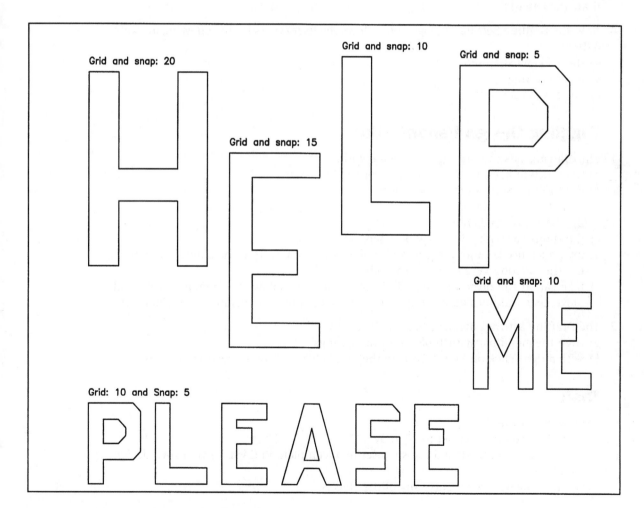

Figure 6.1   Using GRID and SNAP draughting aids.

Grid and snap spacing – dialogue box method

1 From the menu bar select **Tools–Drafting Settings** and:

prompt   Drafting Settings dialogue box
with   *a*) Snap on with X and Y spacing 15
            b) Grid on with X and Y spacing 15 from previous setting – Fig. 6.2
respond   1) alter the Snap X spacing to 10 by:
                 a) click to right of last digit
                 b) back-space until all digits removed
                 c) enter 10
                 d) left click at Snap Y spacing – alters to 10
            2) alter the Grid X spacing by:
                 a) position pick arrow to left of first digit
                 b) hold down left button and drag over all digits – they will be
                 c) enter 10
                 d) left click at Grid Y spacing – alters to 10
            3) pick OK.

2 Use the LINE command to draw the letter L.

3 Use the Drafting Settings dialogue box to set both the grid and snap spacings to 5 and draw the letter P.

4 *Note*: the Drafting Settings dialogue box allows the user access to the following drawing aids:
   a) the grid and snap settings
   b) polar tracking
   c) object snap settings.

Toggling the grid/snap/ortho

1 The drawing aids can be toggled ON/OFF with:
   a) the function keys, i.e. F7 – grid; F8 – ortho; F9 – snap
   b) the Drafting Settings dialogue where:
      1) tick in box – aid ON
      2) blank box – aid OFF
   c) the status bar with a left-click on Snap, Grid, Ortho
   d) my preference is to set the grid and snap spacing values from the dialogue box then use the function keys to toggle the aids on or off
   e) take care if the ortho drawing aid is on. Ortho only allows horizontal and vertical movement and lines may not appear as expected. I tend to ensure that ortho is off.

2 The Drafting Settings dialogue box can be activated:
   a) from the menu bar with Tools–Drafting Settings
   b) with a right-click on SNAP/GRID in the Status bar and then selecting Settings.

Task

Refer to Fig. 6.1 and:
a) with the grid and snap set to 10, draw ME
b) with the grid set to 10 and the snap set to 5, complete PLEASE to your own design specification
c) when complete, do not erase any of the objects.

Drawing with the Polar Tracking aid

1 The screen should still display HELP ME PLEASE?

2 Menu bar with **File–New** and:
  prompt   `Create New Drawing dialogue box`
  respond *a*) pick Start from Scratch
       b) pick Metric
       c) pick OK
       d) blank drawing screen returned.

3 Set the grid and snap on with settings of 20.

4 Right click on POLAR in the Status bar and pick Settings and:
  prompt   `Drafting Settings dialogue box with Polar Tracking`
       `displayed`
  respond *a*) scroll at Incremental angle and pick 45
       b) ensure Track use all polar angle settings is active
       c) ensure Absolute active – Fig. 6.3
       d) pick OK.

5 Activate the LINE command and pick a suitable grid/snap start point.

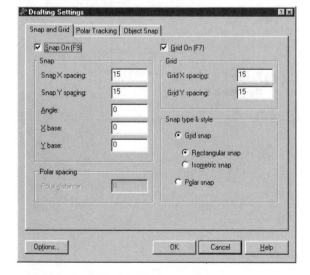

Figure 6.2 Drafting Settings dialogue box
– snap and find.

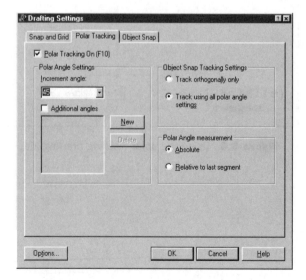

Figure 6.3 Polar Tracking dialogue box.

6 Move the cursor horizontally to the right and observe the polar tracking information displayed. Move until Polar: 100.0000<0 is displayed as Fig. 6.4(a) then left click. This is a line **segment** that you have drawn using the polar tracking drawing aid.

7 Now move the cursor vertically downwards until 40.0000<90 is displayed as Fig. 6.4(b) then left click.

8 Move the cursor downwards and to the right until a 45 degree angle is displayed at any value and left click – Fig. 6.4(c).

9 Complete the fourth line segment as Fig. 6.4(d) then end the line command.

10 *Note*: the polar tracking aid displays information of the format 100.0000<90, i.e. a length and an angle.

11 When this exercise is complete, proceed to the next chapter but try not to exit AutoCAD.

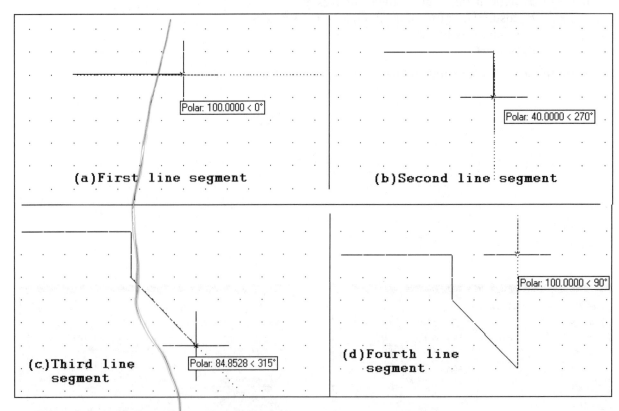

Figure 6.4 Using the polar tracking drawing aid.

Chapter **7**

Saving and opening drawings

It is essential that *all* users know how to save and open a drawing, and how to exit AutoCAD correctly. These operations cause new users to CAD a great deal of concern, and as R2000 allows multiple drawings to be opened during a drawing session, the exit process is slightly different from previous releases. For this chapter it is recommended that you have a blank formatted disk or know how to work with folders/directories on the hard drive. The name of this folder could be **mywork** or something similar. It is easier for me to demonstrate the exercises with the A: floppy drive.

Note: at this time we have two drawings 'opened' in AutoCAD, these being:

a) the four line segments created with Polar tracking
b) the HELP ME PLEASE drawing created with the grid/snap.

Saving a drawing and exiting AutoCAD

1 Place your floppy disk (if that's what is being used) into the drive.

2 Menu bar with **File–Exit** and:
   prompt AutoCAD message dialogue box as Fig. 7.1.

3 This dialogue box is informing the user that since starting the drawing, changes have been made and that these drawing changes have not yet been saved. The user has to respond to one of the three options which are:

   Yes   picking this option will save the drawing with the name displayed, i.e. Drawing2.dwg. The name is drawing2 because it is the second drawing we are working on in this session.
   No   selecting this option means that the alterations made will not be saved, i.e. the four line segments will not be able to be recalled at a later time.
   Cancel returns the user to the drawing screen.

4 At this time pick Cancel, as we want to investigate how to save a drawing.

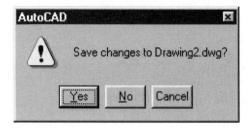

Figure 7.1 AutoCAD message dialogue box.

5   Select from the menu bar **File–Save As** and:
    prompt   Save Drawing As dialogue box
    respond   *a*) scroll at Save in and pick 3¹/₂ floppy (A)
                b) alter File name to DRG2 – Fig. 7.2
                c) note the Save as type
                d) pick Save.

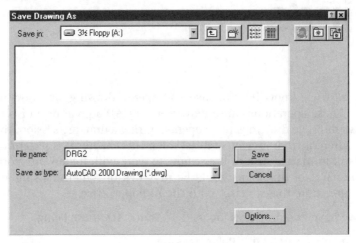

Figure 7.2   The Saving Drawing As dialogue box.

6   The screen drawing will be saved to the floppy disk, but will still be displayed on the
    screen.

7   Menu bar with **File–Exit** and:
    a) the four line segment drawing disappears – it has been saved
    b) the HELP ME PLEASE drawing will be 'returned to the screen'
    c) the AutoCAD message dialogue box will be displayed as we are still trying to exit
        AutoCAD without having saved changes
    d) pick Cancel to the message dialogue box.

8   Menu bar with **File–Save as** and using the Save Drawing As dialogue box:
    a) ensure A: floppy is current
    b) alter File name to MYFIRST
    c) pick Save.

9   Now menu bar with **File–Exit** to exit AutoCAD.

10 *Note*: when multiple drawings have been opened in AutoCAD R2000, the user is required
    to save the changes made to each drawing before AutoCAD can be exited.

Opening, modifying and saving existing drawings

1   Start AutoCAD and:
    prompt   Startup dialogue box
    respond   pick Open a Drawing
    prompt   Select File dialogue box similar to Fig. 7.3
    with   *a*) File names and paths listed
                b) a preview of the highlighted drawing
                c) information about the highlighted drawing
    respond   1) pick MYFIRST.dwg (note the A: path)
                2) note the preview
                3) pick OK.

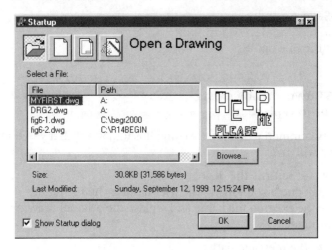

Figure 7.3 Startup dialogue box – open an existing drawing.

2 The HELP ME PLEASE drawing will be displayed.

3 Set the grid and snap to 5 and use the line command to draw a box around each letter/phrase as Fig. 7.4.

Figure 7.4 Modified MYFIRST drawing.

4 Menu bar with **File–Save As** and:

   prompt   Save Drawing As dialogue box
   with   MYFIRST as the File name
   respond pick Save
   prompt   Save Drawing As message dialogue box – Fig. 7.5
   with   **A:\MYFIRST.dwg already exists**
              Do you want to replace it?

5 This dialogue box is very common with AutoCAD and it is important that you understand what the three options will give:

   Cancel   does nothing and returns the dialogue box
   No   returns the dialogue box allowing the user to alter the file name
   Yes   will overwrite the existing file name and replace the original drawing with the modifications made.

6 At this stage, respond to the message with:

   a) pick No
   b) alter the file name to MYFIRST1
   c) pick Save.

7 What have we achieved?

   a) we opened drawing MYFIRST from the A: drive
   b) we altered the drawing layout
   c) we saved the alterations as MYFIRST1
   d) the original MYFIRST drawing is still available and has not been modified.

8 Menu bar with **File–Open** and:

   prompt   Select File dialogue box
   respond 1) pick DRG2 and note the preview
             2) pick Open.

9 The screen will display the four line segments and we now have two opened drawings – DRG2 and MYFIRST1.

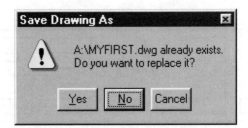

Figure 7.5 Save message dialogue box.

Closing files

AutoCAD R2000 allows multiple opened drawings to be closed and we will use the two opened drawings to demonstrate the process.

1 Erase the four lines with a window selection – easy?

2 Menu bar with **File–Close** and:
prompt   Save changes to A:\DRG2.dwg message
respond   pick No – reason out why?

3 The screen will display the MYFIRST1 modified drawing.

4 Menu bar with **File–Close** and a blank screen will be displayed with a short menu bar – File, View, Window, Help.

5 Menu bar with **File** to display a pull-down menu similar to Fig. 7.6 with the last four opened drawings listed.

6 Respond to the pull down menu by picking **A:\Myfirst1** to display the modified HELP ME PLEASE drawing.

7 *a*) Menu bar with **File** and pick A:\Myfirst
   b) menu bar with **File** and pick A:\DRG2.

8 We have now opened three drawings with DRG2 displayed.

9 Menu bar with:
   a) File–Close to close DRG2 and display MYFIRST
   b) File–Close to close MYFIRST and display MYFIRST1
   c) File–Close to close MYFIRST1 and display a blank screen
   d) File–Exit to exit AutoCAD, all drawings having been closed.

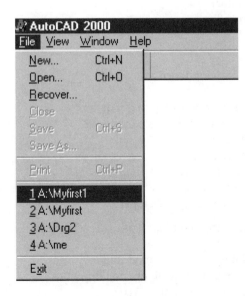

Figure 7.6   Menu bar pull-down.

Save and Save As

The menu bar selection of **File** allows the user to pick either **Save** or **Save As**. The new AutoCAD user should be aware of the difference between these two options.

Save: will save the current drawing with the same name with which the drawing was opened. No dialogue box will be displayed.

Save As: allows the user to enter a drawing name via a dialogue box. If a drawing already exists with the entered name, a message is displayed in a dialogue box.

Assignment

You are now in the position to try a drawing for yourself, so:

1   Start AutoCAD and select Start from Scratch–Metric–OK.

2   Refer to activity drawing 1 (all of the activity drawings are grouped together at the end of the book).

3   Set a grid and snap spacing to suit, e.g. 10 and/or 5.

4   Use only the LINE and CIRCLE commands (and perhaps ERASE if you make a mistake) to draw some simple shapes. The size and position are not really important at this stage, the objective being to give you a chance to practice drawing using the drawing aids.

5   When you have completed the drawing, save it as **A:ACT1**.

Summary

1   The **recommended** procedure for saving a drawing is:
  a) menu bar with **File–Save As**
  b) select A: (or named folder)
  c) enter drawing name in File name box
  d) pick Save.

2   The procedure to open a drawing from **within AutoCAD** is:
  a) menu bar with **File–Open**
  b) select A: (or named folder)
  c) pick drawing name from list
  d) preview obtained
  e) pick Open.

3   The procedure to open a drawing **from start** is:
  a) start AutoCAD R14
  b) pick **Open a Drawing** from Start Up dialogue box
  c) either 1) pick drawing name if displayed then OK
      or   2) pick Browse then:
             i)   scroll at Look in
             ii)   select A: drive or folder name
             iii)   pick the drawing name
             iv)   note preview then pick Open.

4   The **recommended** procedure to end an AutoCAD session is:
  a) complete the drawing
  b) save the drawing to floppy or your named folder
  c) menu bar with **File–Close** to close all opened drawings
  d) menu bar with **File–Exit** to quit AutoCAD.

5 The save and open command can be activated:
   a) by menu bar selection – recommended method
   b) by keyboard entry
   c) from icon selection in the Standard toolbar.

6 The menu bar method for saving a drawing is recommended as it allows the user the facility to enter the drawing name. This may be different from the opened drawing name.

7 The Save icon from the Standard toolbar and entering SAVE at the command line is a **quick save** option, and does not allow an different file name to be entered. These methods save the drawing with the opened name, and therefore overwrite the original drawing. This may not be what you want?

Chapter 8

Standard sheet 1

Traditionally one of the first things that a draughtsperson does when starting a new drawing is to get the correct size sheet of drawing paper. This sheet will probably have borders, a company logo and other details already printed on it. The drawing is then completed to 'fit into' the preprinted layout material. A CAD drawing is no different from this, with the exception that the user does not 'get a sheet of paper'. Companies who use AutoCAD will want their drawings to conform to their standards in terms of the title box, text size, linetypes being used, the style of the dimensions, etc. Parameters which govern these factors can be set every time a drawing is started, but this is tedious and against CAD philosophy. It is desirable to have all standard requirements set automatically, and this is achieved by making a drawing called a **standard sheet** or **prototype drawing** – you may have other names for it. Standard sheets can be 'customized' to suit all sizes of paper, e.g. A0, A1, etc., as well as any other size required by the customer. These standard sheets will contain the company's settings, and the individual draughtsperson can add his or her personal settings as required. It is this standard sheet which is the CAD operator's 'sheet of paper'.

We will create an A3 standard sheet, save it, and use it for all future drawing work. At this stage, the standard sheet will not have many 'settings', but we will continue to refine it and add to it as we progress through the book.

The A3 standard sheet will be created using the Advanced Wizard so:

1 Start AutoCAD and:
   prompt `Startup dialogue box`
   respond *a*) pick Use a Wizard
            b) pick Advanced Setup
            c) pick OK
   prompt `Advanced Setup dialogue box`
   respond to each dialogue box with the following selections:
            1) Units: Decimal with 0.00 precision then Next>
            2) Angle: Decimal degrees with 0.0 precision then Next>
            3) Angle Measure: East for 0 degrees then Next>
            4) Angle Direction: Counter-Clockwise then Next>
            5) Area: Width of 420, Length of 297 then Finish.

2 A blank drawing screen will be returned.

3 Menu bar with **Tools–Drafting Settings** and select:
   a) Snap and Grid Tab with:
      Snap on and spacing set to 5
      Grid on and spacing set to 10
   b) Polar Tracking Tab
      Polar tracking off
   c) pick OK.

4 Menu bar with **Format–Drawing Limits** and:
   prompt Specify lower left corner
   enter   **0,0 <R>**
   prompt Specify upper right corner
   enter   **420,297 <R>**.

5 Menu bar with **View–Zoom–All** and the grid will 'fill the screen'.

6 At the command line enter:
   a) **GRIPS <R>** and set to 0
   b) **PICKFIRST <R>** and set to 0.

7 Display toolbars to suit. I would suggest:
   a) Standard and Object Properties docked at the top as default
   b) Draw and Modify docked to left as default
   c) other toolbars will be displayed as required.

8 Menu bar with **Draw–Rectangle** and:
   prompt Specify first corner point
   enter   **0,0 <R>**
   prompt Specify other corner point
   enter   **420,297 <R>**.

9 This rectangle will represent our 'drawing area'.

10 Menu bar with **File–Save As** and:
   a) scroll and pick the A: drive (or your named folder)
   b) enter the file name as **A3PAPER**
   c) pick Save.

This completes our standard sheet (at this stage). We have created an A3-sized sheet of paper which has the units and screen layout set to our requirements. The Status bar displays the coordinates to two decimal places with both the Snap and Grid ON.

Note

Although we have activated several toolbars in our standard sheet, the user should be aware that these may not always be displayed when your standard sheet drawing is opened. AutoCAD displays the screen toolbars that were active when the system was 'shut down'. If other CAD operators have used 'your machine', then the toolbar display may not be as you left it. If you are the only user on the machine, then there should not be a problem. Anyway you now know how to display toolbars.

Chapter 9

Line creation and coordinate input

The line and circle objects so far created were drawn at random on the screen without any attempt being made to specify position or size. To draw objects accurately, coordinate input is required and AutoCAD R2000 allows different 'types' of coordinate entry, which include:

1 Absolute, i.e. from an origin point.

2 Relative (or incremental), i.e. from the last point entered.

In this chapter we will use our A3PAPER standard sheet to create several squares by different entry methods. The completed drawing will then be saved for future work.

Getting started

1 Still in AutoCAD?

A. **Answer YES**: then menu bar with **File–Open** and:

prompt Select File dialogue box

respond *a*) scroll at Look in
   b) pick 3½ floppy (A:)
   c) pick A3PAPER and note Preview
   d) pick Open

B. **Answer NO**: then Start AutoCAD and:

prompt Startup dialogue box

respond *a*) select Open a Drawing icon
   b) observe Select a File and:
     1) pick A3PAPER.dwg then OK if displayed
     2) pick Browse if A3PAPER not displayed then proceed as step 1(A) above.

2 The A3PAPER standard sheet will be displayed, i.e. a black border with the grid set to 10 and the snap set to 5.

3 Display the Draw and Modify toolbars and position to suit.

4 Decide if you want polar tracking displayed. If not, then pick POLAR from the status bar to toggle it off.

5 Refer to Fig. 9.1.

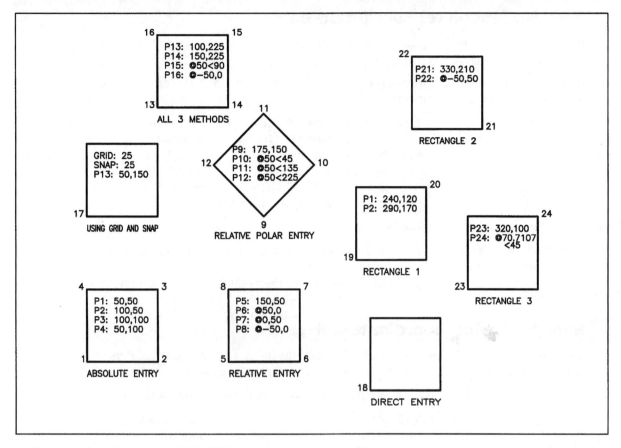

Figure 9.1 Line creation using different entry methods.

Absolute coordinate entry

This is the traditional X–Y Cartesian system, where the origin point is (0,0) at the lower left corner of the drawing area. This origin point can be 'moved' by the user, but this will be investigated in a later chapter.

Select the LINE icon from the Draw toolbar and:

prompt	`Specify first point`	and enter **50,50 <R>**	start point 1
prompt	`Specify next point`	and enter **100,50 <R>**	point 2
prompt	`Specify next point`	and enter **100,100 <R>**	point 3
prompt	`Specify next point`	and enter **50,100 <R>**	point 4
prompt	`Specify next point`	and enter **50,50 <R>**	end point 1
prompt	`Specify next point`	and right-click and enter to end line command.	

Relative (absolute) coordinate entry

Relative coordinates are from the **last point** entered and the @ (at) symbol is used for the incremental entry.

From the menu bar select **Draw–Line** and enter the following X–Y coordinate pairs, remembering <R> after each entry.

prompt	Specify first point	and enter **150,50 <R>**	start point 5
prompt	Specify next point	and enter **@50,0 <R>**	point 6
prompt	Specify next point	and enter **@0,50 <R>**	point 7
prompt	Specify next point	and enter **@–50,0 <R>**	point 8
prompt	Specify next point	and enter **@0,–50 <R>**	end point 5
prompt	Specify next point	and right-click then pick Enter	

The @ (at) symbol has the following effect:

a) @50,0 is 50 units in the positive X direction and 0 units in the Y direction from the last point, which is 150,50

b) @0,–50 is 0 units in the X direction and 50 units in the negative Y direction from the last point on the screen.

Relative (polar) coordinate entry

This also allows coordinates to be specified relative to the last point entered and uses the @ (at) symbol as before, but also introduces angular entry using the < symbol.

Activate the LINE command (icon or menu bar) and enter the following coordinates:

Specify first point	**175,150 <R>**	start point 9
Specify next point	**@50<45 <R>**	point 10
Specify next point	**@50<135 <R>**	point 11
Specify next point	**@50<225 <R>**	point 12
Specify next point	**C <R>**	close the square and end line command

Note

1 The entries can be read as:
  a) @50<45 is 50 units at an angle of 45 degrees from the last point which is 175,150
  b) @50<225 is 50 units at an angle of 225 degrees from the last point.

2 The entry **C <R>** is the **CLOSE** option and:
  a) closes the square, i.e. a line is drawn from the current screen position (point 12) to the start point (point 9)
  b) ends the sequence, i.e. <R> not needed
  c) the close option works for any straight line shape.

3 There is **NO** comma (,) with polar entries.

Using all three entry methods

Activate the LINE command then enter the following:

Specify first point	**100,225 <R>**	start point
Specify next point	**150,225 <R>**	absolute entry
Specify next point	**@50<90 <R>**	relative polar entry
Specify next point	**@–50,0 <R>**	relative absolute entry
Specify next point	**C <R>**	close square and end command.

Grid and snap method

The grid and snap drawing aids can be set to any value suitable for current drawing requirements, so:

a) set the grid and snap spacing to 25
b) with the LINE command, draw a 50 unit square the start point being at **50,150 point**
c) set the grid and snap to original values, of 10 and 5, respectively.

Direct distance entry

This method is used with the on-screen cursor. Activate the LINE command and:

prompt	Specify first point	
enter	**250,30 <R>**	point 18
prompt	Specify next point	
respond	move cursor horizontally to right and enter: **50 <R>**	
prompt	Specify next point	
respond	move cursor vertically upwards and enter: **50 <R>**	
prompt	Specify next point	
respond	move cursor horizontally to left and enter: **50 <R>**	
prompt	Specify next point	
enter	**C <R>**.	

Rectangles

Rectangular shapes can be created by specifying two points on a diagonal of the rectangle, and the command can be used with absolute or relative input.

1 From the menu bar select **Draw–Rectangle** and:

prompt	Specify first corner point	
enter	**240,120 <R>**	point 19
prompt	Specify other corner point	
enter	**290,170 <R>**.	point 20

2 Select the rectangle icon from the Draw toolbar and:

prompt	Specify first corner point	
enter	**330,210 <R>**	point 21
prompt	Specify other corner point	
enter	**@–50,50 <R>**	point 22

3 At the command line enter **RECTANG <R>** and:

prompt	Specify first corner point and enter: **320,100 <R>**	point 23
prompt	Specify other corner point and	
	enter: **@70,7107<45 <R>**.	point 24

Question: why the 70.7107 length entry?

Saving the squares

The drawing screen should now display nine squares positioned as shown in Fig. 9.1, but without the text. This drawing must be saved as it will be used in other chapters, so from the menu bar select **File–Save As** and:

prompt	Save Drawing As dialogue box
respond	1) scroll at Save in and pick 3$\frac{1}{2}$ floppy (A:)
	2) enter file name as **DEMODRG**
	3) pick Save.

Conventions

Coordinate axes

The X–Y axes convention used by AutoCAD is shown in Fig. 9.2(a) and displays four points with their coordinate values. When using the normal X–Y coordinate system:

a) a positive X direction is to the right, and a positive Y direction is upwards
b) a negative X direction is to the left, and a negative Y direction is downwards.

Angles

When angles are being used:

a) positive angles are anti-clockwise
b) negative angles are clockwise.

Figure 9.2(b) displays the angle convention with four points with their polar coordinate values.

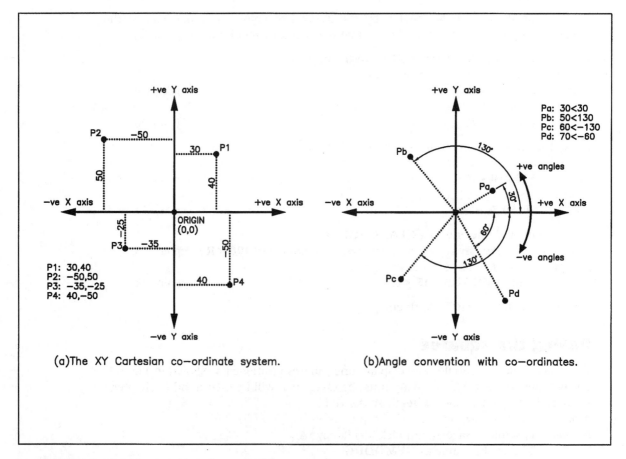

Figure 9.2 Coordinate and angle convention.

Task

Before leaving this exercise, try the following:

1 Make sure you have saved the squares!

2 Erase a square create with a Draw–Rectangle sequence. It is erased with a 'single pick' as it is a polyline – more on this in a later chapter.

3 Now erase all the squares from the screen.

4 Draw a line sequence using the following entries:
Specify first point: 30,40
Specify next point: −100,100
Specify next point: −150,−200
Specify next point: 80,−100
Specify next point: C <R>.

5 Draw four lines, entering the following:
a) specify first point: 0,0; specify next point: 100<30
b) specify first point: 0,0; specify next point: 200<150
c) specify first point: 0,0; specify next point: 250<−130
d) specify first point: 0,0; specify next point: 90<−60.

6 When these eight line segments have been drawn, not all are completely visible on the screen.

7 Menu bar with **View–Zoom–All** and:
a) all eight lines are visible, i.e. we can draw 'off the screen'?
b) move the cursor to the intersection of the four polar lines, and with the snap on, the status bar displays 0,0,0 as the coordinates
c) now **View–Zoom–Previous** from the menu bar.

Notes

1 When using coordinate input with the LINE command, it is very easy to make a mistake with the entries. If the line 'does not appear to go in the direction it should', then either:
a) enter **U <R>** from the keyboard to 'undo' the last line segment drawn, or
b) right-click and pick **undo** from the right button dialogue box
c) this 'undo effect' can be used until all segments are erased.

2 The @ (at) symbol is very useful if you want to 'get to the last point referenced on the screen'. Try the following:
a) draw a line and cancel the command with a <RETURN>
b) re-activate the line command and enter @ **<R>**
c) the cursor 'snaps to' the endpoint of the drawn line.

3 A <RETURN> keyboard press will always activate the last command.

4 A right-click on the mouse will activate a 'pop-up' dialogue box, allowing the last command to be activated.

Assignment

This activity only uses the LINE command (and ERASE?), but requires coordinate entry (and some 'sums') for you to complete the drawing.

1 Open your A:A3PAPER standard sheet.

2 Refer to Activity 2 and draw the three template shapes using coordinate input. Any entry method can be used, but I would recommend that:
   a) position the start points with absolute entry
   b) use relative entry as much as possible.

3 When the drawing is complete, save it as A:ACT2.

4 Read the summary then proceed to the next chapter.

Summary

1 Coordinate entry can be **ABSOLUTE** or **RELATIVE**.

2 ABSOLUTE entry is from an origin – the point (0,0). Positive directions are UP and to the RIGHT, negative directions are DOWN and to the LEFT. The entry format is **X,Y**, e.g. 30,40.

3 RELATIVE entry refers the coordinates to the last point entered and uses the @ symbol. The entry format is:
   a) relative absolute: **@X,Y**, e.g. @50,60
   b) relative polar: **@X<A**, e.g. @100<50 and note – no comma.

4 An angle of –45 degrees is the same as an angle of +315 degrees.

5 The following polar entries are the same:
   a) @–50<30
   b) @50<210
   c) @50<–150.

   Try them if you are not convinced.

6 All entry methods can be used in a line sequence.

7 A line sequence is terminated with:
   a) the <RETURN> key
   b) a right-click and Enter on the mouse
   c) 'closing' the shape.

8 The rectangle command is useful, but it is a 'single object' and not four 'distinct lines'.

9 The LINE command can be activated by:
   a) icon selection from the Draw toolbar
   b) menu bar selection with Draw–Line
   c) entering LINE <R> at the command line.

   It is the user's preference what method is to be used.

Chapter 10

Circle creation

In this chapter we will investigate how circles can be created by adding several to the squares created in the previous chapter, so:

1 Open you A:DEMODRG to display the nine squares.
2 Refer to Fig. 10.1 and ensure the Draw and Modify toolbars are displayed.

AutoCAD R2000 allows circles to be created by six different methods and the command can be activated by icon selection, menu bar selection or keyboard entry. When drawing circles, absolute coordinates are usually used to specify the circle centre, although the next chapter will introduce the user to the Object Snap modes. These Object Snaps allow greater flexibility in selecting existing entities for reference.

Centre-radius

Select the CIRCLE icon from the Draw toolbar and:
prompt Specify center point for circle or [3P/2P/Ttr (tan tan radius)]:
enter **75,75 <R>** – the circle centre point
prompt Specify radius of circle or [Diameter]
enter **20 <R>** – the circle radius.

Centre-diameter

From the menu bar select **Draw–Circle–Center,Diameter** and:
prompt Specify center point for circle or...
enter **175,75 <R>**
prompt Specify diameter of circle
enter **20 <R>**.

Two points on circle diameter

At the command line enter **CIRCLE <R>** and:
prompt Specify center point for circle or ...
enter **2P <R>** – the two-point option
prompt Specify first point on circle's diameter and enter: **280,210 <R>**
prompt Specify second point on circle's diameter and enter: **330,260 <R>**.

Three points on circle circumference

Menu bar selection with **Draw–Circle–3 Points** and:
prompt Specify first point on circle
respond **pick any point within the top left square**
prompt Specify second point on circle
respond **pick another point within the top left square**
prompt Specify third point on circle
respond **drag out the circle and pick a point.**

TTR: tangent–tangent–radius

1 Menu bar with **Draw–Circle–Tan,Tan,Radius** and:
   prompt   Specify point on object for first tangent of circle
   and   pickbox attached to cursor cross-hairs
   respond **move cursor onto the line A and leave for a second**
   and   *a*) a small marker is displayed
              b) Deferred Tangent displayed
   respond **pick line A**, i.e. left click on it
   prompt   Specify point on object for second tangent of circle
   respond **pick line B**
   prompt   Specify radius of circle <??,??>
   enter   **25 <R>**
   and   a circle is drawn as tangent to the two selected lines.

2 At the command line enter **CIRCLE <R>** and:
   prompt   Specify center point for circle or...
   enter   **TTR <R>** – the tan,tan,radius option
   prompt   first tangent point prompt and: **pick line C**
   prompt   second tangent point prompt and: **pick line D**
   and   a circle is drawn tangential to the two selected lines, line C being assumed extended.

TTT: tangent–tangent–tangent

1 Menu bar with **Draw–Circle–Tan,Tan,Tan** and:
   prompt   Specify first point on circle and: **pick line L1**
   prompt   Specify second point on circle and: **pick line L2**
   prompt   Specify third point on circle and: **pick circle C1**.

2 Activate the **Draw–Circle–Tan,Tan,Tan** sequence and:
   prompt   Specify first point on circle and: **pick circle C1**
   prompt   Specify second point on circle and: **pick circle C2**
   prompt   Specify third point on circle and: **pick circle C3**.

Circles are drawn tangentially to the selected objects, these being:

a) two lines and a circle
b) three circles.

Question: how long would this take by conventional methods?

Saving the drawing

Assuming that the CIRCLE commands have been entered correctly, your drawing should resemble Fig. 10.1 (without the text) and is ready to be saved for future work.

From the menu bar select **File–Save As** and:
prompt   Save Drawing As dialogue box
with   File name: DEMODRG
respond **pick Save**
prompt   Drawing already exists message
respond **pick Yes** – obvious?

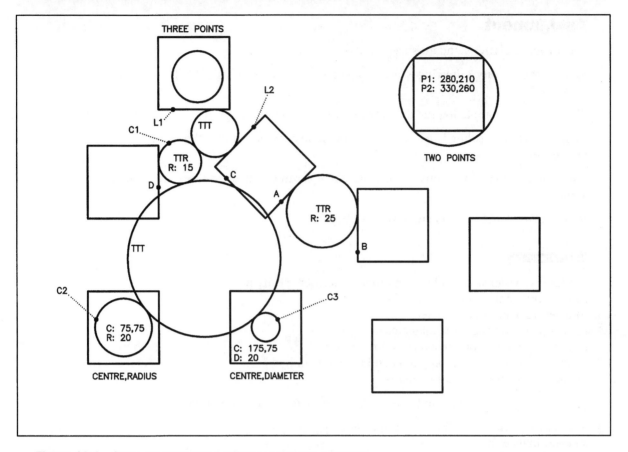

Figure 10.1 Circle creation using different selection methods.

Task

The two Tan,Tan,Tan circles have been created without anything being known about their radii.

1 From the menu bar select **Tools–Inquiry–List** and:
   prompt   Select objects
   respond **pick the smaller TTT circle**
   prompt   1 found and Select objects
   respond **right-click**
   prompt   AutoCAD Text window with information about the circle.

2 Note the information then cancel the text window by picking the right (X) button from the title bar.

3 Repeat the **Tools–Inquiry–List** sequence for the larger TTT circle.

4 The information for my two TTT circles is as follows:

	smaller	*larger*
Centre point	139.52, 208,53	131.88, 122.06
Radius	16.47	53.83
Circumference	103.51	338.21
Area	852.67	9102.42

5 Could you calculate these figures manually as easy as this?

Assignment

1 Open your A:STDA3 standard sheet.

2 Refer to the Activity 3 drawing which can be completed with only the LINE and CIRCLE commands.

3 The method of completing the drawings is at your discretion.

4 Remember that absolute is recommended for circle centres and that the TTR method is very useful.

5 You may require some 'sums' for certain circle centres, but the figures are relatively simple.

6 When the drawing is complete, save it as A:ACT3.

Summary

1 Circles can be constructed by six methods, the user specifying:
   a) a centre point and radius
   b) a centre point and diameter
   c) two points on the circle diameter
   d) any three points on the circle circumference
   e) two tangent specification points and the circle radius
   f) three tangent specification points.

2 The TTR and TTT options can be used with lines, circles, arcs and other objects.

3 The centre point and radius can be specified by:
   a) coordinate entry
   b) picking a point on the screen
   c) referencing existing entities – next chapter.

Chapter 11

Object snap

The lines and circles drawn so far have been created by coordinate input. While this is the basic method of creating objects, it is often desirable to 'reference' existing objects already displayed on the screen, e.g. we may want to:
a) draw a circle, centre at the midpoint of an existing line
b) draw a line, from a circle centre perpendicular to another line.

These types of operations are achieved using **the object snap modes** – generally referred to as **OSNAP** – and are one of the most useful (and powerful) draughting aids.

Object snap modes are used **transparently**, i.e. whilst in a command, and can be activated: *a*) from the Object Snap toolbar or *b*) by direct keyboard entry.

While the toolbar method is the quicker and easier to use, we will investigate both methods. Release 2000 has two new object snap modes, which will become apparent to pre-R2000 users as the exercise progresses. A full explanation of these new additions will be given later in the chapter.

Getting ready

1 Open your A:DEMODRG of the squares and circles.

2 Erase the two TTT circles.

3 Display the Draw, Modify and Object Snap toolbars and position them to suit.

4 Refer to Fig. 11.1.

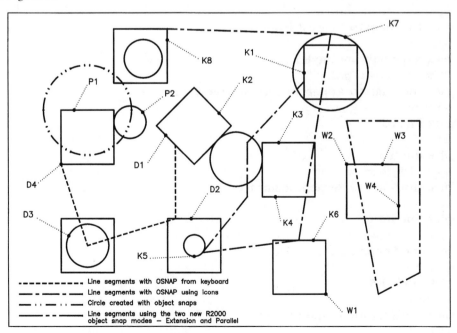

Figure 11.1 Using the object snap modes with A:DEMODRG.

Using object snap from the keyboard

Activate the LINE command and:

prompt	Specify first point
enter	**MID <R>**
prompt	of
and	aperture box on cross-hairs
respond	1) move cursor to line D1 and leave
	2) coloured triangular marker at line midpoint
	3) Midpoint snap tip in colour – yellow?
now	**pick line D1**
and	line 'snaps to' the midpoint of D1
prompt	Specify next point
enter	**PERP <R>**
prompt	to
respond	**pick line D2** – note coloured Perpendicular marker
prompt	Specify next point
enter	**CEN <R>**
prompt	of
respond	**pick circle D3** – note coloured Center marker
prompt	Specify next point
enter	**INT <R>**
prompt	of
respond	**pick point D4** – note blue Intersection marker
prompt	Specify next point and: **right–click–Enter** to end sequence.

Using object snap from the toolbar

Activate the LINE command and:

prompt	Specify first point	
respond	**pick the Snap to Nearest icon**	
prompt	nea to	
respond	**pick any point on line K1**	
prompt	Specify next point	
respond	**pick the Snap to Apparent Intersection icon**	
prompt	appint of	
respond	**pick line K2**	
prompt	and	
respond	**pick line K3**	
prompt	Specify next point	
respond	**pick the Snap to Perpendicular icon**	
prompt	per to	
respond	**pick line K4**	
prompt	Specify next point	
respond	**pick the Snap to Tangent icon**	
prompt	tan to	
respond	**pick circle K5**	
prompt	To point	
respond	**pick the Snap to Midpoint icon**	
prompt	mid of	
respond	**pick line K6**	

prompt	Specify next point
respond	**pick the Snap to Quadrant icon**
prompt	qua of
respond	**pick circle K7**
prompt	Specify next point
respond	**pick the Snap to Endpoint icon**
prompt	endp of
respond	**pick line K8**
prompt	Specify next point
respond	**right-click-Enter** to end sequence.

Object snap with circles

Select the CIRCLE icon from the Draw toolbar and:

prompt	Specify center point for circle or...
respond	**pick the Snap to Midpoint icon**
prompt	mid of
respond	**pick line P1**
prompt	Specify radius of circle or...
respond	**pick the Snap to Center icon**
prompt	cen of
respond	**pick circle P2**.

Note

1 Save your drawing at this stage as A:DEMODRG.

2 The endpoint 'snapped to' depends on which part of the line is 'picked'. The coloured marker indicates which line endpoint.

3 A circle has four quadrants, these being at the 3,12,9,6 o'clock positions. The coloured marker indicates which quadrant will be snapped to.

The two new R2000 object snap modes

Release 2000 has two new object snap modes, these being Extension and Parallel. They are used as follows:

a) extension: used with lines and arcs. Gives a temporary extension line as the cursor is passed over the endpoint of an object

b) parallel: used with straight line objects only. Allows a vector to be drawn parallel to another object.

To demonstrate these new object snap modes:

1 Continue with the A:DEMODRG and turn on the grid and snap, both with 10 settings.

2 Activate the LINE command and:

prompt	Specify first point
respond	**pick the Snap to Extension icon**
prompt	ext of
respond	**move cursor over point W1 then drag to right**
with	1) highlighted extension line dragged out
	2) information displayed about distance from endpoint
respond	1) move cursor until Extension: 50.00<0.0 displayed
	2) left-click
prompt	Specify next point
respond	**pick the Snap to Extension icon**
prompt	ext of
respond	1) move cursor over point W2
	2) move cursor vertically up until Extension: 40.00<90.0 is displayed
	3) left-click
prompt	Specify next point
respond	**pick the Snap to Parallel icon**
prompt	par to
respond	1) move cursor over line W3 and note the display
	2) move cursor to right of last pick point and:
	a) highlighted line
	b) information about distance and angle displayed
	3) move cursor to right until 70.00<0.0 displayed
	4) left-click
prompt	Specify next point
respond	**pick the Snap to Parallel icon**
prompt	par to
respond	1) move cursor over line W4
	2) move cursor vertically below last pick point
	3) move cursor until 140.00<270.0 displayed
	4) left-click
prompt	Specify next point
enter	**C <R>** to close the shape and end the line command.

3 The line segments should be as Fig. 11.1.

4 Save your layout as A:DEMODRG, updating the existing drawing.

Running object snap

Using the object snap icons from the toolbar will increase the speed of the draughting process, but it can still be 'tedious' to have to pick the icon every time an ENDpoint (for example) is required. It is possible to 'preset' the object snap mode to ENDpoint, MIDpoint, CENter, etc., and this is called a **running object snap**. Pre-setting the object snap does not preclude the user from selecting another mode, i.e. if you have set an ENDpoint running object snap, you can still pick the INTersection icon.

The running object snap can be set:

1 From the menu bar with **Tools–Drafting Settings** and pick the Object Snap tab.

2 Entering **OSNAP <R>** at the command line.

3 Picking the Object Snap Settings icon from the Object Snap toolbar.

4 With a right-click on OSNAP in the Status bar and picking Settings.

Each method displays the Osnap Settings dialogue box.

Task

1 Select **Tools–Drafting Settings** from the menu bar and:
   prompt   Drafting Settings dialogue box
   respond   1) pick the Object Snap tab – Fig. 11.2
               2) activate Endpoint, Midpoint and Nearest by picking the appropriate box –
                 tick means active
               3) pick OK.

2 Now activate the LINE command and move the aperture/cross-hairs onto any line and leave it.

3 A coloured marker will be displayed at the Nearest point of the line.

4 Press the **TAB** key to cycle through the set running object snaps, i.e. the line should display the cross, square and triangular coloured markers for the Nearest, Endpoint and Midpoint object snap settings.

5 Cancel the line command with **ESC**.

Figure 11.2 The Object Snap dialogue box.

AutoSnap and AutoTrack

The Object Snap dialogue box allows the user to select **Options** which displays the Drafting tab dialogue box – Fig. 11.3. With this dialogue box, the user can control both the AutoSnap and the AutoTrack settings. The settings which can be altered are:

AutoSnap	*AutoTrack*
Marker	Display polar tracking vector
Magnet	Display full screen tracking vector
Display tool tip	Display autotrack tooltip
Display aperture box	Alter alignment point acquisition
Alter marker colour	Alter aperture size
Alter marker size	

The various terms should be self-explanatory at this stage(?):
Marker: is the geometric shape displayed at a snap point
Magnet: locks the aperture box onto the snap point
Tool tip: is a flag describing the name of the snap location.

The rest of the options should be apparent. It is normal to have the marker, magnet and tool tip active (ticked). The colour of the marker and the aperture box sizes are at the user's discretion, as is having polar tracking 'on'.

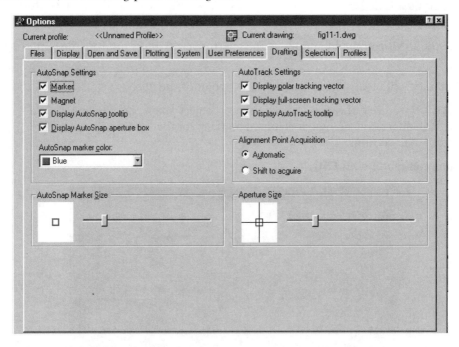

Figure 11.3 Drafting Options dialogue box.

Cancelling a running object snap

A running object snap can be left 'active' once it has been set, but this can cause problems if the user 'forgets' about it. The running snap can be cancelled:

1 From the Object Settings dialogue box with **Clear All**.

2 By entering **-OSNAP <R>** at the command line and:
prompt   Enter list of object snap modes
enter   **NONE <R>**.

3 *Note*:

   a) selecting the Snap to None icon from the Object Snap toolbar will turn of the object snap running modes for the next point selected

   b) using the Object Snap dialogue box is the recommended way of activating and de-activating object snaps.

The Snap From object snap

This is a very useful object snap, allowing the user to reference points relative to existing objects.

1 Using the squares and circles which should still be displayed, erase the lines and circle created with the object snaps. This is to give 'some space'. Ensure the Object Snap toolbar is displayed.

2 Activate the circle command and:

prompt	Specify center point for circle
respond	**pick Snap From icon from the Object Snap toolbar**
prompt	from Base Point
respond	**pick Snap to Midpoint icon**
prompt	mid of
respond	**pick line K8**
prompt	<Offset>
enter	**@50,0 <R>**
prompt	Specify radius of circle
enter	**20 <R>**.

3 A circle is drawn with its centre 50 mm from the midpoint of the selected line.

4 Select the LINE icon and:

prompt	Specify first point
respond	**pick Snap From icon**
prompt	from Base point
respond	**pick Intersection icon**
prompt	int of
respond	**pick point W1**
prompt	<Offset>
enter	**@25,–25 <R>**
prompt	Specify next point
respond	**pick Snap From icon**
prompt	from Base point
respond	**pick Snap to Centre icon**
prompt	cen of
respond	**pick circle K7**
prompt	<Offset>
enter	**@80<–20 <R>**
prompt	Specify next point
respond	**right-click and Enter**.

5 A line is drawn between the specified points, the line end points being 'offset' from the selected objects by the entered values.

6 Do not save these additions to your drawing layout.

Assignment

1   Open your A:A3PAPER standard sheet and refer to Activity 4.

2   Draw the three components using lines and circles.

3   Object snap will require to be used and hints are given.

4   When complete, save as A:ACT4.

5   Read the summary then progress to the next chapter.

Summary

1   Object snap (OSNAP) is used to reference existing objects.

2   OSNAP is an invaluable aid to draughting and should be used whenever possible.

3   The user can 'pre-set' a running objects snap.

4   Geometric markers will indicate the snap points on objects.

5   The Drafting Settings dialogue box allows the user to 'control' the geometric markers.

6   Object snap is an example of a **transparent** command, as it is activated when another command is being used.

7   The object snap mode can be set and cancelled using the dialogue box or toolbar.

Chapter 12

Arc, donut and ellipse creation

These three drawings commands will be discussed in turn using our square and circle drawing. Each command can be activated from the toolbar, menu bar or by keyboard entry and both coordinate entry and referencing existing objects will be demonstrated.

Getting started

1 Open your A:DEMODRG to display the squares, circles and object snap lines, etc.

2 Erase the objects created during the object snap exercise.

3 Refer to Fig. 12.1 and activated the Draw, Modify and Object Snap toolbars.

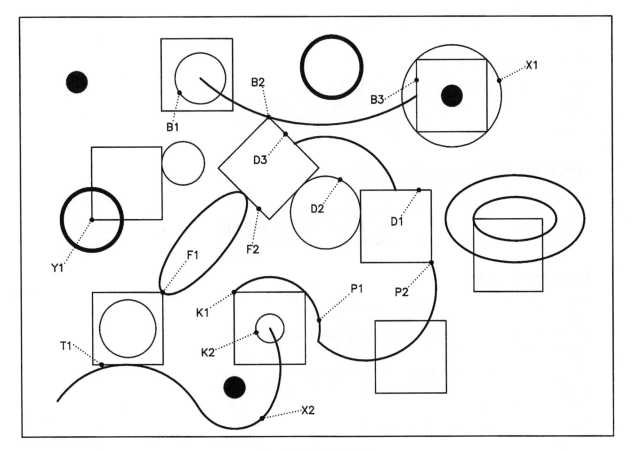

Figure 12.1 Arc, donut and ellipse creation with A:DEMODRG.

Arcs

There are 10 different arc creation methods. Arcs are normally drawn in an anti-clockwise direction with combinations of the arc start point, end point, centre point, radius, included angle, length of arc, etc. We will investigate five different arc creation methods, and you can try the others for yourself.

Start,Center,End

From the menu bar select **Draw–Arc–Start,Center,End** and:
prompt   Specify start point of arc
respond   **Snap to Midpoint icon and pick line D1**
prompt   Specify center point of arc
respond   **Snap to Center icon and pick circle D2**
prompt   Specify end point of arc
respond   **Snap to Midpoint icon and pick line D3.**

Start,Center,Angle

Menu bar with **Draw–Arc–Start,Center,Angle** and:
prompt   Specify start point of arc
respond   **Snap to Intersection icon and pick point K1**
prompt   Specify center point of arc
respond   **Snap to Center icon and pick circle K2**
prompt   Specify included angle
enter   **–150 <R>.**

Note that negative angle entries draw arcs in a clockwise direction.

Start,End,Radius

Menu bar again with **Draw–Arc–Start,End,Radius** and:
prompt   Start point and **snap to Endpoint of line P1**
prompt   End point and **snap to Intersection of point P2**
prompt   Radius and enter **50 <R>.**

Three points (on arc circumference)

Activate the 3 Points arc command and:
prompt   Start point and **snap to Center of circle B1**
prompt   Second point and **snap to Intersection of point B2**
prompt   End point and **snap to Midpoint of line B3.**

Continuous arcs

1 Activate the 3 Points arc command again and:
   prompt   Start point and enter **25,25 <R>**
   prompt   Second point and **snap to Midpoint of line T1**
   prompt   End point and enter **@50,–30 <R>.**

2 Select from the menu bar **Draw–Arc–Continue** and:
   prompt   End point – and snaps to end point of last arc drawn
   enter   **@50,0 <R>.**

3 Repeat the **Arc–Continue** selection and:
   prompt   End point
   respond   **snap to Center of circle K2.**

Donut

A donut (or doughnut) is a 'solid filled' circle or annulus (a washer shape), the user specifying the inside and outside diameters and then selecting the donut centre point.

1 Menu bar with **Draw–Donut** and:
prompt   Specify inside diameter of donut and enter **0 <R>**
prompt   Specify outside diameter of donut and enter **15 <R>**
prompt   Specify center of donut and enter **40,245 <R>**
prompt   Specify center of donut
respond   **Snap to Center of circle X1**
prompt   Specify center of donut
respond   **Snap to Center of arc X2**
prompt   Specify center of donut and **right-click**.

2 Repeat the donut command and:
prompt   Specify inside diameter of donut and enter **40 <R>**
prompt   Specify outside diameter of donut and enter **45 <R>**
prompt   Specify center of donut and enter **220,255 <R>**
prompt   Specify center of donut
respond   **Snap to Intersection of point Y1**
prompt   Specify center of donut and **right-click**.

3 *Note*: the donut command allows repetitive entries, while the circle command only allows one – I don't know why this is!

Ellipse

Ellipses are created by the user specifying:

a) either the ellipse centre and two axes endpoints
b) or three points on the axes endpoints.

1 Select from the menu bar **Draw–Ellipse–Center** and:
prompt   Specify center of ellipse and enter **350,150 <R>**
prompt   Specify endpoint of axis and enter **400,150 <R>**
prompt   Specify distance to other axis or. and enter **350,120 <R>**.

2 Select the ELLIPSE icon from the Draw toolbar and:
prompt   Specify axis endpoint of ellipse or (Arc/Center)
enter   **C <R>** – the center option
prompt   Specify center of ellipse
respond   **Snap to Center icon and pick the existing ellipse**
prompt   Specify endpoint of axis and enter **@30,0 <R>**
prompt   Specify distance to other axis and enter **@0,15 <R>**.

3 Menu bar with **Draw–Ellipse–Axis,End** and:
prompt   Specify axis endpoint of ellipse
respond: **Snap to Intersection of point F1**
prompt   Specify other endpoint of axis
respond   **Snap to Midpoint of line F2**
prompt   Specify distance to other axis or [Rotation]
enter   **R <R>** – the rotation option
prompt   Specify rotation around major axis and enter **70 <R>**.

Note

1 At this stage your drawing should resemble Fig. 12.1 but without the text.

2 Save it as A:DEMODRG for future recall if required. Remember that this will 'over-write' the existing A:DEMODRG file.

3 Arcs, donuts and ellipses have centre points and quadrants which can be 'snapped to' with the object snap modes.

4 It is also possible to use the tangent snap icon and draw tangent lines, etc. between these objects. Try this for yourself.

Solid fill

Donuts are generally displayed on the screen 'solid', i.e. 'filled in'. This solid fill effect is controlled by the FILL system variable and can be activated from the menu bar or the command line.

1 Still with A:DEMODRG on the screen?

2 Menu bar with **Tools–Options** and:
   prompt Options dialogue box
   respond **pick the Display tab**
   then   1) Apply solid fill OFF, i.e. no tick in box
            2) pick OK.

3 Menu bar with **View–Regen** and the donuts will be displayed without the fill effect.

4 At the command line enter **FILL <R>**
   prompt Enter mode [ON/OFF] <OFF>
   enter   **ON <R>**.

5 At the command line enter **REGEN <R>** to 'refresh' the screen and display the donuts with the fill effect.

6 *Note:* this fill effect also applies to polylines, which will be discussed in a later chapter.

Summary

Arcs, donuts and ellipses are Draw commands and can be created by coordinate entry or by referencing existing objects.

General

1 The three objects have a centre point and quadrants.

2 They can be 'snapped to' with the object snap modes.

3 Tangent lines can be drawn to and from them.

Arcs

1 Several different creation options.

2 Normally drawn in an anti-clockwise direction.

3 Very easy to draw in the wrong 'sense' due to the start and end points being selected wrongly.

4 Continuous arcs are possible.

5 A negative angle entry will draw the arc clockwise.

Donuts

1 Require the user to specify the inside and outside diameters.

2 Can be displayed filled or unfilled.

3 An inside radius of 0 will give a 'filled circle'.

4 Repetitive donuts can be created.

Ellipses

1 Two creation methods.

2 Partial ellipses (arcs) are possible.

3 The created ellipses are 'true', i.e. have a centre point.

Chapter 13

Layers and standard sheet 2

All the objects that have been drawn have had a continuous linetype and no attempt has been made to introduce centre or hidden lines, or even colour. All AutoCAD releases have a facility called **LAYERS** that allow the user to assign different linetypes and colours to named layers. For example, a layer may for red continuous lines, another may be for green hidden lines, and yet another for blue centre lines. Layers can also be used for specific drawing purposes, e.g. there may be a layer for dimensions, one for hatching, one for text, etc. Individual layers can be 'switched' on/off by the user to mask out drawing objects which are not required.

The concept of layers can be imagined as a series of transparent overlays, each having its own linetype, colour and use. The overlay used for dimensioning could be switched off without affecting the remaining layers. Figure 13.1 demonstrates the layer concept with:

1 Five layers used to create a simple component. Each 'part' of the component has been created on 'its own' layer.

2 The layers 'laid on top of each other'. The effect is that the user 'sees' one component.

The following points are worth noting when considering layers:

1 All objects are drawn on layers.

2 Layers should be used for each 'part' of a drawing, i.e. dimensions should not be on the same layer as centre lines (for example).

3 New layers must be 'created' by the user, using the Layer Properties Manager dialogue box.

4 Layers are one of the most important concept in AutoCAD.

5 Layers are essential for good and efficient draughting.

As layers are very important, and as the user must have a sound knowledge of how they are used, this chapter is therefore rather long (and perhaps boring). I make no apology for this, as all CAD operators must be able to use layers correctly.

As a point of interest, try and complete this chapter at 'the one sitting' as it is important for all future drawing work.

Getting started

Several different aspects of layers will be discussed in this chapter before we will modify our existing standard sheet, so:

1 Open your A:A3PAPER standard sheet.

2 Draw a horizontal and vertical line each of length 200, and a circle of radius 75 anywhere on the screen.

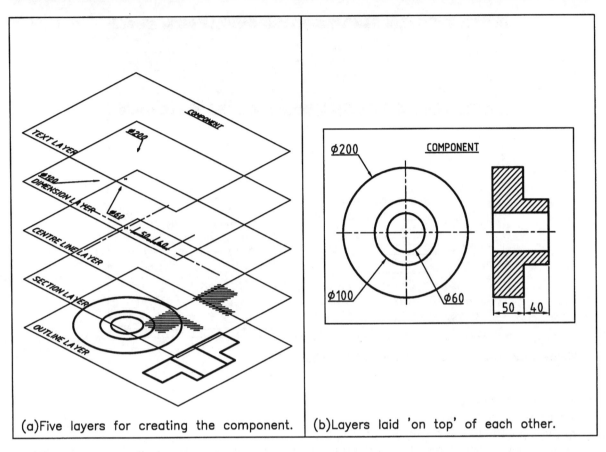

Figure 13.1 Layer concept.

The Layer Properties Manager dialogue box

1   From the menu bar select **Format–Layer...** and:

prompt   Layer Properties Manager dialogue box
respond   Study the layout of the dialogue box

2   The format of the Layer Properties Manager dialogue box is:

   a) named layer filter: Show all layers (generally this option)
   b) four selections: New, Delete, Current, Show Details
   c) current Layer: 0
   d) layer information display:
      i)   layer name: only 0 at present
      ii)   three layer states: On, Freeze, (L)ocked
      iii)   layer colour: White (with a black box)
      iv)   Linetype: Continuous
      v)   Lineweight: Default
      vi)   Plot Style
      vii) Plot.

3   Layer 0 is the layer on which all objects have so far been drawn, and is 'supplied' with AutoCAD. It is the **current** layer and is displayed in the Objects Properties toolbar with the layer state icons.

4   Certain areas of the dialogue box are 'greyed out', i.e. inactive.

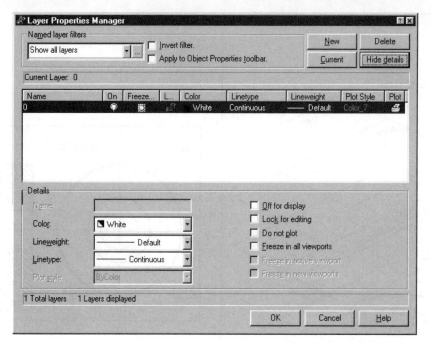

Figure 13.2 Layer Properties Manager dialogue box.

5 Move the pointing device arrow onto the 0 named line and:
  a) pick with a left-click
  b) the 'complete line' is highlighted in colour (mine was blue)
  c) pick Show Details to reveal other information about the selected layer as Fig. 13.2.

6 Move the cursor along the highlighted area and pick the On/Off icon which is a yellow light bulb (indicating ON) and:
  prompt   `AutoCAD layer message box` – Fig. 13.3
  and   On/Off icon now a blue light bulb, indicating OFF
  respond   1) pick OK from the message box
             2) pick OK from the Layer Properties Manager dialogue box
  and   the drawing screen will be returned and no objects are displayed – they were all drawn on layer 0 which has been turned off.

7 Re-activate the Layer Properties Manager dialogue box and:
  a) pick the 0 layer name – highlighted in colour
  b) pick the 'blue light' and it changes to yellow (ON)
  c) pick OK.

8 Line and circle objects displayed – layer 0 is on.

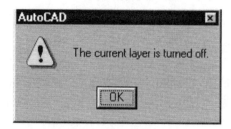

Figure 13.3 Layer message dialogue box.

Linetypes

AutoCAD allows the user to display objects with different linetypes, e.g. continuous, centre, hidden, dotted, etc. Until now, all objects have been displayed with continuous linetype.

1 Activate the menu selection **Format–Layer** and:

prompt	Layer Properties Manager dialogue box
respond	**pick Continuous from layer 0 'line'**
prompt	Select Linetype dialogue box
with	Continuous _____ Solid lines only displayed
respond	**pick Load...**
prompt	Load or Reload Linetype dialogue box
with	1) Filename: **acadiso.lin**
	2) a list of all linetypes in the acadiso.lin file
respond	1) scroll (at right) and **pick CENTER** – Fig. 13.4
	2) pick OK
prompt	Select Linetype dialogue box
with	CENTER linetype displayed, i.e. it has been 'loaded'
respond	**pick Load**
prompt	Load or Reload Linetypes dialogue box
respond	1) scroll and **pick HIDDEN**
	2) pick OK.

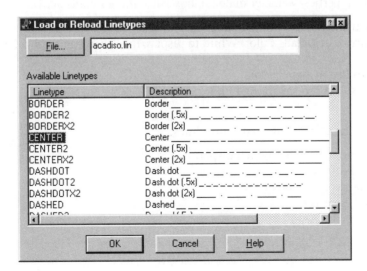

Figure 13.4   Load or Reload Linetypes dialogue box.

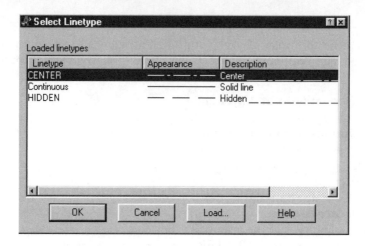

Figure 13.5 Select Linetype dialogue box.

prompt	`Select Linetype dialogue box`
with	HIDDEN linetype displayed, i.e. loaded
respond	1) **pick CENTER** – Fig. 13.5
	2) pick OK
prompt	`Layer Properties Manager dialogue box`
with	layer 0 – CENTER linetype
respond	pick OK.

2 The drawing screen will display the three objects with center linetype – remember it is an American package, i.e. *center* and not *centre*.

Colour

Individual objects can be displayed on the screen in different colours, but I prefer to use layers for the colour effect. This is achieved by assigning a specific colour to a named layer.

1 Activate the Layer Properties Manager dialogue box with Show Details active.

2 *a*) Pick line 0 to activate the layer information
   b) pick the scroll arrow at Details Color: White to display the seven standard colours
   c) pick Red and:
      i) White alters to Red at Details Color
      ii) layer 0 line displays red square Red under Color
   d) pick OK.

3 The screen displays the objects with red centre lines.

4 Note the Object Properties toolbar which displays:
   a) layer 0 with a red square
   b) the ByLayer colour is a red square
   c) the ByLayer linetype is centre.

Task

By selecting the Layers icon from the Object Properties toolbar:
a) set layer 0 linetype to Continuous
b) set layer 0 colour to White/Black
c) screen should display continuous white/black objects
d) note the Object Properties toolbar.

A note on colour

1   The default AutoCAD colour for objects is dependent on your screen configuration (preference):
a) white background – black lines
b) black background – white lines.

2   The white/black linetype can be confusing?

3   All colours in AutoCAD are numbered. There is a total of 255 colours, but the seven standard colours are:

1 red	2 yellow	3 green	4 cyan
5 blue	6 magenta	7 black/white	

4   The number or colour name can be used to select a colour. The numbers are associated with colour pen plotters.

5   The complete 255 'colour palette' can be activated from:
a) Layer Program Manager dialogue box by picking the coloured square under Color
b) from the Details by scrolling and picking Others...

6   Generally only the seven standard colours will be used, but there may be the odd occasion when a colour from the palette will be selected.

Creating new layers

Layers should be made to suit individual or company requirements, but for our purposes the layers which will be made for all future drawing work are:

Usage	Layer name	Layer colour	Layer linetype
General	0	white/black	continuous
Outlines	OUT	red	continuous
Centre lines	CL	green	center
Hidden detail	HID	yellow	hidden
Dimensions	DIMEN	magenta	continuous
Text	TEXT	blue	continuous
Hatching	SECT	cyan	continuous
Construction	CONS	to suit	continuous

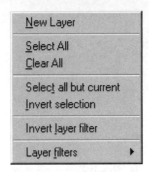

Figure 13.6 Layer Properties Manager right button pop-up menu.

1 Menu bar with **Format–Layer** and:

prompt   `Layer Properties Manager dialogue box`

respond   either 1) pick New

           or   2) right-click the mouse to display the pop-up menu as Fig. 13.6 and pick New Layer

and   Layer1 added to layer list with the same properties as layer 0, i.e. white and continuous

respond   pick New until 7 new layers are added to the layer list, i.e. 8 layers in total, named 0 and layer1–layer7

a) names

respond   1) move pick arrow onto layer1 and pick it – highlighted

          2) pick Show details

          3) at Details, highlight Layer1 name and enter OUT

          4) Layer1 is renamed OUT in the layer list

          5) repeat the above steps and rename layer2-layer7 with the following names:

              layer2: CL   layer3: HID   layer4: DIMS

              layer5: TEXT layer6: SECT   layer7: CONS

b) linetypes

respond   1) pick layer line CL

          2) move pick arrow to Linetype-Continuous and pick it

          3) from the Select Linetype dialogue box, pick CENTER then OK. Note: the linetype CENTER should be loaded from an earlier exercise in this chapter. If it is not, refer back to Linetypes and load the CENTER and HIDDEN linetypes.

          4) pick layer line HID

          5) from the Select Linetype dialogue box, pick HIDDEN then OK

c) colours

respond   1) pick layer line OUT

          2) scroll at Details–Color and pick Red

          3) pick the other layer lines and set the following colours:

          CL: green   HID: yellow   DIMS: magenta

          TEXT: blue   SECT: cyan   CONS: colour to suit.

2 At this stage the Layer Properties Manager dialogue box should resemble Fig. 13.7.

3 Pick OK from the Layer Properties Manager dialogue to save the layers (with linetypes and colours) which have been created.

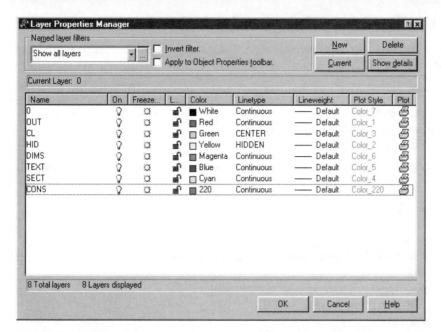

Figure 13.7 Layer Properties Manager dialogue box with created new layers.

The current layer

The current layer is the one on which all objects are drawn. The current layer name appears in the Layer Properties Manager section of the Object Properties toolbar, which is generally docked below the Standard toolbar at the top of the screen. The current layer is also named in the Layer Properties Manager dialogue box when it is activated. The current layer is 'set' by the user.

1   Activate the Layer Properties Manager dialogue box and:
   prompt   `Layer Properties Manager dialogue box`
   with   the layers created earlier displayed in numeric then alphabetical order, i.e. 0, CL, CONS ... TEXT
   respond 1) pick layer line OUT – becomes highlighted
             2) pick Current
             3) pick OK.

2   The drawing screen will be returned, and the Object Properties dialogue box will display OUT with a red box, and ByLayer will also display a red box.

   The Layer Properties Manager dialogue box is used to create new layers with their colours and linetypes. Once created, the current layer can be set:
   a) from the Layer Properties Manager dialogue box
   b) from the Object Properties toolbar by scrolling at the right of the layer name and selecting the name of the layer to be current.

   I generally start a drawing with layer OUT current, but this is a personal preference. Other users may want to start with layer CL or 0 as the current layer, but it does not matter, as long as the objects are eventually 'placed' on their correct layers.

   Having created layers it is now possible to draw objects with different colours and linetypes, simply by altering the current layer. All future work should be completed with layers used correctly, i.e. if text is to be added to a drawing, then the TEXT layer should be current.

Saving the layers to the standard sheet

1 Erase the two lines and circle from the screen, but leave the black border – created as a rectangle on layer 0 in Chapter 8.

2 Use the Layer Properties Manager dialogue box and make layer OUT current.

3 Select one of the following:
   a) the Save icon from the Standard toolbar
   b) menu bar with **File–Save**.

4 This selection will automatically update the **A:A3PAPER** standard sheet drawing opened at the start of the chapter.

5 Menu bar with **File–Save As** and:
   prompt   Save Drawing As dialogue box
   respond 1) scroll at Save as type
              2) pick **AutoCAD Drawing Template File (*.dwt)**
              3) scroll at Save in
              4) pick 3¹/₂ floppy (A) **or** your named folder
              5) enter File name as **A3PAPER**
              6) pick Save
   prompt   Template Description dialogue box
   enter   1) MY A3 TEMPLATE – Fig. 13.8
              2) pick OK.

6 The standard sheet has now been saved with:
   a) units set to metric
   b) sheet size A3
   c) grid, snap, etc. set as required
   d) several new layers
   e) a border effect on layer 0.

7 With the layers having been saved to A:A3PAPER, the layer creation process does not need to be undertaken every time a drawing is started. Additional layers can be added to the standard sheet at any time – the process is fairly easy?

8 The A3PAPER standard sheet has been saved:
   a) as a drawing file with extension .dwg
   b) as a template file with extension .dwt.

9 We will discuss these two file formats in the next chapter.

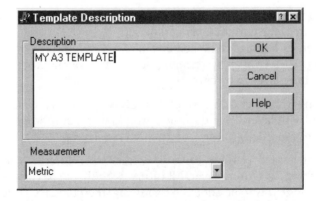

Figure 13.8   Template Description dialogue box.

Layer states

Layers can have four 'states' these being:
a) ON or OFF
b) THAWED or FROZEN
c) LOCKED or UNLOCKED
d) PLOTTABLE or NON-PLOTTABLE.

The layer states are displayed both in the Layer Control box of the Objects Properties dialogue box as well as in the Layer Properties Manager dialogue box itself. In both, the layer states are displayed in icon form. Theses icon states are:
a) yellow – ON, THAWED
b) bluey grey – OFF, FROZEN
c) lock and unlock should be obvious?

Figure 13.9 displays the pull-down icons from the scroll arrow of the Object Properties dialogue box with:
a) layer CL: non-plottable
b) layer HID: frozen
c) layer OUT: current
d) layer SECT: off
e) layer TEXT: locked.

The following exercise will investigate layers:

1　A:A3PAPER on screen with black border and layer Out current?

2　Using the seven layers (our created six and layer 0):
　　a) make each layer current in turn
　　b) draw a 50 radius circle on each layer
　　c) make layer 0 current
　　d) toggle the grid of to display eight coloured circles.

3　The green circle will be displayed with center linetype and the yellow circle with hidden linetype.

4　Activate the Layer Properties Manager dialogue box, activate Show details and:
　　a) pick On/Off icon on CL layer line – highlighted
　　b) note the Details – tick at Off for display
　　c) pick OK – no green circle.

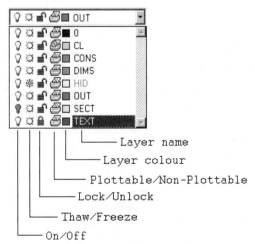

Figure 13.9　Layer state icons.

5 Layer Properties Manager dialogue box and:
   a) pick Freeze/Thaw icon on DIMS layer line – highlighted
   b) note the Details – tick at Freeze in all viewports
   c) pick OK – no magenta circle.

6 Pick the scroll arrow at Layer in Object Properties toolbar and:
   a) note CL and DIMS display information!
   b) pick Lock/Unlock icon on HID layer line – note appearance
   c) left-click to side of pull-down menu
   d) yellow circle still displayed.

7 With the pull-down layer control menu from the Object Properties toolbar:
   a) pick Freeze and Lock icons for SECT
   b) left-click to side
   c) no cyan circle.

8 Using the pull down layer menu:
   a) turn off, freeze and lock the TEXT layer
   b) no blue circle.

9 Activate the Layer Properties Manager dialogue box and:
   a) note the icon display
   b) make layer OUT current
   c) pick Freeze icon
   d) Warning message – **Cannot freeze the current layer**
   e) pick OK
   f) turn layer 0 OFF
   g) Warning message – **The current layer is turned off**
   h) pick OK then OK – no red circle displayed.

10 The screen should now display:
   a) a black circle – drawn on layer 0
   b) a yellow hidden linetype circle – on frozen layer HID
   c) a circle on layer CONS coloured to your own selection.

11 Thus objects will not be displayed if their layer is OFF or FROZEN.

12 Make layer 0 current.

13 Erase the yellow circle – you cannot. The prompt line displays: *1 was on a locked layer*.

14 Draw a line from the centre of the yellow circle to the centre of the black circle. You can reference the yellow circle, although it is on a locked layer.

15 *a*) Make layer OUT current
   b) warning message? – pick OK
   c) draw a line from 50,50 to 200,200 – no line obviously?

16 Erase the coloured circle on layer CONS then use the Layer Properties Manager dialogue box, investigate the Named layer filters:
   a) Show all layers – 8 displayed
   b) show all used layers – 7 displayed – no CONS layer
   c) show all Xref dependent layers – 0 layers displayed
   d) display Show all layers then pick OK.

17 With the Layer Properties Manager dialogue box:
   a) all layers to be – ON, THAWED and UNLOCKED
   b) 7 circles and 2 lines displayed – CONS circle was erased.

18 The layer states can be activated using the Layer Properties Manager dialogue box, or the Object Properties pull-down menu.

The Object Properties toolbar

The Object Properties toolbar is generally displayed at all times and is usually docked below the Standard toolbar at the top of the drawing screen under the title bar. This toolbar gives information about layers and their states, and Fig. 13.10 displays the complete toolbar details for our A3PAPER standard sheet. The various 'areas' of the toolbar are:

a) Make Object's Layer Current icon. When this icon is selected:
  prompt Select object whose layer will become current
  respond **pick the green circle**
  prompt CL is now the current layer
  and   CL (green) displayed in the Object Properties toolbar.
b) Layers icon. Selecting this icon will display the Layer Properties Manager dialogue box,
  i.e. an alternative to the menu bar selection Format–Layer.
c) Pull-down layer information. Allows the user to quickly set a new current layer, or activate one of the layer states, e.g. off, freeze, lock, etc.
d) Color control. By scrolling at the colour control arrow, the user can select one of the standard colours. By selecting *Other* from the colour pull-down menu, the Select Color dialogue box is displayed allowing access to all colours available in AutoCAD. Selecting a colour by this method will allow objects to be drawn with that colour, irrespective of the current layer colour. This is not recommended but may be useful on certain occasions.
e) Linetype control. Similar to colour control, the scroll arrow display all linetypes loaded in the current drawing. By selecting *Other* the Linetype Manager dialogue box will be displayed, allowing the user to load any other linetype from a named file – usually **acadiso.lin**. By selecting a linetype from the pull down menu, the user can create objects with this linetype, independent of the current layer linetype. Again this is not recommended. Layers should be used to display a certain linetype, but it may be useful to have different linetypes displayed an the one layer occasionally.
f) Lineweight control. Lineweight allows objects to be displayed (and plotted) with different thicknesses from 0 to 2.11 mm and the lineweight control scroll arrow allows the user to select the required thickness. We will be investigating this topic in greater detail in a later chapter, and will not discuss at this stage.

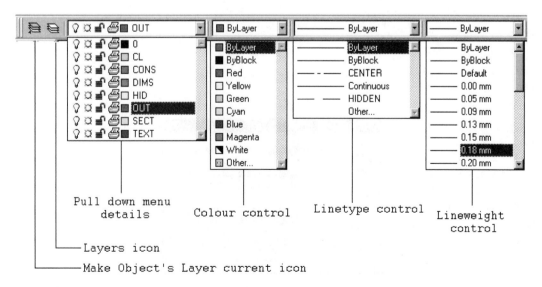

Figure 13.10 The Object Properties toolbar information.

Renaming and deleting layers

Unwanted or wrongly named layers can easily be deleted or renamed in AutoCAD Release 2000.

1　Still have the A3PAPER drawing on the screen with seven coloured circles (the circle on layer CONS was erased) and two lines.

2　Make layer OUT current.

3　Activate the Layer Properties Manager dialogue box by picking the Layer icon from the Object Properties toolbar and:
a) pick New twice to add two new layers to the list – Layer1 and Layer2
b) rename Layer1 as NEW1 and Layer2 as NEW2
c) pick **Show all used layers** and CONS, NEW1 and NEW2 will not be listed
d) pick **Show all layers** then pick OK.

4　Making each new layer current in turn, draw a circle anywhere on the screen on each new layer.

5　Make layer OUT current.

6　*a*) Activate the Layer Properties Manager dialogue box and:
　　respond　**pick NEW1 layer line then Delete**
　　prompt　AutoCAD message – The selected layer was not deleted
b) Pick OK from this message box (Fig. 13.11) then pick OK from the Layer Properties Manager dialogue box.

7　*a*) Erase the two added circles
b) activate the Layer Properties Manager dialogue box
c) pick NEW1–Delete
d) pick NEW2–Delete.

This completes this chapter, so exit AutoCAD (do **not** save changes). Hopefully your A:A3PAPER standard sheet was saved with the layers and border earlier in the chapter?

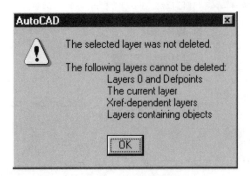

Figure 13.11　The Layer warning dialogue box.

Assignment

There is no activity specific to layers, but all future drawings will be started with the A:A3PAPER drawing or the A:A3PAPER template, both of which were created with layers during this chapter. More of this in the next chapter.

Summary

1 Layers are one of the most important concept in AutoCAD. Perhaps even the most important?

2 Layers allow objects to be created with different colours and linetypes.

3 Layers are created using the Layer Properties Manager dialogue box – often called layer control.

4 There are 255 colours available, but the seven Standard colours should be sufficient for most users' needs.

5 Linetypes are loaded by the user as required.

6 Layers saved to a standard sheet need only be created once.

7 New layers can easily be added as and when required.

8 Layer states are:
   ON: all objects are displayed and can be modified
   OFF: objects are not displayed
   FREEZE: similar to OFF, but allows faster regeneration of screen
   THAW: undoes a frozen layer
   LOCK: objects are displayed but **cannot** be modified
   UNLOCK: undoes a locked layer
   PLOTTABLE: layers will be plotted
   NON-PLOTTABLE: layers with this active will not be plotted.

9 Layer states are displayed and activated in icon form from the Layer Properties Manager dialogue box or using Layer Control from the Object Properties toolbar.

10 Care must be taken when modifying a drawing with layers which are turned off or frozen. More on this later.

11 Layers can be renamed at any time.

12 Unused layers can be deleted at any time.

Chapter 14

User exercise 1

By now you should have the confidence and ability to create line and circle objects by various methods, e.g. coordinate entry, referencing existing objects, etc.

Before proceeding to other draw and modify commands, we will create a working drawing which will be used to introduce several new concepts, as well as reinforcing your existing draughting skills. The exercise will also demonstrate how:

a) to open a drawing or a template
b) a 'new' drawing can be created from an existing standard sheet.

1   A) *Using the A3PAPER drawing*
      Start AutoCAD and:

   prompt   Startup dialogue box
   respond   1) select Open a Drawing icon
                2) pick A3PAPER.dwg
                3) pick OK
   and   the standard sheet is displayed with the black border and layer OUT current.
   respond   now exit AutoCAD.

   B) *Using the A3PAPER template*
      Start AutoCAD and:

   prompt   Startup dialogue box
   respond   1) pick Use a Template icon
                2) pick Browse
   prompt   Select a template file dialogue box
   respond: *a*) scroll and pick 3^1/$_2$ floppy (A:) or your named folder
                b) pick A3PAPER
                c) pick Open
   and   the A3 standard sheet is displayed with layer OUT current.

   C) *Note*:   *a*) whether the A3PAPER drawing or the A3PAPER template is opened, both
                   methods will display the standard sheet with the layers created from the
                   previous chapter. The difference is noticed when the completed drawing is
                   to be saved
                b) now continue with the exercise with the A3PAPER template opened.

2   Refer to Fig. 14.1 and:
      a) draw full size the component given. Only layer OUT is used
      b) a start point is given – **use it, as it is important**
      c) *do not attempt to add the dimensions*
      d) use absolute coordinates for the start point then relative coordinates for the outline
      e) use absolute coordinates for the circle centres – some 'sums' needed!

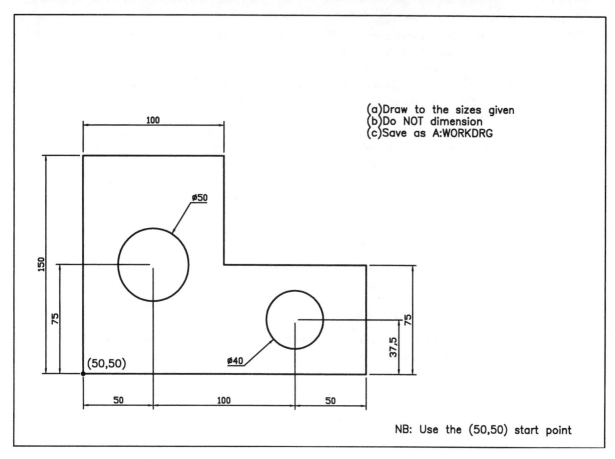

Figure 14.1 User exercise 1.

3 When the drawing is complete, select either (a) or (b) following:
  a) if you opened A3PAPER template file
  Menu bar with **File–Save As** and:
  prompt   Save Drawing As dialogue box
  with   File name: Drawing1 (or similar) but NOT A3PAPER
  respond 1) ensure A: (or named folder) is current
          2) enter file name as: **WORKDRG**
          3) pick Save.
  b) If you opened A3PAPER drawing file
    Menu bar with **File–Save As** and:
    prompt Save Drawing As dialogue box
    with   File name: A3PAPER
    respond 1) ensure A: (or named folder) is current
           2) alter file name to: **WORKDRG**
           3) pick Save.

4 Either method (3a or 3b) will have saved the drawing with the file name **A:WORKDRG**.

5 *Opening a template vs Opening a drawing*
Whether to open a template file or a drawing file is always something of a worry to new AutoCAD users. As we saved our A3PAPER as both a template file and a drawing file, there would appear to be no difference when the standard sheet was displayed on the screen. The main difference is when a completed drawing is to be saved. When the **File–Save As** sequence is activated from the menu bar, the Save Drawing As dialogue box is displayed and if:

a) template opened: the file name is Drawing1 or similar but is not A3PAPER and the user can enter a new file name (always recommended) if required. The original A3PAPER template file remains 'untouched', i.e. is not affected by the drawing which has just been completed

b) drawing opened: the file name is A3PAPER and the user **must** enter a new file name. If a new name is not entered, the drawing which has just been completed will be saved as A3PAPER overwriting the existing A3PAPER drawing. This could result in information being 'lost' from the standard sheet.

6 It is user preference as to whether to open the A3PAPER template or drawing file with a new exercise/activity. Opening a template is probably 'more technically correct' but the decision is yours. I will generally open the A3PAPER template file but will still start some exercises with the A3PAPER drawing file.

Hopefully you now understand the template/drawing file difference and are now ready to investigate other draw and modify commands.

Chapter 15

Fillet and chamfer

In this chapter we will investigate how the fillet and chamfer commands can be used to modify an existing drawing. Both commands can be activated by icon, menu bar selection or keyboard entry.

1 Open the **A:WORKDRG** created in the previous chapter.

2 Ensure layer OUT is current and display the Draw and Modify toolbars.

3 Refer to Fig. 15.1.

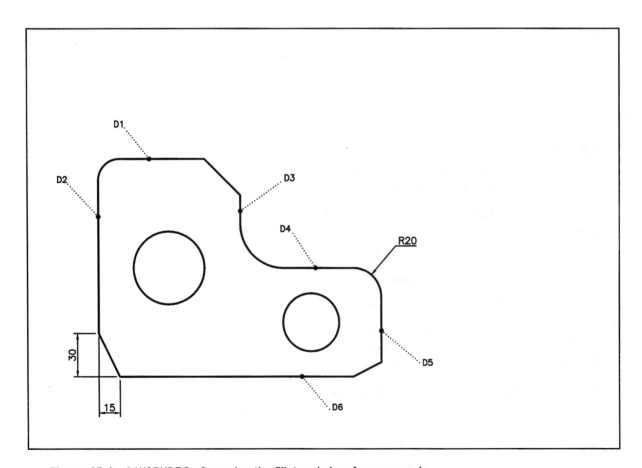

Figure 15.1   A:WORKDRG after using the fillet and chamfer commands.

Fillet

A fillet is a radius added to existing line/arc/circle objects. The fillet radius must be specified before the objects to be filleted can be selected.

1 Select the FILLET icon from the Modify toolbar and:
   prompt   Current settings: MODE=TRIM, Radius=??
               Select first object or [Polyline/Radius/Trim]
   enter   **R <R>** – the radius option
   prompt   Specify fillet radius<??>
   enter   **15 <R>**.

2 Right-click the mouse and pick Repeat Fillet to re-activate the fillet command and:
   prompt   Select first object
   respond **pick line D1**
   prompt   Specify second line
   respond **pick line D2**.

3 The corner selected will be filleted with a radius of 15, and the two 'unwanted line portions' will be erased.

4 From the menu bar select **Modify–Fillet** and:
   prompt   Select first object or...
   enter   **R <R>** – the radius option
   prompt   Specify fillet radius<15.00>
   enter   **30 <R>**.

5 Right-click and activate the fillet command and:
   prompt   Select first object and: **pick line D3**
   prompt   Select second object and: **pick line D4**.

6 At the command line enter **FILLET <R>** and:
   a) set the fillet radius to 20
   b) fillet the corner indicated.

Chamfer

A chamfer is a straight 'cut corner' added to existing line objects. The chamfer distances must be 'set' prior to selecting the object to be chamfered.

1 Select the CHAMFER icon from the Modify toolbar and:
   prompt   (TRIM mode) Current chamfer Dist1=?? Dist2=??
               Select first line or [Polyline/Distance/Angle/Trim/
               Method]
   enter   **D <R>** – the Distance option
   prompt   Specify first chamfer distance<??> and enter: **25 <R>**
   prompt   Specify second chamfer distance<25.00> and enter: **25 <R>**.

2 Right-click to repeat the Chamfer command and:
   prompt   Select first line and: **pick line D1**
   prompt   Select second line and: **pick line D3**.

3 The selected corner will be chamfered and the unwanted line portions removed.

4 Menu bar selection with **Modify–Chamfer** and:
prompt   `Select first line or...`
enter   **D <R>**
prompt   `Specify first chamfer distance` and enter: **10 <R>**
prompt   `Specify second chamfer distance` and enter: **20 <R>**.

5 Right-click to repeat the Fillet command and:
prompt   `Select first line` and: **pick line D5**
prompt   `Select second line` and: **pick line D6**.

Note that the pick order is important when the chamfer distances are different. The first line picked will have the first chamfer distance set.

6 At the command line enter **CHAMFER <R>** and:
a) set first chamfer distance: 15
b) set second chamfer distance: 30
c) chamfer the corner indicated.

Saving

When the three fillets and three chamfers have been added to the component, save it as **A:WORKDRG**.

Error messages

The fillet and chamfer commands are generally used without any problems, but the following error messages may be displayed at the command prompt:

1 Radius is too large.

2 Distance is too large.

3 Chamfer requires 2 lines (not arc segments).

4 No valid fillet with radius ??

5 Lines are parallel – chamfer error.

These error messages should be self-evident(?).

Fillet and chamfer options

Although simple to use, the fillet and chamfer commands have several options. It is in your own interest to attempt the following exercises, so:

1 Erase all objects from the screen but ensure A:WORKDRG has been saved.

2 Refer to Fig. 15.2.

3 *Fillet/Chamfer with inclined lines.*
 Our working drawing demonstrated the fillet and chamfer commands with lines which were at right angles to each other. This was not deliberate – just the way the component was drawn. Draw three to four inclined lines then use the fillet and chamfer commands. You only have to be careful with the fillet radius and chamfer distance values entered. The effect is displayed:
 a) fillet effect – fig. (a)
 b) chamfer effect – fig. (b).

4 Both commands have a Polyline option. This will be covered after we have investigated the polyline command.

5 The commands have a TRIM option and the effect is displayed in fig. (c). The option is obtained by entering **T <R>** at the prompt line and:
 prompt Enter trim mode option [Trim/No Trim]<Trim>
 enter   *a*) T: corner removed. This is the default
       b) N: corners not removed.

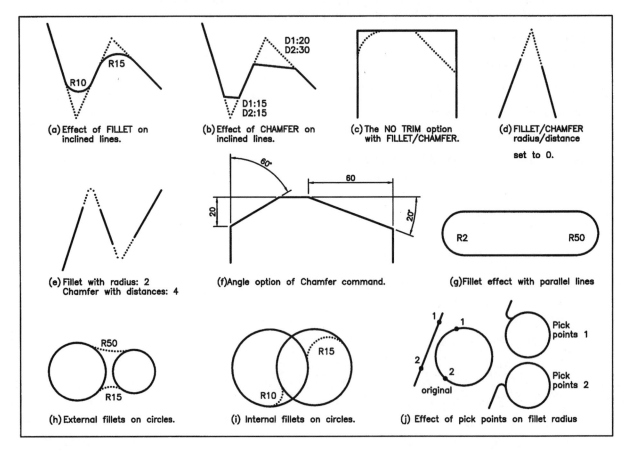

Figure 15.2 The fillet and chamfer options.

6 The two commands can be used to extend two inclined lines to a point – fig. (d) – if:
   a) the fillet radius is set to 0
   b) both chamfer distances are set to 0.

7 Chamfer with one distance set to 20 and the other set to 0. Think about this!

8 Interesting effect with inclined lines if the fillet radius and the chamfer distances are 'small'. The lines are extended if required, and the fillet/chamfer effect 'added at the ends' as displayed in fig. (e).

9 Chamfer has an angle option and when the command is selected:
   prompt Select first line or [Polyline/Distance/Angle/Trim/ Method]
   enter **A <R>** – the angle option
   prompt Specify chamfer length on the first line and enter: **20<R>**
   prompt Specify chamfer angle from the first line and enter: **60<R>**.

   The required lines can now be chamfered as fig. (f) which displays:
   a) length of 20 and angle of 60
   b) length of 60 and angle of 20.

10 The fillet command can be used with parallel lines, the effect being to add 'an arc' to the ends selected. This arc is added independent of the set fillet radius as fig. (g) demonstrates. The fillet radius was set to 2 and 50, but the added 'arc' is the same at both ends.

11 Circles can be filleted:
   a) externally as fig. (h)
   b) internally as fig. (i).

12 Circles cannot be chamfered. If any circle is selected:
   prompt Chamfer requires 2 lines (not arc segments).

13 Lines–circles–arcs can be filleted, but the position of the pick points is important as displayed in fig. (j).

14 Chamfer has a Method option and when **M** is entered:
   prompt Enter trim method [Distance/Angle]
   and *a*) entering **D** sets the two distance method – the default
         b) entering **A** sets the length and angle method.

Summary

1 FILLET and CHAMFER are Modify commands, activated from the menu bar, by icon selection or by keyboard entry.

2 Both commands require the radius/distances to be set before they can be used.

3 When values are entered, they become the defaults until altered by the user.

4 Lines, arcs and circles can be filleted.

5 Only lines can be chamfered.

6 A fillet/chamfer value of 0 is useful for extending two inclined lines.

7 Both commands have several useful options.

Chapter 16

Offset, extend, trim and change commands

In this chapter we will investigate OFFSET, EXTEND and TRIM – three of the most commonly used draughting commands. We will also investigate the CHANGE command as well the LTSCALE system variable.

To demonstrate these new commands:

1 Open A:WORKDRG – easy by now?

2 Ensure layer OUT is current and display the Draw and Modify toolbars.

Offset

The offset command allows to user to draw objects parallel to other selected objects and lines, circles and arcs can all be offset. The user specifies:
a) an offset distance
b) the side to offset the selected object.

1 Refer to Fig. 16.1.

2 Select the OFFSET icon from the Modify toolbar and:

prompt	Specify offset distance or [Through]
enter	**50 <R>** – the offset distance
prompt	Select object to offset or <exit>
respond	**pick line D1**
prompt	Specify point on side to offset
respond	**pick any point to right of line D1 as indicated**
and	line D1 will be offset by 50 units to right
prompt	Select object to offset, i.e. any more 50 offsets
respond	**pick line D2**
prompt	Specify a point on side to offset
respond	**pick any point to left of line D2 as indicated**
and	line D2 will be offset 50 units to left
prompt	Select object to offset, i.e. any more 50 offsets
respond	**right-click** to end command.

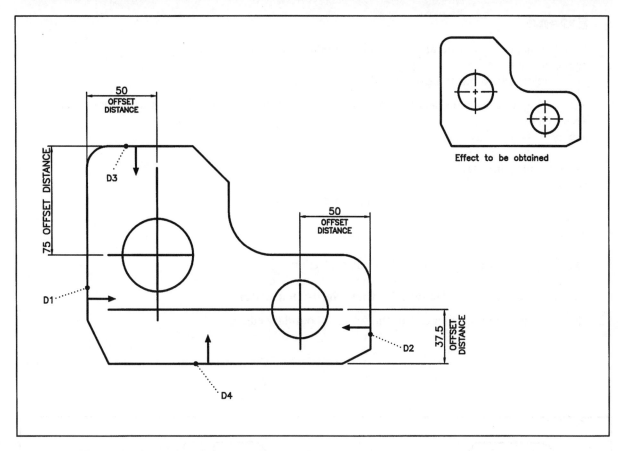

Figure 16.1 A:WORKDRG after the OFFSET command.

3 Menu bar with **Modify–Offset** and:
   prompt Specify offset distance or [Through]<50.00>
   enter **75 <R>**
   prompt Select object to offset and **pick line D3**
   prompt Specify a point on side to offset and **pick as indicated**.

4 At the command line enter **OFFSET <R>** and:
   a) set an offset distance of 37.5
   b) offset line D4 as indicated.

5 We have now created centre lines (of a sort) through the two circles. Later in the chapter we will investigate how these lines can be modified to be 'real centre lines'.

6 Continue to the next part of the exercise.

Extend

This command will extend an object 'to a boundary edge', the user specifying:

a) the actual boundary – an object

b) the object which has to be extended.

1 Refer to Fig. 16.2(a) and select the EXTEND icon from the Modify toolbar and with the SNAP OFF:

prompt	Select boundary edges ...
	Select objects
respond	**pick line D1**
prompt	1 found
	Select objects, i.e. any more boundary edges
respond	**pick line D2**
prompt	1 found, 2 total
	Select objects
respond	**right-click** to end boundary edge selection
prompt	Select object to extend or [Project/Edge/Undo]
respond	**pick lines D3, D4 and D5 then right-click-Enter**.

2 The three lines will be extended to the selected boundary edges.

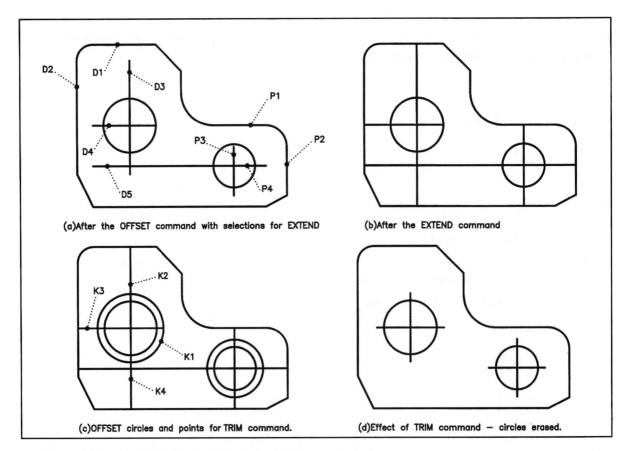

(a)After the OFFSET command with selections for EXTEND

(b)After the EXTEND command

(c)OFFSET circles and points for TRIM command.

(d)Effect of TRIM command – circles erased.

Figure 16.2 A:WORKDRG with EXTEND and TRIM commands.

3 From the menu bar select **Modify–Extend** and:
   prompt   Select objects, i.e. the boundary edges
   respond **pick lines P1 and P2 then right-click**
   prompt   Select object to extend
   respond **pick lines P3 and P4 then right-click–Enter**.

4 At the command line enter **EXTEND <R>** and extend the two vertical 'centre lines' to lower horizontal outline.

5 When complete, the drawing should resemble Fig. 16.2(b).

Trim

Allows the user to trim an object 'at a cutting edge', the user specifying:
a) the cutting edge – an object
b) the object to be trimmed.

1 Refer to Fig. 16.2(c)and OFFSET the two circles for a distance of 5 'outwards' – easy?

2 Extend the top horizontal 'circle centre line' to the offset circle – should be obvious?

3 Select the TRIM icon from the Modify toolbar and:
   prompt   Select cutting edges...
                Select objects
   respond **pick circle K1 then right-click**
   prompt   Select object to trim or [Project/Edge/Undo]...
   respond **pick lines K2, K3 and K4 then right-click–Enter**

4 From menu bar select **Modify–Trim** and:
   prompt   Select objects, i.e. the cutting edge
   respond **pick the other offset circle then right-click**
   prompt   Select object to trim
   respond **pick four circle centre lines then right-click**.

5 Now have 'neat centre lines' as Fig. 16.2(d).

6 At this stage select the Save icon from the Standard toolbar to automatically update A:WORKDRG. We will recall it shortly.

Additional exercises

Offset, extend and trim are powerful commands and can be used very easily. To demonstrate some additional uses for the commands:

1 Erase all objects from the screen – have you saved?

2 Refer to Fig. 16.3 and attempt the exercise which follows.

3 *Offset for circle centre point.*
Using OFFSET to obtain a circle centre point is one of the most common uses for the command. Figure 16.3(a) demonstrates offsets of 18.5 horizontally and 27.8 vertically to position the circle centre point.

Question: what about inclined line offsets?

4 *Offset through.*
This is a very useful option of the command, as it allows an object to be offset through a specified point. When the command is activated:

prompt	Specify offset distance or [Through]
enter	**T <R>** – the through option
prompt	Select object to offset
respond	**pick the required object, e.g. a line**
prompt	Specify through point
respond	**Snap to Center icon and pick the circle**

The line will be offset through the circle centre – fig. (b).

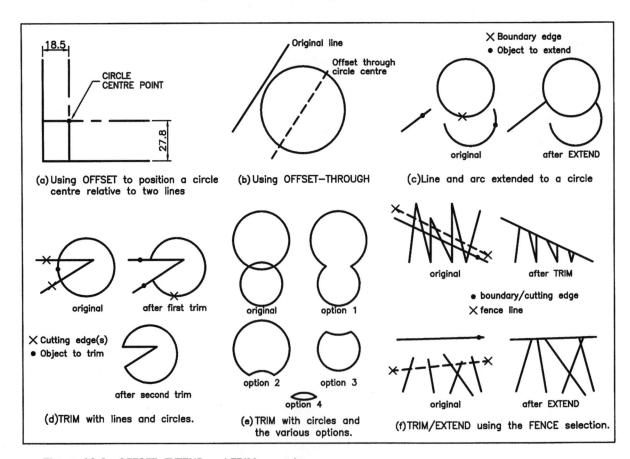

(a) Using OFFSET to position a circle centre relative to two lines

(b) Using OFFSET–THROUGH

(c) Line and arc extended to a circle

(d) TRIM with lines and circles.

(e) TRIM with circles and the various options.

(f) TRIM/EXTEND using the FENCE selection.

Figure 16.3 OFFSET, EXTEND and TRIM examples.

5 *Extending lines and arcs.*
Lines and arcs can be extended to other objects, including circles – fig.(c).

6 *Trim lines and circles.*
Lines, circles and arcs can be trimmed to 'each other' and fig.(d) demonstrates trimming lines with a circle.

7 *Trimming circles.*
Circles can be trimmed to each other, but the selected objects to be trimmed can give different effects. Can you obtain the options in fig.(e)?

8 *Trim/Extend with a fence selection.*
When several objects have to be trimmed or extended, the fence selection option can be used – fig.(f). The effect is achieved by:
a) activating the command
b) selecting the boundary (extend) or cutting edge (trim)
c) entering **F <R>** – the fence option
d) draw the fence line then right-click.

9 These exercise do not need to be saved.

Changing the offset centre lines

The WORKDRG drawing was saved with 'centre lines' obtained using the offset, extend and trim commands. These lines pass through the two circle centres, but they are continuous lines and not centre lines. We will modify these lines to be centre lines using the CHANGE command. This command will be fully investigated in a later chapter, but for now:

1 Re-open A:WORKDRG saved earlier in this chapter.

2 At the command line enter **CHANGE <R>** and:
prompt Select objects
respond **pick the four offset centre lines then right-click**
prompt Specify change point or [Properties]
enter **P <R>** – the properties option
prompt Enter property to change [Color/Elev/LAyer/LType/ltScale/LWeight/Thickness]
enter **LA <R>** – the layer option
prompt Enter new layer name<OUT>
enter **CL <R>**
prompt Enter property to change, i.e. any more?
respond **right-click–Enter** to end command.

3 The four selected lines will be displayed as green centre lines, as they were changed to the CL layer. This layer was made with centre linetype and colour green. Confirm with Format–Layer if you are not convinced!

4 Although the changed lines are centre lines, their 'appearance' may not be ideal and an additional command is required to 'optimize' the centre line effect. This command is LTSCALE.

5 The CHANGE command will be investigated in more detail in a later chapter.

LTSCALE

LTSCALE is a system variable used to 'alter the appearance' of non-continuous lines on the screen. It has a default value of 1.0 and this value is altered by the user to 'optimize' centre lines, hidden lines, etc. To demonstrate its use:

1 At the command line enter **LTSCALE <R>** and:
   prompt   Enter new linetype scale factor<1.0000>
   enter   **0.6 <R>**.

2 The four centre lines should now be 'better defined'.

3 The value of LTSCALE entered depends on the type of lines being used in a drawing, and can be further refined – more on this in a later chapter.

4 Try other LTSCALE values until you are satisfied with the appearance of the four centre lines, then save the drawing as **A:WORKDRG**.

5 *Note*:
   a) LTSCALE must be entered from the command line. There is no icon or menu bar sequence for it
   b) the LTSCALE system variable is **global**. This means that when its value is altered, all linetypes (centre, hidden, etc.) will automatically be altered to the new value. In a later chapter we will discover how this can be 'overcome'.

Question

In our offset exercise we obtained four circle centre lines using the offset command. These lines were then changed to the CL layer to display then as 'real centre lines'.

The question I am repeatedly asked by new AutoCAD users is: **'Why not use offset with the CL layer current?'** This question is reasonable so:

1 A:WORKDRG still on the screen?

2 Make layer CL current.

3 Set an offset distance of 30 and offset:
   a) any red perimeter line
   b) any green centre line.

4 The effect of the offset command is:
   a) the offset red outline is a red outline
   b) the offset green centre line is a green centre line.

5 The offset command will offset an object 'as it was drawn' and is independent of the current layer.

Assignment

It is now some time since you have attempted any activities on your own. Refer to the Activity 5 drawing and create the two template shapes as given. Use the commands already investigated and make particular use of FILLET, CHAMFER, OFFSET and TRIM as much as possible. **Do not attempt to add dimensions**.

Start with your A:A3PAPER template file and save the completed drawing as A:ACT5.

Summary

1 OFFSET, TRIM and EXTEND are modify commands and can be activated by icon select, from the menu bar or by keyboard entry.

2 Lines, arcs and circles can be offset by:
a) entering an offset distance and selecting the object
b) selecting an object to offset through a specific point.

3 Extend requires:
a) a boundary edge
b) objects to be extended.

4 Trim requires:
a) a cutting edge
b) objects to be trimmed.

5 Lines and arcs can be extended to other lines, arcs and circles

6 Lines, circles and arcs can be trimmed.

Chapter 17

User exercise 2

In this chapter we will create another working drawing using previous commands, save it and then list all drawings which have so far been completed.

1 Open your A:A3PAPER template file standard sheet with layer OUT current and display the Draw and Modify toolbars.

2 Refer to Fig. 17.1 and complete the drawing using:
   a) the basic shape from four lines: **use the 140,100 start point**
   b) three offset lines
   c) four extended lines
   d) trim to give the final shape.

3 When complete save as **A:USEREX**.

4 Do not exit AutoCAD.

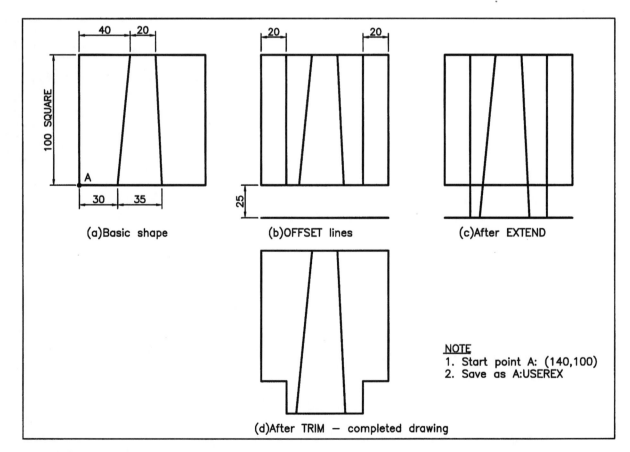

Figure 17.1 A:USEREX construction.

So far, so good

At this stage of our learning process, we have completed the following drawings:

1 A demonstration drawing A:DEMODRG, used in the creation of lines, circles, arcs and for object snap.

2 A standard sheet with layers saved as:
   a) a drawing file A3PAPER.dwg
   b) a template file A3PAPER.dwt.

3 A working drawing A:WORKDRG which was used to demonstrate several new topics. This drawing will still be used to investigate other new topics as they are discussed.

4 A new working drawing A:USEREX, which will also be used to demonstrate new topics.

5 Five activity exercises, ACT1 to ACT5, which you have been completing and saving as the book progresses. Or have you?

And now ...

Proceed to the next chapter in which we will discuss how text can be added to a drawing.

Chapter 18

Text

Text should be added to a drawing whenever possible. This text could simply be a title and date, but could also be a parts list, a company title block, notes on costing, etc. AutoCAD Release 2000 has text suitable for:

a) short entries, i.e. a few lines

b) larger entries, i.e. several lines.

In this chapter we will consider the short entry type text, and leave the other type (multiple line entry) to a later chapter, so:

1 A:USEREX still on the screen? – it should be. If it is not, then open the appropriate drawing file.

2 Make layer Text (blue) current and refer to Fig. 18.1.

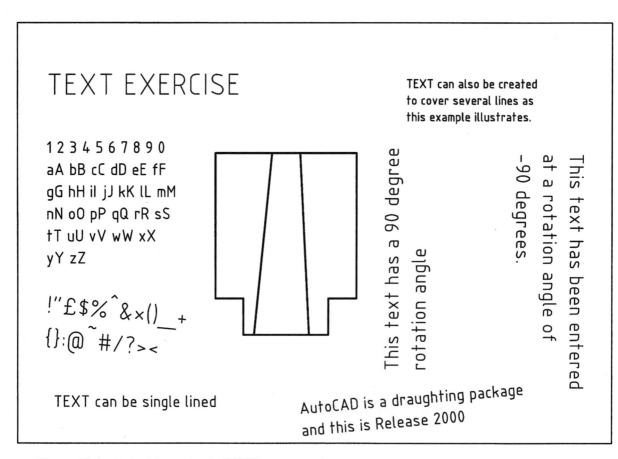

Figure 18.1 Text addition with A:USEREX.

One line of text

1 Menu bar with **Draw–Text–Single line text** and:
   prompt Specify start point of text or [Justify/Style]
   enter   **25,25 <R>**
   prompt Specify height<??> and enter: **8 <R>**
   prompt Specify rotation angle of text<0.0> and enter **0 <R>**
   prompt Enter text
   enter   **TEXT can single lined <R>**
   prompt Enter text
   respond **press the <RETURN> key** to end the command.

2 The entered text item will be displayed at the entered point and must be ended with a return key press.

3 Repeat the Draw–Text–Single line text sequence with:
   a) start point: 20,240
   b) height: 15
   c) rotation: 0
   d) text: TEXT EXRECISE – this misspelling is deliberate!

4 *Note:* the text is displayed on the screen as you enter it from the keyboard. This is *dynamic* text.

Several lines of text

1 Select from the menu bar **Draw–Text–Single Line Text** and:
   prompt Specify start point of text and enter **275,245 <R>** and:
   prompt Specify height and enter **6 <R>**
   prompt Specify rotation angle of text and enter **0 >R>**
   prompt Enter text and enter **TEXT can also be created <R>**
   prompt Enter text and enter **to cover several lines as <R>**
   prompt Enter text and enter **this example illustrates <R>**
   prompt Enter text and respond **<RETURN>**

2 At the command line enter **TEXT <R>** and:
   prompt Specify start point of text and enter **200,20 <R>**
   prompt Specify height and enter **8 <R>**
   prompt Specify rotation angle of text and enter **10 <R>**
   prompt Enter text and enter **AutoCAD is a draughting package<R>**
   prompt Enter text and enter **and this is Release 2000 <R>**
   prompt Enter text and enter **<R>** – to end command.

3 Using the menu bar sequence Draw–Text–Single line text or the command line entry TEXT, add the other items of text shown in Fig. 18.1. The start point and height are at your discretion.

Editing existing screen text

Text can be edited as it is being entered from the keyboard if the user notices the mistake. Screen text that needs to be edited requires a command.

1 From the menu bar select **Modify–Text** and:

prompt `Select an annotation object or [Undo]`
respond **pick the TEXT EXRECISE item**
prompt `Edit Text dialogue box` – Fig. 18.2 with the text phrase highlighted
either 1) retype the phrase correctly then pick OK
or 2) *a*) left-click at right of the text item
        b) backspace to remove error
        c) retype correctly
        d) pick OK
or 3) *a*) move cursor to TEXT EXR|ECISE and left-click
        b) backspace to give TEXT EX|ECISE
        c) move cursor to TEXT EXE|CISE and left-click
        d) enter R to give TEXT EXER|CISE
        e) pick OK
prompt `Select an annotation object`, i.e. any more selections?
respond **right-click and Enter**.

2 The text item will now be displayed correctly.

3 *Note.*
You could always erase the text item and enter it correctly?

4 AutoCAD has a built in spell check which can be activated with the menu bar sequence **Tools–Spelling** and:

prompt `Select object`
respond **pick AutoCAD is a draughting package then right-click**
prompt `Check Spelling dialogue box` as Fig. 18.3
with Current word: draughting
      Suggestion: draught
respond **pick Ignore**
prompt `AutoCAD Message box` as Fig. 18.4
respond pick OK – spell check is complete.

5 Save the screen layout if required, **but not as A:USEREX**.

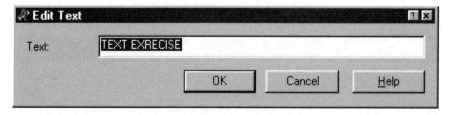

Figure 18.2 Edit Text dialogue box.

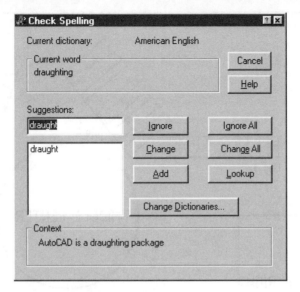

Figure 18.3 Check Spelling dialogue box.

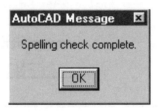

Figure 18.4 AutoCAD Message dialogue box.

Text justification

Text items added to a drawing can be 'justified' (i.e. positioned) in different ways, and Release 2000 has several justification positions, these being:
a) six basic: left, aligned, fitted, centred, middled, right
b) nine additional: TL, TC, TR, ML, MC, MR, BL, BC, BR.

1 Open your A:A3PAPER template file and refer to Fig. 18.5.

2 With layer OUT current, draw the following objects:
   a) a 100 sided square, the lower left point at (50,50)
   b) a circle of radius 50, centred at (270,150)
   c) five lines:
     1) start point: 220,20 end point: 320,20
     2) start point: 220,45 end point: 320,45
     3) start point: 120,190 end point: 200,190
     4) start point: 225,190 end point: 275,250
     5) start point: 305,250 end point: 355,100.

3 Make layer TEXT (blue) current and display the Draw, Modify and Object Snap toolbars.

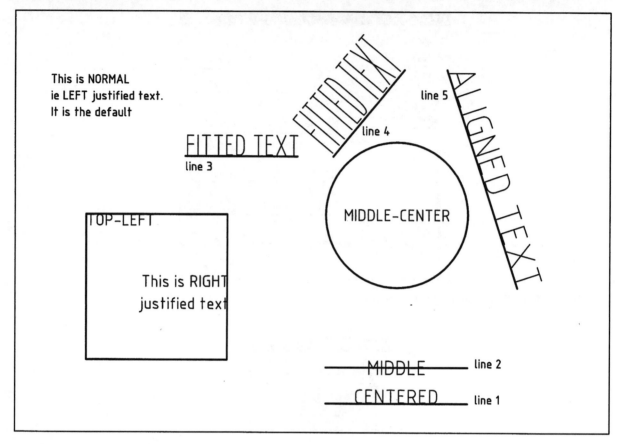

Figure 18.5 Text justification exercise.

4 At the command line enter **TEXT <R>** and:

prompt Specify start point of text or [Justify/Style] and enter **25,240 <R>**

prompt Specify height and enter: **6 <R>**

prompt Specify rotation angle of text and enter **0 <R>**

prompt Enter text and enter **This is NORMAL <R>**

prompt Enter text and enter, i.e. **LEFT justified text. <R>**

prompt Enter text and enter **It is the default <R>**

prompt Enter text and enter **<R>**.

5 Menu bar with **Draw–Text–Single Line Text** and:

prompt Specify start point of text or [Justify/Style]

enter **J <R>** – the justify option

prompt Enter an option [Align/Fit/Center/Middle/Right...

enter **R <R>** – the right justify option

prompt Specify right endpoint of text baseline

respond **Snap to Midpoint icon and pick right vertical line of the square**

prompt Specify height and enter **8 <R>**

prompt Specify rotation angle of text and enter **0 <R>**

prompt Enter text and enter **This is RIGHT <R>**

prompt Enter text and enter **justified text <R> and <R>**.

6 Repeat the single line text command and:
   prompt   `Specify start point of text or [Justify/Style]` and enter **J <R>**
   prompt   `Enter an option [Align/Fit..` and enter **C <R>** – center option
   prompt   `Specify center point of text`
   respond **Snap to Midpoint icon and pick line 1**
   prompt   `Specify height` and enter **10 <R>**
   prompt   `Specify rotation angle of text` and enter: **0 <R>**
   prompt   `Enter text` and enter **CENTERED <R> and <R>**

7 Enter **TEXT <R>** at the command line then:
   a) enter J <R> for justify
   b) enter M <R> for middle option
   c) Middle point: Snap to Midpoint icon and pick line 2
   d) Height: 10 and Rotation: 0
   e) Text: MIDDLE <R><R>

8 Activate the single line text command with the Fit justify option and:
   prompt   `Specify first endpoint of text baseline`
   respond **Snap to Endpoint icon and pick left end of line 3**
   prompt   `Specify second endpoint of text baseline`
   respond **Snap to Endpoint icon and pick right end of line 3**
   prompt   `Specify height` and enter **15 <R>**
   prompt   `Enter text` and enter **FITTED TEXT <R><R>**

   Note: this option has no rotation prompt!

9 Using the TEXT command with the Fit justify option, add the text item FITTED TEXT with a height of 40 to line 4.

10 With TEXT again:

    a) select the Align justify option
    b) pick 'top' of line 5 as first endpoint of text baseline
    c) pick 'bottom' of line 5 as second endpoint of text baseline
    d) text item: ALIGNED TEXT.

    Note: this option has no height or rotation prompt!

11 Activate the single line text command and:
    a) justify with TL option
    b) Top/Left point: snap to Intersection icon of top left of square
    c) Height of 8 and rotation of 0
    d) text item: TOP-LEFT.

12 Finally with the TEXT command and:
    a) justify with MC option
    b) Middle point: Snap to center of circle
    c) height of 8 and rotation of 0
    d) text item: MIDDLE-CENTER.

13 Your drawing should now resemble Fig. 18.3. It can be saved, but we will not use it again.

14 The text justification options are easy to use. Simply enter the appropriate letter for the justification option. The letters used are:

A: Align   F: Fit   C: Center
M: Middle   R: Right   TL: Top left
MC: Middle center   BR: Bottom right   etc., etc.

Text style

When the single line text command is activated, one of the options available is *Style*. This option allows the user to select any one of several previously created text styles. This will be discussed in a later chapter which will investigate text styles and fonts.

Assignment

Attempt Activity 6 which has four simple components for you to complete. Text should be added, but not dimensions.

The procedure is:

1 Open A:A3PAPER template file.

2 Complete the drawings using layers correctly.

3 Save as A:ACT6.

4 Read the summary then progress to the next chapter.

Summary

1 Text is a draw command which allows a single or several lines of text to be entered from the keyboard.

2 The command is activated:
   a) from the keyboard with TEXT <R>
   b) from the menu bar with Draw–Text–Single line text.

3 The entered text is dynamic, i.e. the user 'sees' the text on the screen as it is entered from the keyboard.

4 Text can be entered with varying height and rotation angle.

5 Text can be justified to user specifications, and there are 15 justification options.

6 Screen text can be modified with:
   a) menu bar Modify–Text
   b) keyboard entry: DDEDIT.

7 Fitted and aligned text are similar, the user selecting both the start and end points of the text item, but:
   a) fitted: allows the user to enter a text height
   b) aligned: text is automatically 'adjusted' to suit the selected points
   c) neither has a rotation option.

8 Centered and middled text are similar, the user selecting the center/middle point, but:
   a) centered: is about the text baseline
   b) middled: is about the text middle point.

9 *a*) Text styles can be set by the user
   b) multiple line (or paragraph) text can be set by the user.

These two topics will be investigated in later chapters.

Chapter 19

Dimensioning

AutoCAD has both automatic and associative dimensioning, the terms meaning:

Automatic: when an object to be dimensioned is selected, the actual dimension text, arrows, extension lines, etc. are added.

Associative: the arrows, extension lines, dimension text, etc. which 'make up' a dimension are treated as a single object.

AutoCAD has different 'types' of dimensions which can be added to a drawing these being:

1 Linear: horizontal, vertical and aligned.

2 Baseline and Continue.

3 Ordinate: both X- and Y-datum.

4 Angular.

5 Radial: diameter and radius.

6 Leader: taking the dimension text 'outside' the object.

Figure 19.1 displays the different dimension types.

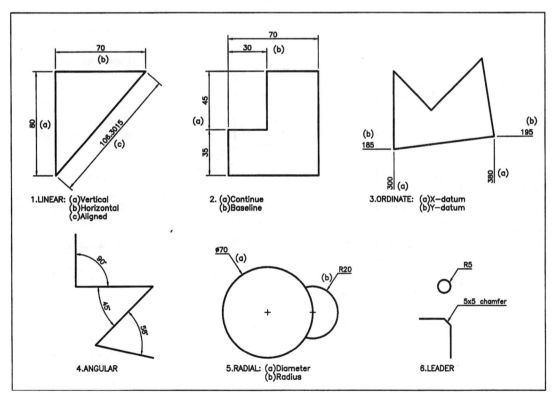

Figure 19.1 Dimension types.

Dimension exercise

To demonstrate how dimensions are added to a drawing, we will use one of our working drawings, so:

1 Open A:USEREX and with layer OUT current add the following three circles:
   a) centre: 220,180, radius: 15
   b) centre: 220,115, radius: 3
   c) centre: 190,75, radius: 30
   d) trim the large circle to the line as Fig. 19.2.

2 Make layer DIMS current and activate the Object Snap and Dimension toolbars.

3 From the Dimension toolbar, scroll at the Dim Style Control icon and pick ISO_25. This will be the dimension style which will be used with the added dimensions.

Linear dimensioning

1 Select the LINEAR DIMENSION icon from the Dimension toolbar and:
   prompt   Specify first extension line origin or <select object>
   respond **Endpoint icon and pick line D1**
   prompt   Specify second extension line origin
   respond **Endpoint icon and pick the other end of line D1**
   prompt   Specify dimension line location or [Mtext/Text...
   respond **pick any point to the left of line D1**.

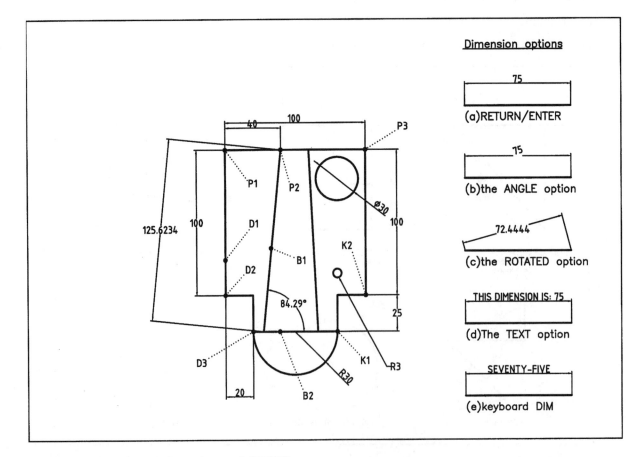

Figure 19.2 Adding dimensions to A:USEREX.

2 From the menu bar select **Dimension–Linear** and:
prompt   Specify first extension line origin or <select object>
respond **Intersection icon and pick point D2**
prompt   Specify second extension line origin
respond **Intersection icon and pick point D3**
prompt   Specify dimension line location or...
respond **pick any point below object.**

Baseline dimensioning

1 Select the LINEAR DIMENSION icon and:
prompt   Specify first extension line origin
respond **Intersection icon and pick point P1**
prompt   Specify second extension line origin
respond **Intersection icon and pick point P2**
prompt   Specify dimension line location
respond **pick any point above the line.**

2 Select the BASELINE DIMENSION icon from the Dimension toolbar and:
prompt   Specify a second extension line origin
respond **Intersection icon and pick point P3**
prompt   Specify a second extension line origin
respond **press the ESC key** to end command.

3 The menu bar selection Dimension–Baseline could have been selected for step 2.

Continue dimensioning

1 Select the LINEAR DIMENSION icon and:
prompt   Specify first extension line origin
respond **Intersection icon and pick point K1**
prompt   Specify second extension line origin
respond **Intersection icon and pick point K2**
prompt   Specify dimension line location
respond **pick any point to right of the line.**

2 Menu bar with **Dimension–Continue** and:
prompt   Specify a second extension line origin
respond **Intersection icon and pick point P3**
prompt   Specify a second extension line origin
respond **press ESC.**

3 The menu bar selection Dimension–Continue could have been selected for step 2.

Diameter dimensioning

Select the DIAMETER DIMENSION icon from the Dimension toolbar and:
prompt   Select arc or circle
respond **pick the larger circle**
prompt   Specify dimension line location
respond **pick a suitable point.**

Radius dimensioning

Select the RADIUS DIMENSION icon and:

prompt	Select arc or circle
respond	**pick the arc**
prompt	Specify dimension line location
respond	**pick a suitable point**.

Angular dimensioning

Select the ANGULAR DIMENSION icon and:

prompt	Select arc, circle, line or...
respond	**pick line B1**
prompt	Select second line
respond	**pick line B2**
prompt	Specify dimension arc line location
respond	**pick a point to suit**.

Aligned dimensioning

Select the ALIGNED DIMENSION icon and:

prompt	Specify first extension line origin
respond	**Endpoint icon and pick line B1**
prompt	Specify second extension line origin
respond	**Endpoint icon and pick other end of line B1**
prompt	Specify dimension line location
respond	**pick any point to suit**.

Leader dimensioning

Select the LEADER DIMENSION icon and:

prompt	Specify first leader point
respond	**Nearest icon and pick any point on smaller circle**
prompt	Specify next point
respond	**drag to a suitable point and pick**
prompt	Specify next point
respond	**right-click**
prompt	Enter text width and: **right-click**
prompt	Enter first line of annotation text
enter	**R3 <R>**
prompt	Enter next line of annotation text
respond	**right-click** to end leader dimension command.

Dimension options

When using the dimension commands, the user may be aware of various options when the prompts are displayed. To investigate these options:

1 Make layer OUT current and draw five horizontal lines of length 75 at the right-side of the screen then make layer DIMS current.

2 *The RETURN option.*
Select the LINEAR DIMENSION icon and:
prompt Specify first extension line origin or <select object>
respond **press the RETURN/ENTER key**
prompt Select object to dimension
respond **pick the top line**
prompt Specify dimension line location
respond **pick above the line** – fig. (a).

3 *The ANGLE option.*
Select the LINEAR DIMENSION icon, press RETURN, pick the second top line and:
prompt Specify dimension line location
and [Mtext/Text/Angle...
enter **A <R>** – the angle option
prompt Specify angle of dimension text
enter **15 <R>**
prompt Specify dimension line location
respond **pick above the line** – fig. (b).

4 *The ROTATED option.*
LINEAR icon, right-click, pick third line and:
prompt Specify dimension line location
enter **R <R>** – the rotated option
prompt Specify angle of dimension line<0>
enter **15 <R>**
prompt Specify dimension line location
respond **pick above the line** – fig. (c).

5 *The TEXT option.*
LINEAR icon, right-click, pick the fourth line and:
prompt Specify dimension line location
enter **T <R>** – the text option
prompt Enter dimension text<75>
enter **THIS DIMENSION IS: 75 <R>**
prompt Specify dimension line location
respond **pick above the line** – fig. (d).

6 *Dimensioning with keyboard entry.*
At the command line enter **DIM <R>** and:
prompt Dim
enter **HOR <R>** – horizontal dimension
prompt Specify first extension line origin
respond **right-click and pick the fifth line**
prompt Specify dimension line location
respond **pick above the line**
prompt Enter dimension text<75>
enter **SEVENTY-FIVE <R>** – fig. (e)
prompt Dim and **ESC** to end command.

Note

1 At this stage your drawing should resemble Fig. 19.2.

2 The dimensions in Fig. 19.2 may differ in appearance from those which have been added to your drawing. This is because I have used the 'default AutoCAD dimension style' and made no attempt to alter it. The object of the exercise was to investigate the dimensioning process and dimension styles will be discussed in the next chapter.

3 The <RETURN> selection is useful if a single object is to be dimensioned. It is generally not suited to baseline or continue dimensions.

4 Object snap is used extensively when dimensioning. This is one time when a running Object Snap (e.g. Endpoint) will assist, but remember to cancel the running object snap!

5 From the menu bar select Format–Layer to display the Layer Control dialogue box. Note the layer **Defpoints**. We did not create this layer. It is *automatically* made by AutoCAD any time a dimension is added to a drawing. This layer can be turned off or frozen but cannot be deleted. **It is best left untouched**.

Dimension terminology

All dimensions used with AutoCAD objects have a terminology associated with them. It is important that the user has an understanding if this terminology especially when creating dimension styles. Figure 19.3 explains the basic dimension terminology for:

1 *The dimension and extension lines*. These are made up of:
  a) dimension line   *b*) extension line
    – the actual line   – an origin offset from the object
    – the dimension text   – an extension beyond the line
    – arrowheads   – spacing (for baseline)
    – extension lines.

2 *Centre marking*. This can be:
  a) a mark
  b) a line
  c) nothing.

3 *Dimension text*. It is possible to:
  a) have interior dimension line drawn or not drawn
  b) display alternative units, i.e. (imperial)
  c) draw a frame around the dimension text.

4 *Arrowheads*. Release 2000 has 19 arrowheads for selection and has the facility for user-defined arrowheads. A selection is displayed.

5 *Dimension text alignment*. It is possible to align the dimension relative to the dimension line by altering certain dimension variables. A selection of dimension text positions is displayed.

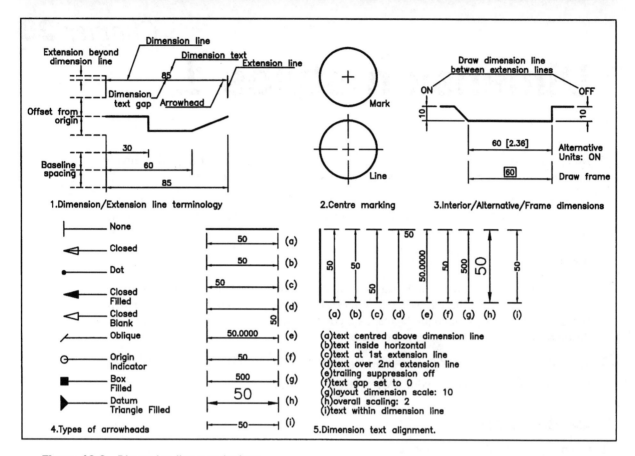

Figure 19.3 Dimension line terminology.

Summary

1 AutoCAD 2000 has automatic, associative dimensions.

2 Dimensioning can be linear, radial, angular, ordinate or leader.

3 The diameter and degree symbol are automatically added when using radial or angular dimensions.

4 Object snap modes are useful when dimensioning.

5 A layer DEFPOINTS is created when dimensioning. The user has no control over this layer.

6 Dimensions should be added to a drawing using a Dimension Style.

Chapter 20

Dimension styles 1

Dimension styles allow the user to set dimension variables to individual/company requirements. This permits various styles to be saved for different customers.

To demonstrate how a dimension style is 'set and saved', we will create a new dimension style called **A3DIM**, use it with our A:WORKDRG drawing and then save it to our standard sheet.

Note

1 The exercise which follows will display several new dialogue boxes and certain settings will be altered within these boxes. It is important for the user to become familiar with these Dimension Style dialogue boxes, as a good knowledge of their use is essential if different dimension styles have to be used.

2 The settings used in the exercise are my own, designed for our A3PAPER standard sheet.

3 You can alter the settings to your own values at this stage.

Getting started

1 Open your A:WORKDRG drawing to display the component created from a previous chapter, i.e. red outline with green centre lines.

2 Activate the Draw, Modify, Dimension and Object Snap toolbars.

Setting dimension style A3DIM

1 Either *a*) menu bar with **Dimension–Style**
     or *b*) Dimension Style icon from Dimension toolbar
   prompt   Dimension Style Manager dialogue box
   with   *a*) Current Dimstyle: ISO-25 or similar
           b) Styles for selection
           c) Preview of current dimstyle
           d) Description of current dimstyle
   respond **pick New**
   prompt   Create New Dimension Style dialogue box
   respond 1) alter New Style Name: **A3DIM**
           2) Start with: ISO-25 or similar
           3) Use for: All dimensions – Fig. 20.1
           4) Pick Continue
   prompt   New Dimension Style: A3DIM dialogue box
   with   tab selections.

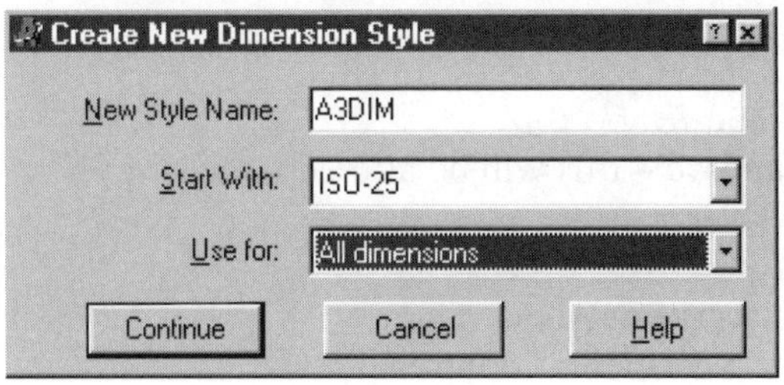

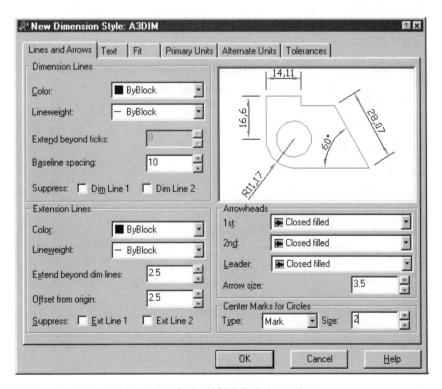

Figure 20.1 Create New Dimension Style dialogue box.

2 Lines and Arrows

respond   pick Lines and Arrows tab

prompt   `Lines and Arrows tab dialogue box` – probably active?

alter
1) Baseline Spacing: 10
2) Extend beyond dim lines: 2.5
3) Offset from origin: 2.5
4) Arrowheads: both Closed Filled
5) Leader: Close Filled
6) Arrow size: 3.5
7) Center mark for Circle; Type: Mark; Size: 2
8) dialogue box as Fig. 20.2.

Figure 20.2 Lines and Arrows Dimension Style (A3DIM) dialogue box.

3 **Text**

respond pick Text tab

prompt Text tab dialogue box

alter 1) Text Style: Standard – this will be altered later
   2) Text Color: Bylayer
   3) Text height: 4
   4) Vertical text placement: Above
   5) Horizontal text placement: Centered
   6) Offset from dim line: 1.5
   7) Text Alignment: ISO Standard
   8) dialogue box as Fig. 20.3.

4 **Fit**

respond pick Fit tab

prompt Fit tab dialogue box

alter 1) Fit options: Either the text or the arrows, whichever fits best active, i.e. black
      dot
   2) Text Placement: Beside the dimension line
   3) Scale for Dimension Feature: Overall scale: 1
   4) Fine tuning: both not active, i.e. no black dots
   5) dialogue box as Fig. 20.4.

5 **Primary Units**

respond pick Primary Units tab

prompt Primary Units tab dialogue box

alter Linear Dimensions   Angle Dimensions
   1) Unit Format: Decimal   1) Units Format: Decimal Degrees
   2) Precision: 0.00   2) Precision: 0.00
   3) Decimal separator: '.' Period   3) Zero Suppression: Trailing active
   4) Round off: 0   4) dialogue box as Fig. 20.5.
   5) Zero Suppression: Trailing active, i.e. tick in box.

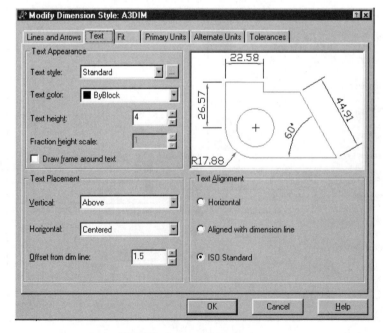

Figure 20.3 Text Dimension Style (A3DIM) dialogue box.

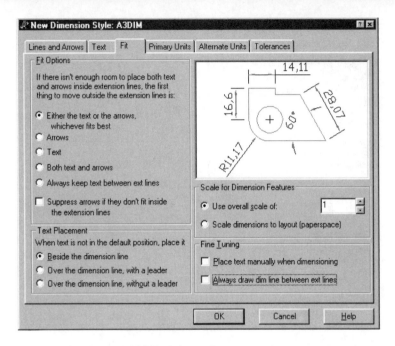

Figure 20.4 Fit Dimension Style (A3DIM) dialogue box.

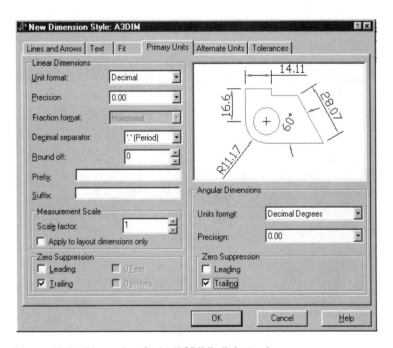

Figure 20.5 Primary Units Dimension Style (A3DIM) dialogue box.

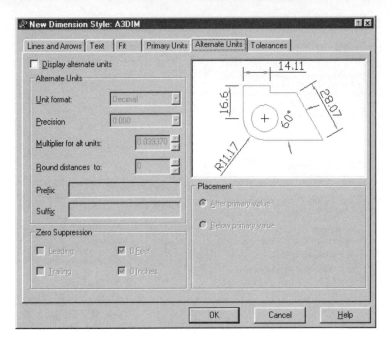

Figure 20.6 Alternate Units Dimension Style (A3DIM) dialogue box.

6 **Alternate Units**

    respond   pick Alternate Units tab

    prompt   `Alternate Units tab dialogue box`

    and   do not display alternate units as Fig. 20.7.

7 **Tolerances**

    respond   pick Tolerances tab

    prompt   `Tolerances tab dialogue box`

    and   do not alter anything – Fig. 20.8.

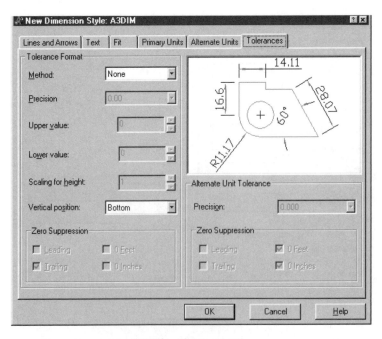

Figure 20.7 Tolerances Dimension Style (A3DIM) dialogue box.

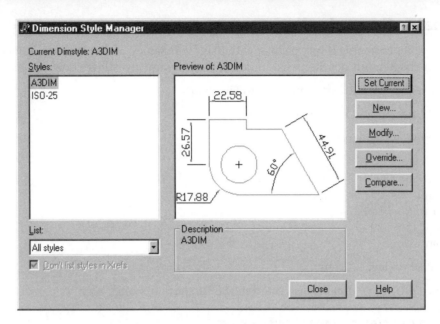

Figure 20.8 Dimensions Style Manager dialogue box for A3DIM.

8 **continue:**

respond pick OK from New Dimension Style dialogue box

prompt Dimension Style Manager dialogue box

with 1) A3DIM added to styles list

2) Preview of the A3DIM style

3) Description of the A3DIM style

respond 1) pick A3DIM – becomes highlighted

2) pick Set Current – note description

3) dialogue box similar to Fig. 20.8

4) pick Close

note if you have been altering other dimension styles during this process, the AutoCAD over-ride alert message may be displayed. If it is, respond as necessary.

9 *Note:* we have still to 'set' a text style for our A3DIM dimension style. This will be covered in a later chapter. For the present, our A3DIM dimension style is 'complete', and will be used for all future dimensioning work.

Using the A3DIM dimension style

1 A:WORKDRG drawing still on the screen?

2 Make layer DIMS current

3 Refer to Fig. 20.9 and add the following dimensions as indicated:

a) linear baseline

b) linear continue

c) diameter

d) radius

e) angular

f) leader.

4 With layer TEXT current add suitable text, the height being at your discretion.

5 When all dimensions have been added save the drawing as A:WORKDRG.

Ordinate dimensioning

This type of dimensioning is very popular with many companies, and as it was mentioned in the last chapter, but not discussed in detail, we will now investigate how it is used.

1   Continue using A:WORKDRG and refer to Fig. 20.6.

2   Layer OUT current and toolbars to suit.

3   Draw the following objects:

LINE	*CIRCLE*
First point: 300,200	centre: 335,235
Next point: @90,25	radius: 10
Next point: @−30,30	
Next point: @−50,0	
Next point: close.	

4   Make the DIMS layer current.

5   Select the ORDINATE dimension icon from the Dimension toolbar and:

prompt	Specify feature location
respond	**pick point A** – osnap helps
prompt	Specify leader endpoint or [Xdatum/Ydatum...
enter	**X <R>** – the Xdatum option
prompt	Specify leader endpoint
enter	**@0,−10 <R>**

6   Menu bar with **Dimension–Ordinate** and:

prompt	Specify feature location
respond	**pick point A**
prompt	Specify leader endpoint or [Xdatum/Ydatum...
enter	**Y <R>**
prompt	Specify leader endpoint
enter	**@−10,0 <R>**

7   Now add ordinate dimensions to the other named points, using the following X and Y datum leader endpoint values:

Point B:	Xdatum:	@0,−35	Point C:	Xdatum:	@0,10
	Ydatum:	@10,0		Ydatum:	@40,0
Point D:	Xdatum:	@0,10	Point E:	Xdatum:	@0,−45
	Ydatum:	@−20,0		Ydatum:	@−45,0.

8   Result as Fig. 20.9 – save if required but it will not be used again and do not use the name A:WORKDRG.

Saving the A3DIM dimension style to the standard sheet

The dimension style which we have created will be used for all future work when dimensioning is required. This means that we want to have this style incorporated in our A:A3PAPER standard sheet – both the drawing file and the template file. We could always open the standard sheet and redefine the A3DIM dimension style, but this seems a waste of time.

1   Make layer OUT current.

2   Erase all objects from the screen **except** the black border.

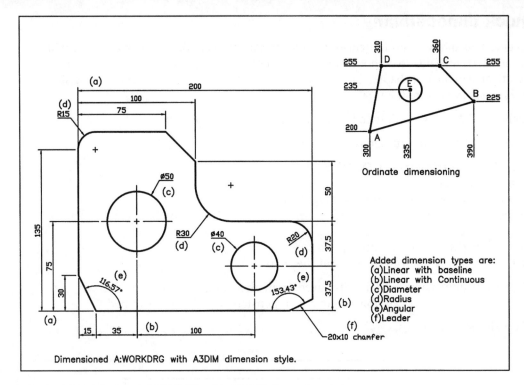

Dimensioned A:WORKDRG with A3DIM dimension style.

Figure 20.9 Dimensioning A:WORKDRG with A3DIM dimension style.

3 *Saving the drawing file*
Menu bar with **File–Save As** and:
prompt Save Drawing As dialogue box
respond 1) ensure type: AutoCAD 2000 Drawing (*.dwg)
         2) scroll and pick: 3½ floppy (A:) or named folder
         3) enter file name: A3PAPER
         4) pick Save
prompt AutoCAD message
with A:A3PAPER.dwg already exists
         Do you want to replace it?
respond pick Yes.

4 *Saving the template file*
Menu bar with **File–Save As** and:
prompt Save Drawing As dialogue box
respond 1) pick type: AutoCAD Drawing Template File(*.dwt)
         2) scroll and pick: 3½ floppy (A:)
         3) enter name: A3PAPER
         4) pick Save
prompt AutoCAD message
respond pick Yes
prompt Template Description dialogue box
enter My A3PAPER standard sheet with A3DIM dimension style
then pick OK.

5 We now have the A3PAPER saved as a drawing file and a template file, both with the A3DIM dimension style. This means that we do not have to set layers or dimension styles every time we start a new drawing. The A3PAPER standard sheet (drawing or template) should be used for all new drawing work.

Quick dimensioning

AutoCAD 2000 has a new dimensioning facility called quick dimensioning and we will use our A:WORKDRG to demonstrate how it is used. This topic should really have been investigated in the last chapter, but I decided to leave it until we had discussed dimension styles. To demonstrate the topic:

1 Open the A:WORKDRG drawing and erase all dimensions and text.

2 Make layer DIMS current and refer to Fig. 20.10.

3 Menu bar with **Dimension–QDIM** and:
prompt Select geometry to dimension
respond **window the shape then right-click**
prompt Specify dimension line position or [Continuous/ Staggered/Baseline...
enter   **B <R>** – the baseline option
then   pick any point to the right of the shape.

4 All vertical dimensions will be displayed from the horizontal base of the shape as Fig. 20.10(a). The user can now delete any dimensions which are unwanted.

5 Erase all the dimensions.

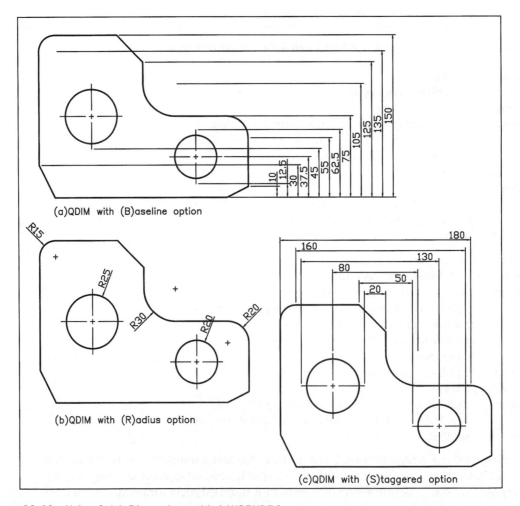

Figure 20.10 Using Quick Dimensions with A:WORKDRG.

6 Select the QUICK DIMENSION icon from the Dimension toolbar and:

prompt   `Select geometry to dimension`
respond   **window the shape then right-click**
prompt   `Specify dimension line position or [Continuous/`
                `Staggered/Baseline...`
enter   **R <R>** – the radius option
then   pick any point to suit.

7 All radius dimensions for the component will be displayed with the A3DIM dimension style as Fig. 20.10(b).

8 Erase the radius dimensions then use QDIM to add staggered dimensions to the component as Fig. 20.10(c).

9 The user should realize that it is now possible to dimension a component with the QDIM command. It may be necessary to use the command several times and delete unwanted dimensions every time the command is used before the required dimensions are displayed. This is an alternative to adding dimensions to individual objects.

10 Do not save this part of the dimension exercise.

Assignments

As dimensioning is an important concept, I have included four activities which will give you practice with:

a) using the standard sheet with layers
b) using the draw commands with coordinates
c) adding suitable text
d) adding dimensions with the A3DIM dimension style.

In each activity the procedure is the same:

1 Open the A:A3PAPER standard sheet – drawing or template?

2 Using layers correctly, complete the drawings.

3 Save the completed work as A:ACT?

The four activities are:

1 Activity 7: two simple components to be drawn and dimensioned. The sizes are more awkward than usual.

2 Activity 8: two components created mainly from circles and arcs. Use offset as much as possible. The signal arm is interesting.

3 Activity 9: a component which is much easier to complete than it would appear. Offset and fillet will assist.

4 Activity 10: components to be drawn and dimensioned. Remember that practice makes perfect.

Summary

1 Dimension styles are created by the user to 'individual' standards.

2 Different dimension styles can be created and 'made current' at any time.

3 The standard A:A3PAPER sheet has a 'customized' dimension style named A3DIM which will be used for all future drawing work including dimensioning.

Chapter 21

Modifying objects

The draw and modify commands are probably the most commonly used of all the AutoCAD commands and we have already used several of each. The modify commands discussed previously have been Erase, Offset, Trim, Extend, Fillet and Chamfer. In this chapter we will use A:WORKDRG to investigate several other modify commands as well as some additional selection set options.

Getting ready

1 Open A:WORKDRG to display the red component with green centre lines. There should be no dimensions displayed.

2 Layer OUT current, with the Draw, Modify and Object Snap toolbars.

3 Freeze layer CL – you will find out why shortly.

Copy

Allows objects to be copied to other parts of the screen. The command can be used for single or multiple copies. The user specifies a start (base) point and a displacement (or second point).

1 Refer to Fig. 21.1.

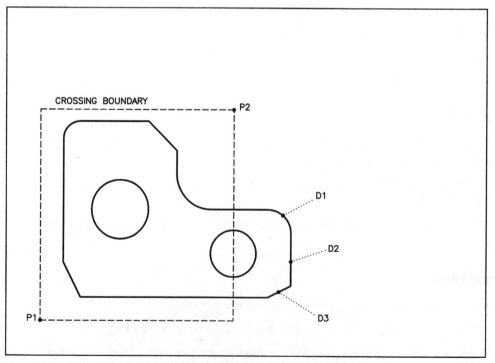

Figure 21.1 A:WORKDRG with selection points for the COPY command.

2 Select the COPY OBJECTS icon from the Modify toolbar and:

prompt	Select objects
enter	**C <R>** – the crossing selection set option
prompt	Specify first corner and: **pick a point P1**
prompt	Specify opposite corner and: **pick a point P2**
prompt	11 found – note objects not highlighted
then	Select objects
enter	**A <R>** – the add selection set option
prompt	Select objects
respond	**pick objects D1, D2 and D3 then right-click**
prompt	Specify base point or displacement or [Multiple]
enter	**50,50 <R>** – note copy image as mouse moved!
prompt	Specify second point of displacement
enter	**300,300 <R>**.

3 The original component will be copied to another part of the screen and **may** not all be visible (if at all?)

4 Don't panic! Select from the menu bar **View–Zoom-All** to 'see' the complete copied effect – Fig. 21.2. You may have to reposition your toolbars.

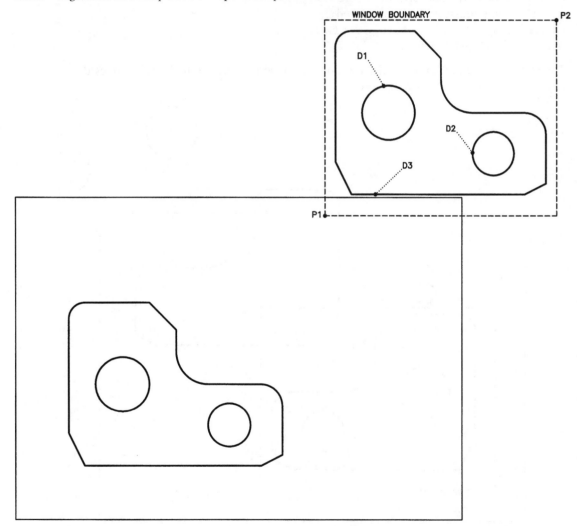

Figure 21.2 A:WORKDRG after the COPY command with selection points for the MOVE command.

Move

Allows selected objects to be moved, the user defining the start and end points of the move by:

a) entering coordinates
b) picking points on the screen
c) referencing existing entities.

1 Refer to Fig. 21.2 and select the MOVE icon from the Modify toolbar:

prompt	Select objects
enter	**W <R>** – the window selection set option
prompt	Specify first corner and: **pick a point P1**
prompt	Specify opposite corner and: **pick a point P2**
prompt	14 found
and	Select objects
enter	**R <R>** – the remove selection set option
prompt	Remove objects
respond	**pick circles D1 and D2 then right-click**
prompt	Specify base point or displacement
respond	**Endpoint icon and pick line D3** (at left end)
	(note image as cursor is moved)
prompt	Specify second point of displacement
enter	**@–115,–130 <R>**.

2 The result will be Fig. 21.3, i.e. the red outline shape is moved, but the two circles do not move, due to the Remove option.

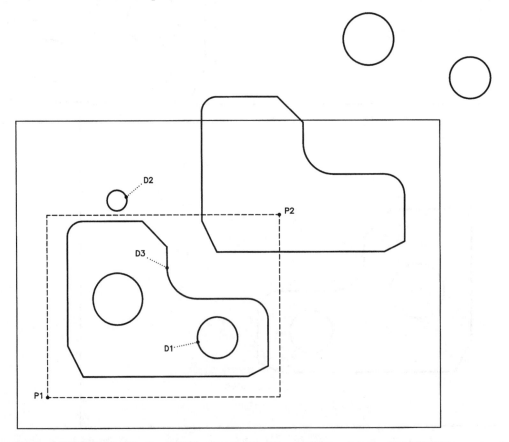

Figure 21.3 A:WORKDRG after the MOVE command with selection points for the ROTATE command.

3 *Task*

Using the Layer Properties Manager dialogue box, THAW layer CL and the centre lines are still in their original positions. They have not been copied or moved. This can be a problem with objects which are on frozen or off layers.

Now:

a) freeze layer Cl

b) erase the copied-moved objects to leave the original shape

c) View–Zoom–All to 'restore' the original screen.

Rotate

Selected objects can be 'turned' about a designated point in either a clockwise (−ve angle) or counter-clockwise (+ve angle) direction. The base point can be selected as a point on the screen, entered as a coordinate or referenced to existing objects.

1 Refer to Fig. 21.3 and draw a circle, centre: 100,220, radius: 10.

2 Menu bar with **Modify–Rotate** and:

prompt	Current positive angle in UCS: ANGDIR=counterclockwise: ANGBASE=0.0
then	Select objects
respond	**window from P1 to P2** – but **NO** right-click yet
prompt	14 found then: Select objects
enter	**R <R>**
prompt	Remove objects and: **pick circle D1**
prompt	1 found, 1 removed, 13 total
then	Remove objects
enter	**A <R>**
prompt	Select objects and: **pick circle D2**
prompt	1 found, 14 total
then	Select objects and **right-click** to end selection
prompt	Specify base point
respond	**Endpoint icon and pick line D3** – at 'lower end'
prompt	Specify rotation angle or [Reference]
enter	**−90 <R>**.

3 The selected objects will be rotated as displayed in Fig. 21.4 on the next page. Note that Fig. 21.4 does not display the two circles 'outside the shape'. They have been erased for the next part of the exercise.

4 Note that two selection set options were used in the sequence:

a) R – removed a circle from the selection set

b) A – added a circle to the selection set.

5 The ROTATE icon could have been selected for this sequence.

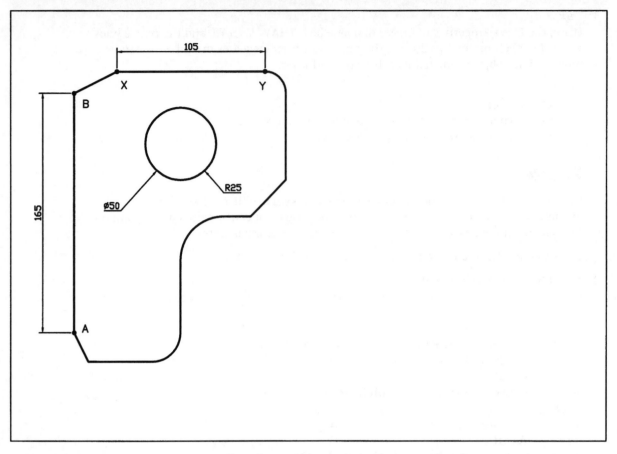

Figure 21.4 A:WORKDRG after the ROTATÉ command, with dimensions for the SCALE command.

Scale

The scale command allows selected objects or complete 'shapes' to be increased/decreased in size, the user selecting/entering the base point and the actual scale factor.

1 Refer to Fig. 21.4 and erase the two circles 'outside the shape'.

2 Make layer DIMS current and with the Dimension command (icon or menu bar):
   a) linear dimension line AB
   b) diameter dimension the circle.

3 At the command line enter **DIM <R>** and:
   prompt   Dim and enter: **HOR <R>**
   prompt   Specify first extension line origin and: **Endpoint of X**
   prompt   Specify second extension line origin and: **Endpoint of Y**
   prompt   Specify dimension line location and: **pick above line**
   prompt   Enter dimension text<105> and enter: **105 <R>**
   prompt   Dim and enter: **RAD <R>**
   prompt   Select arc or circle and: **pick the circle**
   prompt   Enter dimension text<25> and enter: **R25 <R>**
   prompt   Specify dimension text location and: **pick to suit**
   prompt   Dim and **ESC** to end sequence.

4 Make layer OUT current.

5 Select the SCALE icon from the Modify toolbar and:

prompt Select objects

respond **window the complete shape with dimensions then right-click**

prompt Specify base point

respond **Endpoint of line AB at 'B' end**

prompt Specify scale factor or [Reference]

enter **0.5 <R>**.

6 The complete shape will be scaled as Fig. 21.5.

7 Note the dimensions:
   a) the vertical dimension of 165 is now 82.5
   b) the diameter value of 50 is now 25
   c) the horizontal dimension of 105 is still 105
   d) the radius of 25 is still 25.

8 *Questions:*
   a) Why have two dimensions been scaled by 0.5 and two have not? Answer: the scaled dimensions are those which used the icon or menu bar selection and those not scaled had their dimension text values entered from the keyboard.
   b) Which of the resultant dimensions are correct? Is it the 82.5 and 25, or the 105 and 25?

   Answer: I will let you think this one for yourself!

Multiple copy

This is an option of the COPY command and does what it says – it produces as many copies of selected objects as you want.

1 Refer to Fig. 21.5.

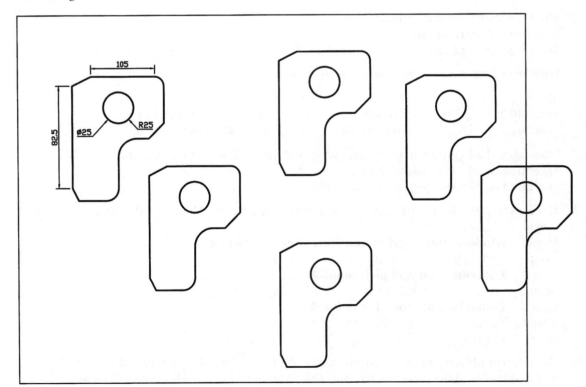

Figure 21.5 A:WORKDRG after the SCALE and MULTIPLE COPY commands.

2   Using the Layer Properties Manager dialogue box, LOCK layer DIMS

3   From menu bar select **Modify–Copy** and:

   prompt   Select objects
   respond   **window the shape and dimensions then right-click**
   prompt   17 found and 4 were on a locked layer
   then   Specify base point or displacement or [Multiple]
   enter   M <R> – the multiple copy option
   prompt   Specify base point
   respond   **Center icon and pick the circle**
   prompt   Specify second point of displacement and enter: **145,150 <R>**
   prompt   Specify second point and enter: **@170,20 <R>**
   prompt   Specify second point and enter: **@170,–135 <R>**
   prompt   Specify second point and enter: **@275,0 <R>**
   prompt   Specify second point
   respond   **Midpoint icon and pick right vertical line of the black 'border'**
   prompt   Specify second point and: **right-click** to end sequence.

4   Result as Fig. 21.5, the 'shape' being multiple-copied, but the dimensions not being copied, due to the locked layer effect.

Mirror

A command which allows objects to be mirror imaged about a line designated by the user. The command has an option for deleting the original set of objects – the source objects.

1   Erase the five multiple copied shapes to leave the original shape and dimensions. Unlock layer DIMS.

2   Move the shape and dimensions:
Base point: **Centre of circle**
Second point: **@120,20**.

3   With layer OUT current, draw the following lines:

AB	MN	PQ	XY
first: 140,270	first: 260,200	first: 240,150	first: 155,150
next: @0,–100	next: @0,70	next: @50<45	next: @60<0.

4   With layer TEXT current, draw the following text items all with 0 rotation and:
   a) centred on 200,255; height: 6; item: AutoCAD
   b) centred on 185,180; height: 7, item: R2000.

5   Make layer OUT current and select the MIRROR icon from the Modify toolbar and:
   prompt   Select objects
   respond   **window shape and dimensions then right-click**
   prompt   Specify first point of mirror line
   respond   **Endpoint icon and pick point A**
   prompt   Specify second point of mirror line
   respond   **Endpoint icon and pick point B**
   prompt   Delete source objects [Yes/No]<N>
   enter   **N <R>**.

6   The selected objects are mirrored about the line AB. Note the text has also been mirrored but the dimension text has not. The positioning of the radial dimensions are interesting?

7   At the command line enter **MIRRTEXT <R>**
    prompt   Enter new value for MIRRTEXTT<1>
    enter   **0 <R>**.

8   Menu bar with **Modify–Mirror** and:
    prompt   Select objects
    enter   **P <R>** – previous election set option
    prompt   19 found and Select objects
    respond   **right-click** to end selection
    prompt   Specify first point of mirror line and: **endpoint of point M**
    prompt   Specify second point of mirror line and: **endpoint of point N**
    prompt   Delete source objects and enter: **N <R>**.

9   The shape is mirrored – what about text?

10 At the command line enter **MIRROR <R>** and:
    a) select objects: enter P <R><R> – yes two returns – why?
    b) first point – pick point P
    c) second point – pick point Q
    d) delete – N.

11 Set the MIRRTEXT variable to 1 and mirror the original shape about line XY.

12 The final result should be Fig. 21.6.

13 *Task:* before leaving the exercise, thaw layer CL. The circle centre lines are still in their original positions.

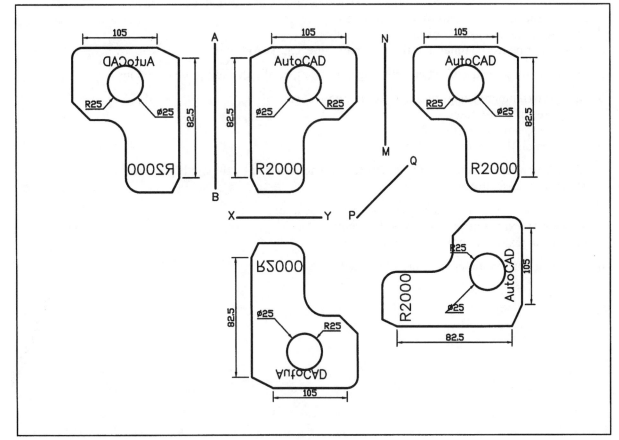

Figure 21.6   A:WORKDRG after the MIRROR command.

Assignments

Four 'relatively easy' activities have been included for the chapter. Each activity should be completed on the A:A3PAPER standard sheet (drawing or template?) and layers should be used correctly. The components do not need to be dimensioned, unless you are feeling adventurous. Remember to save your completed drawings as A:ACT??, etc. and always use your discretion for sizes which are not given. The four activities are:

1 Activity 11: a vent cover plate.
   The original component has to be drawn and then copied into the rectangular plate. Commands could be rotate and multiple copy, but that is your decision.

2 Activity 12: a well-known symbol.
   Easy to draw and construct. Several ways of using the modify commands, e.g. copy/rotate or mirror.

3 Activity 13: a template.
   This is easier to complete than you may think. Draw the quarter template using the sizes, then MIRROR. The text item is to be placed at your discretion. Multiple copy and scale by half, third and quarter. Additional: add the given dimensions to a quarter template.

4 Activity 14: two additional components.
   No help with these two, as one of them is virtually identical to Activity 13.

Summary

1 The commands COPY, MOVE, ROTATE, MIRROR and SCALE can all be activated:
   a) from the menu bar with Modify–Copy, etc.
   b) by selecting the icon from the Modify toolbar
   c) by entering the command at the command line, e.g. SCALE <R>.

2 The selection set is useful when selecting objects, especially the add/remove options.

3 All of the commands require a base point, and this can be:
   a) entered as coordinates
   b) referenced to an existing object
   c) picked on the screen.

4 Objects on layers which are OFF or FROZEN are not affected by the modify commands. This could cause problems!

5 MIRRTEXT is a system variable with a 0 or 1 value and:
   a) value 1: text is mirrored – this is the default
   b) value 0: text is not mirrored.

6 Keyboard entered dimensions are not scaled.

Chapter 22

Grips

Grips are an aid to the draughting process, offering the user a limited number of modify commands. In an earlier chapter we 'turned grips off with the command line entry of GRIPS: 0. This was to allow the user to become reasonably proficient with using the draw and modify commands. Now that this has been achieved, we will investigate how grips are used.

Toggling grips on/off

Grips can be toggled on/off using:

a) the Selection tab from the Options dialogue box
b) command line entry.

1   Open your A:A3PAPER standard sheet with layer OUT current.

2   From the menu bar select **Tools–Options** and:
prompt	Options dialogue box
respond	**pick Selection tab**
prompt	Selection tab dialogue box
with	*a*) Selection modes
	b) Grips
respond	1) Enable grips active, i.e. tick in box
	2) Unselected grip color: Blue
	3) Selected grip color: Red
	4) Grip size: adjust to suit – Fig. 22.1
	5) pick OK.

3   The drawing screen is returned, with the grip box 'attached' to cursor cross-hairs.

4   At the command line enter **GRIPS <R>** and:
prompt	Enter new value for GRIPS<1>
respond	**<RETURN>**, i.e. leave the 1 value.

5   The command entry is GRIPS: 1 are ON; GRIPS: 0 are OFF.

6   *Note:*
    a) the grip box attached to the cross-hairs should not be confused with the pick box used with modify commands. Although similar in appearance they are entirely different
    b) when any command is activated (e.g. LINE), the grips box will disappear from the cross-hairs, and re-appear when the command is terminated.

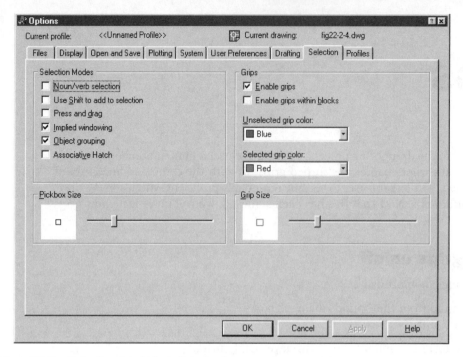

Figure 22.1 Selection tab (grips) dialogue box.

What do grips do and how do they work?

1 Grips provide the user with five modify commands which can also be activated in icon form or from the menu bar. The five commands are Stretch, Move, Rotate, Scale and Mirror.

2 Grips work in the 'opposite sense' from normal command selection:
   a) the usual sequence is to activate the command then select the objects, e.g. COPY, then pick object to be copied
   b) with grips, the user selects the objects and then activates one of the five commands.

3 Draw a line, circle, arc and text item anywhere on the screen.

4 Ensure grips are on, i.e. GRIPS: 1 at command line.

5 Refer to Fig. 22.2 and move the cursor to each object and 'pick them' with the grip box and:
   a) blue grip boxes appear at each object 'snap point' and the object is highlighted – fig. (b)
   b) move the grip box to any one of the blue boxes and 'pick it'. The box becomes red solid in appearance and the object is still highlighted. The red box is the **BASE GRIP** – fig. (c)
   c) press the ESC key – blue grips with highlighted object
   d) press ESC – blue grips with objects not highlighted – fig. (a)
   e) ESC again to cancel the grips operation.

6 *Note:* a useful way of remembering the 'grip types' is the pre-R2000 names of cold, warm and hot. These three names are not generally used in R2000, but I still find them a very useful way of describing the type of grip active at any time.
   a) Cold grip: appear on selected objects in blue, but the object itself is not highlighted as fig. (a). The grip options cannot be used in this state.
   b) Warm grip: appear as blue boxes and the selected objects are highlighted – dashed appearance as fig. (b). The grip options still cannot be used in this state.
   c) Hot grip: appear as solid red boxes when a cold or warm box is 'picked' as fig. (c). The selected hot grip acts as the base grid and the grid options can be used.

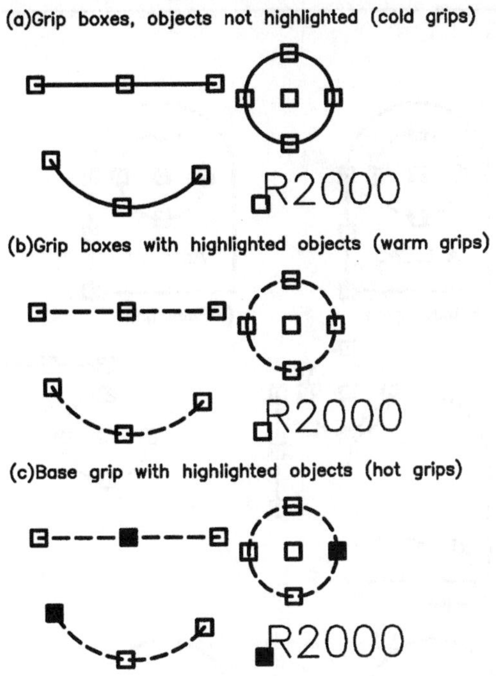

(a)Grip boxes, objects not highlighted (cold grips)

R2000

(b)Grip boxes with highlighted objects (warm grips)

R2000

(c)Base grip with highlighted objects (hot grips)

R2000

Figure 22.2 Grip 'states' or types.

Grip exercise 1

This demonstration is relatively simple but rather long. It is advisable to work through the exercise without missing out any of the steps.

1 Erase all objects from the screen, or re-open A:A3PAPER.

2 Refer to Fig. 22.3 and draw the original shape using the sizes given – fig. (a). Make the lower left corner at the point (100,100).

3 Grips on?

4 Move the cursor to the circle and pick it, then move to the right vertical line and pick it. Blue grip boxes appear and the two objects are highlighted – fig. (b).

5 Move the cursor grip box to the grip box at the circle centre and left-click, i.e. pick it. The selected box will be displayed in red as it is now the base grip – fig. (c). Observe the command line:

prompt   `** STRETCH **`
         `Specify stretch point or [Base point/Copy/Undo/eXit]`
respond **\<RETURN\>**
prompt   `** MOVE **`
         `Specify move point or [Base point/Copy/Undo/eXit]`
enter   **@25,25 \<R\>**.

6 Three things should have happened:
   a) the circle and line are moved
   b) the command prompt line is returned
   c) the grips are still active – fig. (d).

7 Move the cursor and pick the text item to add it to the grip selection – fig. (e).

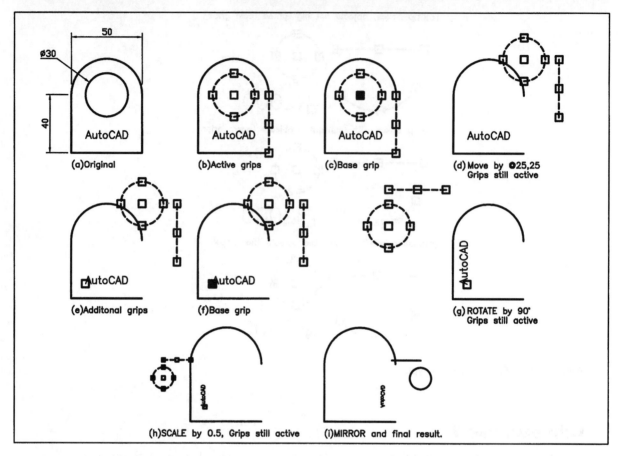

Figure 22.3 Grip exercise 1.

8   Make the grip box of the text item the base grip, by moving the cursor pick box onto it
    and left-clicking – fig. (f), and:
    prompt   ** STRETCH **
              Specify stretch point or [Base point/Copy...
    enter   **<RETURN>**
    prompt   ** MOVE **
              Specify move point or [Base point/Copy...
    enter   **<RETURN>**
    prompt   ** ROTATE **
              Specify rotation angle or [Base point/Copy...
    enter   **90 <R>**.

9   The circle, line and text item will be rotated and the grips are still active – fig. (g).

10 Make the same text item grip box the base grip (easy!) and:
    prompt   **STRETCH**
              Specify stretch point or...
    enter   **SC <R>** – the scale grip option
    prompt   ** SCALE **
              Specify scale factor or [Base point...
    enter   **0.5 <R>**.

11 The three objects are scaled and the grips are still active as fig. (h).

12 Make the right box on the line hot and:
>   *prompt*   `**STRETCH**`
>   *enter*   **MI <R>** – the mirror option
>   *prompt*   `** MIRROR**`
>   `Specify second point or [Base point...`
>   *enter*   **B <R>** – the base point option
>   *prompt*   `Specify base point`
>   *respond* **Midpoint icon and pick the original horizontal line**
>   *prompt*   `** MIRROR **`
>   `Specify second point or...`
>   *respond* **Midpoint icon and pick the arc.**

13 The three objects are mirrored about the selected 'line' and the grips are still active (warm) – fig. (i).

14 Press ESC – grips on the three objects, but objects are not highlighted, i.e. cold grips.

15 Press ESC – removes the grips and ends the sequence.

16 The exercise is now complete. Do not exit yet.

Selection with grips

Selecting individual objects for use with grips can be tedious. It is possible to select a window/crossing option when grips are on.

1 Your screen should display the line, circle and text item after the grips exercise has been completed?

2 Refer to Fig. 22.4(a) and move the cursor and pick a point 'roughly' where indicated. Move the cursor down and to the right, and pick a second point.

3 All complete objects within the window will display grip boxes with highlighted objects, i.e. warm grip.

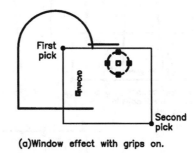

(a)Window effect with grips on.

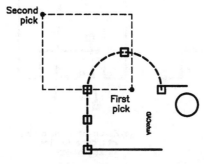

(b)Crossing effect with grips on.

Figure 22.4 Window/crossing selection with grips.

4 Two ESC presses to cancel the grip effect.

5 Move the cursor to about the same point as step 2, and pick a point – Fig. 22.4(b). Move the cursor upwards and to the left and pick a second point.

6 All objects within or which cross the boundary will display grip boxes with highlighted objects.

7 Two ESC presses.

8 The effect can be summarized as:
 a) window effect to the right of first pick
 b) crossing effect to the left of the first pick.

Grips exercise 2

1 Open A:USEREX to display the component used in the offset and text exercises and refer to Fig. 22.5.

2 Ensure only the red objects displayed – fig. (a).

3 Grips on. Pick a point 1 and drag out a window and pick a point 2. Five lines will display grip boxes and be highlighted as fig. (b).

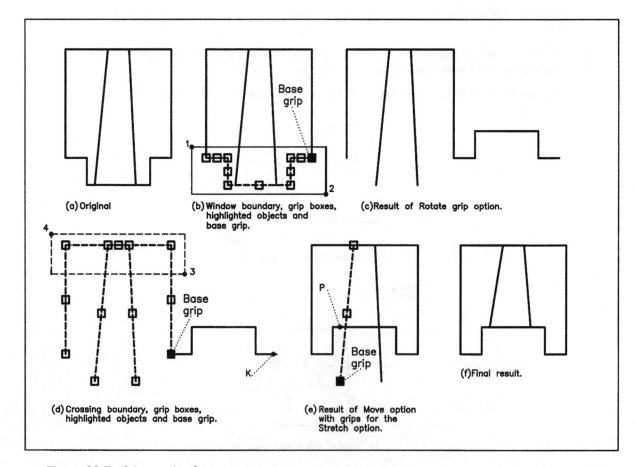

Figure 22.5 Grip exercise 2.

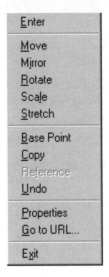

Figure 22.6 Grips option menu.

4 Make the rightmost grip the base grip and:
  prompt ** STRETCH**..
  respond **right-click** to display the grip options menu as Fig. 22.6
  then **pick Rotate**
  prompt Specify rotation angle or...
  enter **180 <R>**.

5 Now two ESC's to cancel the grips – fig. (c).

6 Pick a point 3 and drag out a crossing window and pick a point 4 to display five highlighted lines with grip boxes as fig. (d).

7 Make the lowest grip box on the right vertical line hot and:
  prompt ** STRETCH **...
  respond right-click to display the grip options menu
  then **pick Move**
  prompt Specify move point or...
  respond **Endpoint icon and pick line K**.

8 The lines are moved 'onto' the rotated lines – fig. (e).

9 Two ESC's to cancel the grips.

10 Pick one of the inclined lines and:
  a) make the lowest grip box the base grip
  b) activate the STRETCH option
  c) stretch the grip box perpendicular to line P
  d) repeat for the other inclined line
  e) final result – fig. (f).

11 *Note:* this exercise could have been completed using the modify commands, e.g. rotate and trim. It demonstrates that there is no one way to complete a drawing.

12 Save this exercise if required, but not as A:USEREX.

Assignment

Activity 15 involves the re-positioning of a robotic arm, which has proved relatively successful in my previous 'Beginning books'.

1 Refer to Activity 15 and create the robotic arm in the original position using the sizes given – fig. (a). Use your discretion for sizes not given.

2 Upper arm rotate by 45 degrees – fig. (b). Two circles and two lines need to be 'picked' with the base grip at the larger circle centre.

3 Both arms mirrored about line through large circle centre. Two more lines and a circle added to the grip selection – fig. (c).

4 Both arms rotated to a horizontal position – fig. (d).

5 Finally – fig. (e) – three grip operations:
   a) lower arm stretch by 50
   b) upper arm move
   c) upper arm rotate.

6 Save when completed.

Summary

1 Grips allow the user access to the STRETCH, MOVE, ROTATE, SCALE and MIRROR modify commands without icon or menu bar selection.

2 Grips work in the 'opposite sense' from the normal AutoCAD commands, i.e. select object first then the command.

3 Grips *do not have to be used*. They give the user another draughting tool.

4 Grips are toggled on/off using the Grips dialogue box or by keyboard entry. The dialogue box allows the grip box colours and size to be altered.

5 Grips can be cold, warm or hot – pre-R2000 names.

6 If grips are not being used, I would always recommend that they be toggled off, i.e. GRIPS: 0 at the command line.

7 When a grip box is the base grip, the options can be activated by:
   a) return at the keyboard
   b) entering SC, MO, MI, etc.
   c) right-click the mouse to display the grip option menu.

Chapter 23

Drawing assistance

All objects have been created by picking points on the screen, entering coordinate values or by referencing existing objects, e.g. midpoint, endpoint, etc.

There are other methods which enable objects to be positioned on the screen, and in this chapter we will investigate three new concepts, these being:
a) point filters
b) construction lines
c) ray lines.

Point filters

This allows objects to be positioned by referencing the X and Y coordinate values of existing objects.

Example 1

1   Open the A:A3PAPER standard sheet and refer to Fig. 23.1.

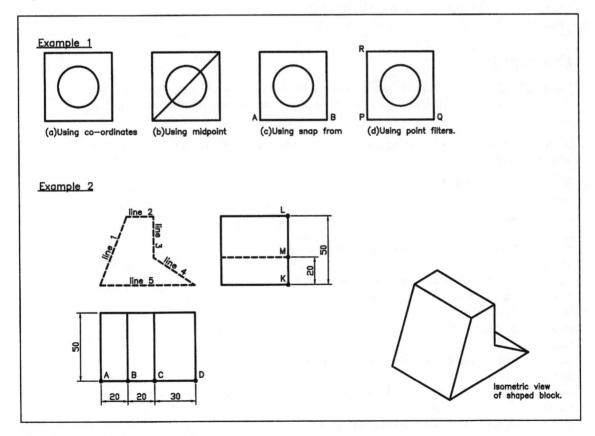

Figure 23.1   Point filter examples.

2 Draw a 50 side square, lower left corner at 20,220.

3 Multiple copy this square to three other positions.

4 A circle of diameter 30 has to be created at the 'centre' of each square and this will be achieved by four different methods:
   a) Coordinates
      Activate the circle command with centre: 45,245; radius: 15.
   b) Object snap midpoint
      – draw in a diagonal of the square
      – pick the centre icon
      – centre point: snap to Midpoint of diagonal
      – radius: enter 15
   c) Object snap from
      – pick the circle icon
      – centre: pick the snap from icon
      – base point: endpoint icon and pick left end of line AB
      – offset: enter @25,25
      – radius: enter 15
   d) Point filters
      Activate the circle command and:

prompt	Specify center point
enter	**.X <R>**
prompt	of
respond	**Midpoint icon and pick line PQ**
prompt	(need YZ)
respond	**Midpoint icon and pick line PR**
prompt	Specify radius and enter: **15 <R>**.

Example 2

Figure 23.1 displays the top, end and isometric views of a shaped block. The front view has to be created from the two given views, and we will use the point filter technique to achieve this.

1 Draw the top and end views using the sizes given. Use the lower part of the screen. Draw with the snap on.

2 Select the line icon and:

prompt	Specify first point
enter	**.X <R>**
prompt	of
respond	**Intersection icon and pick point A**
prompt	(need YZ)
respond	**Intersection icon and pick point K**
and	cursor 'snaps' to a point on the screen
prompt	Specify next point
enter	**.X <R>**
prompt	of
respond	**Intersection icon and pick point B**
prompt	(need YZ)
respond	**Intersection icon and pick point L** – line 1 is drawn
prompt	Specify next point
enter	**.X <R>** and: **Intersection of point C**
prompt	(need YZ) and: **Intersection of point L** – line 2 is drawn

prompt	Specify next point
enter	**.X <R>** and: **Intersection of point C**
prompt	(need YZ) and: **Intersection of point M** – line 3 is drawn
prompt	Specify next point
enter	**.X <R>** and: **Intersection of point D**
prompt	(need YZ) and: **Intersection of point K** – line 4 is drawn
prompt	To point and: **C <R>** to draw line 5.

3 The front view of the shaped block is now complete.

4 This exercise does not need to be saved.

5 *Note*: the point filter method of creating objects can be rather 'cumbersome' to use. Point filters are another aid to draughting.

Construction lines

Construction lines are lines that extend to infinity in both directions from a selected point on the screen. They can be referenced to assist in the creation of other objects.

1 Open the A:A3PAPER standard sheet, layer OUT current and display toolbars Draw, Modify and Object Snap. Refer to Fig. 23.2(a).

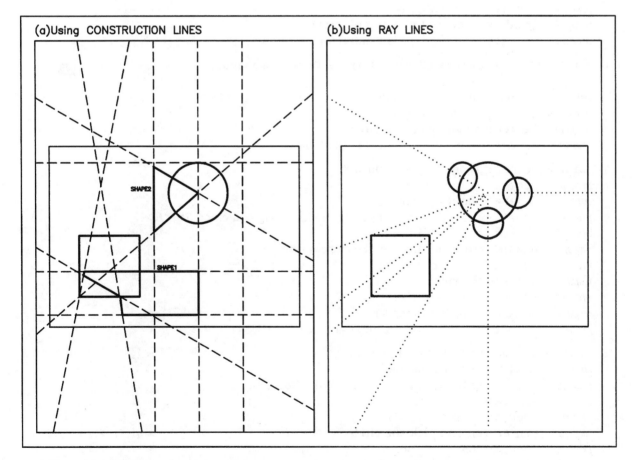

Figure 23.2 Construction and ray lines.

2 With layer OUT current, draw:
  a) a 100 sided square, lower left corner at 50,50
  b) a circle, centred on 250,220 with radius 50.

3 Make a new layer (Format–Layer) named CONLINE, colour to suit and with a DASHED
  linetype. This layer is to be current.

4 Menu bar with **Draw–Construction Line** and:
prompt	`Specify a point or [Hor/Ver/Ang/Bisect/Offset]`
enter	**50,50 <R>**
and	line 'attached' to cursor through the entered point and 'swings' as the mouse is moved
prompt	`Specify through point`
enter	**80,200 <R>**
prompt	`Specify through point`
respond	**Center icon and pick the circle**
prompt	`Specify through point` and right-click.

5 At the command line enter **XLINE <R>** and:
prompt	`Specify a point or...`
enter	H <R> – the horizontal option
prompt	`Specify through point`
enter	**100,20 <R>**
prompt	`Specify through point`
respond	Midpoint icon and pick a vertical line of square
prompt	`Specify through point`
respond	**Quadrant icon and pick top of circle**
prompt	`Specify through point` and right-click.

6 Select the CONSTRUCTION LINE icon from the Draw toolbar and:
prompt	`Specify a point or...`
enter	**V <R>** – the vertical option
prompt	`Specify through point`
respond	**Center icon and pick the circle**
prompt	`Specify through point` and right-click.

7 Activate the construction line command and:
prompt	`Specify a point or...`
enter	**O <R>** – the offset option
prompt	`Specify offset distance or [Through]` and enter: **75 <R>**
prompt	`Select a line object`
respond	pick the vertical line through the circle centre
prompt	`Select side to offset`
respond	**offset to the right**
prompt	`Select a line object`
respond	offset the same line to the left
prompt	`Select a line object` and right-click.

8 Construction line command and at prompt:
enter	**A <R>** – the angle option
prompt	`Enter angle of xline (0.0) or [Reference]`
enter	**–30 <R>**
prompt	`Specify through point`
respond	**Center icon and pick the circle**
prompt	`Specify through point`
enter	**135,40 <R>** then right-click.

9 Construction line command for last time and at prompt:
enter **B <R>** – the bisect option
prompt Specify angle vertex point
respond **Midpoint icon and pick top line of square**
prompt Specify angle start point
respond **pick lower left vertex of square**
prompt Specify angle end point
respond **Midpoint icon and pick square right vertical line**
prompt Specify angle end point and right-click.

10 Construction lines can be copied, moved, referenced to create other objects as SHAPE1 and SHAPE2 in Fig. 23.2(a).

11 *Note:*
   a) Think of how construction lines could have been used to create the front view of the point filters example completed earlier in this chapter.
   b) I would recommend that construction lines are created on their own layer, and that this layer is frozen to avoid 'screen clutter' when not in use. I would also recommend that they are given a colour and linetype not normally used.

12 *Task*: try the following:
   a) at the command line enter LIMITS <R> and:
      prompt Specify lower left corner and enter: **0,0 <R>**
      prompt Specify upper right corner and enter: **10000,10000 <R>**
   b) from menu bar select **View–Zoom-All** and:
      i) our drawing appears very small at bottom of screen
      ii) the construction lines 'radiate outwards' to the screen edges
   c) Enter LIMITS <R> and:
      i) −10000,−10000 as the lower left corner
      ii) 0,0 as the upper right corner
   d) View–Zoom-All to 'see' the construction lines
   e) return limits to 0,0 and 420,297 then View–Zoom-All to restore the original drawing screen. A REGEN <R> may be required?

13 The construction line exercise is now complete. The drawing can be saved if required, but we will not use it again.

Rays

Rays are similar to construction lines, but they only extend to infinity in one direction from the selected start point.

1 Make a new layer called RAYLINE, colour to suit and with a dotted linetype. Make this layer current and refer to Fig. 23.2(b).

2 Freeze layer CONLINE and erase any objects to leave the original square and circle.

3 Menu bar with **Draw–Ray** and:
   prompt Specify start point
   respond **Center icon and pick the circle**
   prompt Specify through point and enter: **@100<150 <R>**
   prompt Specify through point and enter: **@100<0 <R>**
   prompt Specify through point and enter: **@100<−90 <R>**
   prompt Specify through point and right-click.

4 With layer OUT current, draw three 25 radius circles at the intersection of the ray lines and circle.

5   Make layer RAYLINE current and at the command line enter **RAY <R>** and:
    prompt   Specify start point
    respond **pick the circle centre point**
    prompt   Specify through point
    respond **Intersection icon and pick the four vertices of the square** then right-click.

6   Use the LIMITS command and enter:
    a) lower left: −10000,−10000
    b) upper right: 0,0.

7   Menu bar with View–Zoom-All and note position of 'our drawing'.

8   Return limits to 0,0 and 420,297 the Zoom–Previous to restore the original drawing screen. Is a REGEN needed?

9   *Note:* As with construction lines, it is recommended that ray lines be drawn on 'their own layer' with a colour and linetype to suit. This layer can then be frozen when not in use.

Summary

1   Point filters allow the user a method of creating objects by referencing existing object coordinates.

2   Point filters are activated by keyboard entry.

3   Construction and ray lines are aids to draughting. They allow lines to be created from a selected point and:
    a) construction lines extend to infinity in both directions from the selected start point
    b) ray lines extend to infinity in one direction only from the selected start point.

4   Both construction and ray lines can be activated from the menu bar or by keyboard entry. XLINE is the construction line entry and RAY the ray line entry.

5   The default Draw dialogue box only displays the Construction Line icon, although this can be altered to include the ray line icon.

6   Both construction and ray lines are very useful aids for the CAD operator, but it is personal preference if they are used.

Chapter 24

Viewing a drawing

Viewing a drawing is important. This may be to enlarge a certain part of the screen for more detailed work or perhaps to return the screen to a previous display. AutoCAD allows the user several methods of altering the screen display, and these include the scroll bars, the Pan and Zoom commands and the Aerial view option. Realtime pan and zoom are also possible.

Getting ready

1 Open A:WORKDRG to display the red outline, two red circles, four green centre lines and a black border.

2 With layer TEXT current, menu bar with **Draw–Text–Single Line Text** and:
   a) start point: centred on 90,115
   b) height: 0.1 – yes 0.1
   c) rotation: 0
   d) text item: AutoCAD.

3 With layer OUT current, draw a circle centred on 89.98,115.035 and radius 0.01. The awkward coordinate entries are deliberate.

4 These two objects cannot yet be 'seen' on the screen.

5 Ensure the Zoom toolbar is displayed and positioned to suit.

Pan

Allows the graphics screen to be 'moved', the movement being controlled by the user by coordinate entry or by selecting points on the screen.

1 From the Standard toolbar select the PAN REALTIME icon and:
   prompt   Press Esc or Enter to exit, or right-click to display shortcut menu
   and   cursor changes to a hand
   respond 1) hold down the left button of mouse
              2) move mouse and complete drawing moves
              3) note that scroll bars also move
              4) move image roughly back to original position
              5) right-click and:
                 a) pop-up shortcut menu displayed – Fig. 24.1
                 b) Pan is active – tick
                 c) pick Exit.

2 Menu bar with **View–Pan–Point** and:
   prompt   Specify base point or displacement and enter: **0,0 <R>**
   prompt   specify second point and enter: **500,500 <R>**.

3 No drawing on screen – don't panic!

4 Use PAN REALTIME to pan down and to the left, and 'restore' the drawing roughly in its original position, then right-click and exit.

Figure 24.1 Shortcut menu.

Zoom

This is one of the most important and widely used of all the AutoCAD commands. It allows parts of a drawing to be magnified/enlarged on the screen. The command has several options, and it is these options which will now be investigated. To assist us in investigating the zoom options:

a) use the COPY command and copy the red/green component from 50,50 to 210,260
b) refer to Fig. 24.2.

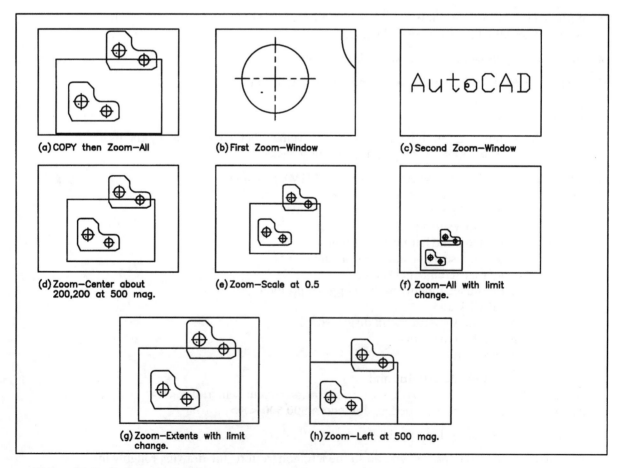

Figure 24.2 Various zoom options.

Zoom All

Displays a complete drawing including any part of the drawing which is 'off' the current screen.

1 From menu bar select **View–Zoom-All**.

2 The two components and the black border are displayed – fig. (a).

Zoom Window

Perhaps the most useful of the zoom options. It allows areas of a drawing to be 'enlarged' for clarity or more accurate work.

1 Select the ZOOM WINDOW icon from the Zoom toolbar and:
   prompt   `Specify first corner`
   respond   window the original left circle – fig. (b).

2 At the command line enter **ZOOM <R>** and:
   prompt   `Specify corner of window, enter a scale factor...`
   enter   **W <R>** – the window option
   prompt   `Specify first corner` and enter: 89.6,114.9 <R>
   prompt   `Specify opposite corner` and enter: **90.4,115.2 <R>**.

3 The text item and circle will now be displayed – fig. (c).

Zoom Previous

Restores the drawing screen to the display before the last view command.

1 Menu bar with **View–Zoom–Previous** – restores fig. (b).

2 At command line enter **ZOOM <R>** then **P <R>** – restores fig. (a).

Zoom Center

Allows a drawing to be centred about a user-defined centre point.

1 Select the ZOOM CENTER icon and:
   prompt   `Specify center point` and enter: **200,200 <R>**
   prompt   `Enter magnification or height<?>` and enter **500 <R>**.

2 The complete drawing is centred on the drawing screen about the entered point – fig. (d).

3 *Note*:
   a) the 'size' of the displayed drawing depends on the magnification/height value entered by the user and is relative to the displayed default <?> value and:
      i) a value less than the default – magnifies drawing on screen
      ii) a value greater than the default – reduces the size of the drawing on the screen
   b) toggle the grid ON and note the effect with the centre option.

4 Menu bar with **View–Zoom–Center** and enter the following centre points, all with 1000 magnification:
   a) 200,200
   b) 0,0
   c) 500,500.

5 Now Zoom–Previous four times to restore fig. (a).

Zoom Scale

Centres a drawing on the screen at a scale factor entered by the user. It is similar (and easier?) than the Zoom–Center option.

1 Select the ZOOM SCALE icon and:
  prompt `Enter a scale factor (nX or nXP)` and enter: **0.5 <R>**.

2 Drawing is displayed centred and scaled – fig. (e).

3 Menu bar with **View–Zoom–Scale** and enter a scale factor of 0.25.

4 Zoom to a scale factor of 1.5.

5 Zoom–Previous three times to restore fig. (a).

Zoom Extents

Zooms the drawing to extent of the current limits.

1 At command line enter **LIMITS <R>** and:
  prompt `Specify lower left corner` and enter: **0,0 <R>**
  prompt `Specify upper right corner` and enter: **1000,1000 <R>**.

2 Menu bar with **View–Zoom-All** – fig. (f).

3 Select the ZOOM EXTENTS icon – fig. (g).

4 Set limits back to 0,0 and 420,297 then Zoom-All to restore fig. (a).

Zoom Dynamic

This option will not be discussed. The other zoom options and the realtime pan and zoom should be sufficient for all users needs?

Zoom Realtime

1 Menu bar with **View–Zoom–Realtime** and:

  prompt `Press ESC or ENTER to exit, or right click to display shortcut menu`
  and cursor changes to a magnifying glass with a + and –
  respond *a*) hold down left button on mouse and move upwards to give a magnification effect
  b) move downwards to give a decrease in size effect
  c) left-right movement – no effect
  d) right-click to display pop-up menu with Zoom active
  e) pick Exit.

2 Zoom-All to display fig. (a).

3 The Zoom Realtime icon is in the Standard Toolbar

Zoom Left

An old zoom option not displayed in icon form or in the menu bar but still available at the command line.

1 At the command line enter **ZOOM <R>** then **L <R>** and:
   prompt   Lower left corner point and enter: **0,0 <R>**
   prompt   Enter magnification or height and enter: **500 <R>**

2 Complete drawing is moved to left of drawing screen and displayed at the entered magnification – fig. (h).

3 Zoom–Previous to restore fig. (a).

Aerial view

The aerial view is a navigation tool (AutoCAD expression) and allows the user to pan and zoom a drawing interactively.

1 The A:WORKDRG drawing should still be displayed from the zoom exercise?

2 Menu bar with **View–Aerial View** and:
   prompt   Aerial View dialogue box as Fig. 24.3
   respond   **position on screen to suit**.

3 The black border displayed in the dialogue box is the aerial view window which the user 'can control'. As the aerial view is altered, the actual screen drawing is interactively altered. The aerial view dialogue box has user selections of:
   View: Zoom In, Zoom Out, Global
   Options: Auto Viewport, Dynamic Update, Realtime Zoom

4 *Task*: using the Aerial View dialogue box:
   a) left-click within the aerial view window – the black border
   b) move the mouse and the aerial view window will move as will the actual screen drawing
   c) hold down the left mouse button and move the mouse to the left and right to 're-sizes' the aerial view window. As the aerial view window is altered in size, the actual drawing also alters in size
   d) position and re-size the aerial view window to suit then right-click the mouse
   e) the aerial view window will be re-sized and the screen drawing will be displayed at the aerial view size
   f) a zoom all in the screen drawing will also be displayed in the aerial view window.

5 Experiment with the Aerial View dialogue box, and decide if it would be useful for you, then cancel the dialogue box.

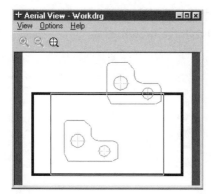

Figure 24.3   Aerial View dialogue box.

Transparent Zoom

A **transparent** command is one which can be activated while using another command and zoom has this facility.

1   Restore the original Fig. 23.2(a) – zoom all?

2   Select the LINE icon and:
    prompt   Specify first point
    enter   **'ZOOM <R>** – the transparent zoom command
    prompt   All/Center/Dynamic... – the zoom options
    enter   **W <R>** – the window zoom option
    and   window the leftmost circle
    prompt   Specify first point, i.e. back to the line command
    enter   **89,115 <R>**
    prompt   Specify next point
    enter   **'ZOOM <R>**
    then   **P <R>** – the previous zoom option
    prompt   Specify next point, i.e. back to the line command
    respond   **pick any point then right-click**.

3   The transparent command is activated by entering **'ZOOM** at the command line.

4   Only certain commands have transparency, generally those which alter a drawing display, e.g. GRID, SNAP and ZOOM.

5   Do not save this drawing modification.

Summary

1   Pan and Zoom are VIEW commands usually activated by icon.

2   Pan does 'not move a drawing' – it 'moves' the complete drawing screen.

3   The zoom command has several options, the most common being:

    All: displays the complete drawing
    Window: allows parts of a drawing to be displayed in greater detail
    Center: centres a drawing about a user-defined point at a user-specified magni-
        fication – very useful with multiple viewports
    Previous: displays the drawing screen prior to the last pan/zoom command
    Extents: zooms the drawing to the existing limits

4   Both the pan and zoom commands have a REALTIME option.

5   The Aerial View allows interactive pan and zoom.

6   The Aerial View is more suited to large drawings.

Chapter 25

Hatching

AutoCAD R2000 has associated boundary hatching. The hatching (sectioning) must be added by the user, and there are three types:
a) predefined, i.e. AutoCAD's stored hatch patterns
b) user defined
c) custom – not considered in this book.

When applying hatching, the user has two methods of defining the hatch pattern boundary:
a) by selecting objects which make the boundary
b) by picking a point within the boundary.

There are two hatch commands available:
a) HATCH: command line entry only
b) BHATCH: activated by icon, menu bar or command line entry. This command displays a dialogue box.

Getting ready

1 Open the A:A3PAPER standard sheet and refer to Fig. 25.1.

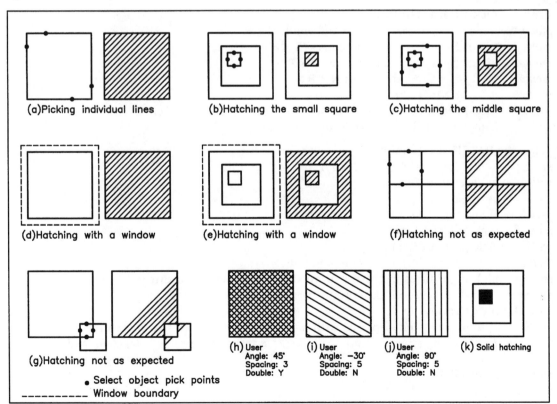

Figure 25.1   User-defined hatching using the select objects method.

2 Draw a 50 unit square on layer OUT and multiple copy it to 10 other parts of the screen. Add the other lines within the required squares. Note that I have included additional squares to indicate appropriate object selection.

3 Make layer SECT current.

User-defined hatch patterns – select objects method

User-defined hatching consists of straight line patterns, the user specifying:
a) the hatch angle relative to the horizontal
b) the distance between the hatch lines – spacing
c) whether single or double (cross) hatching.

1 At the command line enter **HATCH <R>** and:
   prompt   Enter a pattern name or [?/Solid/User defined]<ANGLE>
   enter   U <R> – user-defined option
   prompt   Specify angle for crosshatch lines<0.0>
   enter   **45 <R>**
   prompt   Specify spacing between lines<1.0000>
   enter   **3 <R>**
   prompt   Double hatch area [Yes/No]<N>
   enter   **N <R>**
   prompt   Select objects
   respond **pick the four lines of first square and right-click**
   and   hatching added to the square – fig. (a).

2 Immediately after the hatching has been added, **right-click** and:
   prompt   Shortcut pop-up menu
   respond **pick Repeat HATCH**
   prompt   Enter a pattern name and enter: **U <R>**
   prompt   Specify an angle and enter: **45 <R>**
   prompt   Specify spacing and enter: **3 <R>**
   prompt   Double hatch and enter: **N <R>**
   prompt   Select objects
   respond **pick four lines indicated in second square then right-click**
   and   hatching added to the small square – fig. (b).

3 Select the HATCH icon from the Draw toolbar and:
   prompt   Boundary Hatch dialogue box as Fig. 25.2
   with   *a*) Type: User-defined
             b) Angle: 45
             c) Spacing: 3, i.e. our previous entries!
   respond **pick Select Objects**
   and   dialogue box disappears
   prompt   Select objects at command line
   respond **pick eight lines in third square then right-click and Enter**
   prompt   Boundary Hatch dialogue box returned
   respond **pick Preview**
    and   1) drawing screen displayed with hatching added – check that it is correct
             2) <Hit enter or right-click to return to dialog> at command line
   respond **right-click**
   prompt   Boundary Hatch dialogue box
   respond **pick OK**
   and   hatching added as fig. (c).

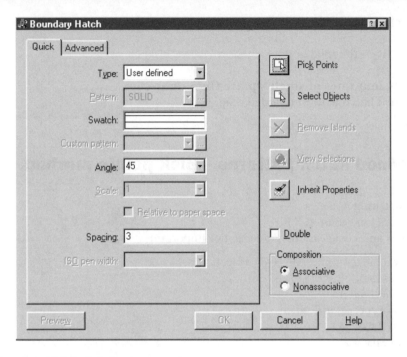

Figure 25.2 Boundary Hatch dialogue box.

4 Menu bar with **Draw–Hatch** and:

prompt	Boundary Hatch dialogue box – settings as before?
respond	**pick Select Objects**
prompt	Select objects
enter	**W <R>** – the window selection option
then	**window the fourth square, right-click and Enter**
prompt	Boundary Hatch dialogue box
respond	**Preview-right click-OK**
and	square hatched – fig. (d).

5 At the command line enter **HATCH <R>** then:
   a) pattern name: U
   b) angle: 45
   c) spacing: 3
   d) double: N
   e) Select objects: window the fifth square then right-click
   f) hatching as fig. (e).

6 Using HATCH from the keyboard, accept the four defaults of U,45,3,N and pick the four lines of the sixth square to give hatching as fig. (f). Not as expected?

7 Repeat the hatch command and select the four lines indicated in the seventh square – fig. (g).

8 With HATCH <R> at the command line, add hatching to the next three squares using the following entries:

	I	*II*	*III*
Pattern:	U	U	U
Angle:	45	−30	90
Spacing:	3	5	5
Double:	Y	N	N
	fig. (h)	fig. (i)	fig. (j)

9 Finally enter **HATCH <R>** and:

   prompt   Enter a pattern name ...
   enter   **S <R>** – the solid option
   prompt   Select objects
   respond **pick four lines of small square then right-click**
   and   a solid hatch pattern is added – fig. (k).

10 This drawing does not need to be saved.

User-defined hatch patterns – pick points method

1 Refer to Fig. 25.3 and:
   a) erase all hatching
   b) erase squares not required
   c) add squares and circles as shown – size not important.

2 With layer Sect current, pick the HATCH icon and:
   prompt   Boundary Hatch dialogue box
   respond 1) check/alter:
               a) Type: User-defined
               b) Angle: 45
               c) Spacing: 3

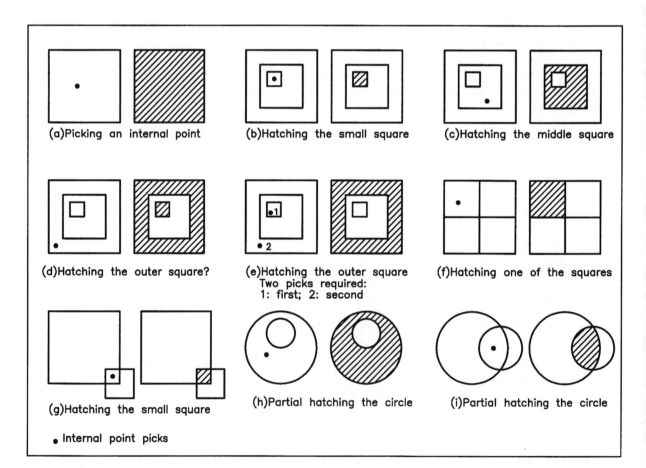

Figure 25.3 User-defined hatching using the pick points method.

2) **pick Pick Points**

prompt	Select internal point
respond	**pick any point within first square**
prompt	Various prompts at command line
then	Select internal point
respond	**right-click and Enter**
prompt	Boundary Hatch dialogue box
respond	**Preview-right click-OK**
and	hatching added to square – fig. (a).

3 Using the HATCH icon with the Pick Points option from the Boundary Hatch dialogue box, add hatching using the points indicated in Fig. 25.3. The only 'problem' is hatching the outer square – figs (d) and (e) – two pick points are required.

Select Objects vs Pick Points

With two options available for hatching, new users to this type of boundary hatch command may be confused as to whether they should Select Objects or Pick Points. In general the Pick Points option is the simpler to use, and will allow complex shapes to be hatched with a single pick within the area to be hatched. To demonstrate the effect:

1 Erase all objects from the screen and refer to Fig. 25.4.

2 Draw two sets of intersecting circles – any size. We want to hatch the intersecting area of the three circles.

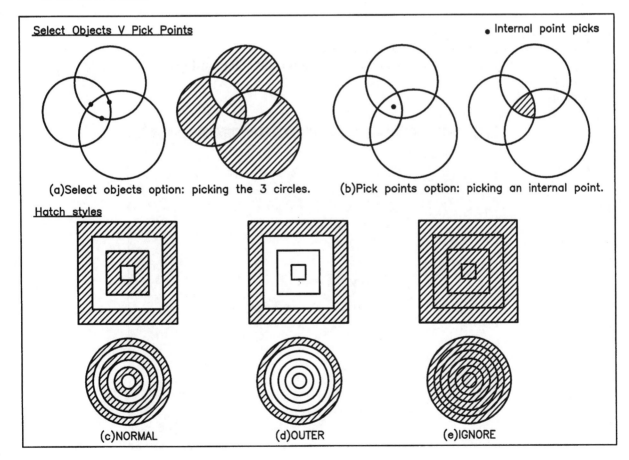

Select Objects V Pick Points

• Internal point picks

(a)Select objects option: picking the 3 circles.

(b)Pick points option: picking an internal point.

Hatch styles

(c)NORMAL

(d)OUTER

(e)IGNORE

Figure 25.4 Using the Hatch command.

3 Select the HATCH icon and from the Boundary Hatch dialogue box set: User-defined, Angle of 45, Spacing of 3, then:
   a) pick the Select Objects option
   b) pick the three circles
   c) preview–right click–OK and hatching as fig. (a).

4 Select the HATCH icon again and:
   a) pick Pick Points option
   b) pick any point within the area to be hatched
   c) preview–right click–OK and hatching as fig. (b).

Hatch Style

AutoCAD has a hatch style option which allows the user to control three 'variants' of the hatch command. To demonstrate the hatch style, refer to Fig. 25.4 and draw:
a) a 70 sided square with three smaller squares 'inside it'
b) six concentric circles, smallest radius being 5
c) copy the squares and circles to two other areas of the screen.

1 Select the HATCH icon and:
   prompt   Boundary Hatch dialogue box
   ensure   User-defined, Angle: 45, Spacing: 3
   then ~   **pick Advanced tab**
   prompt   Boundary Hatch dialogue box with Advanced tab displayed
   note   *a*) Island detection style 'picture'
                b) Style: Normal active – Fig. 25.5
   respond   **pick Select Objects**
   prompt   Select objects at the command line
   respond   **window the first square and circle then right-click and Enter**
   prompt   Advanced boundary hatch dialogue box
   respond   pick Preview–right click–OK
   and   Hatching added as fig. (c).

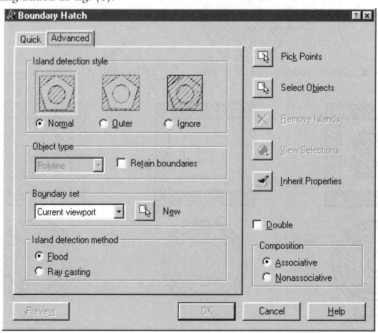

Figure 25.5   Boundary Hatch (advanced) dialogue box.

2 Repeat the HATCH icon and with the Advanced tab:
  a) alter Island detection style to Outer
  b) pick Select Objects and window the second square and circle
  c) preview then OK – hatching as fig. (d).

3 Using the Advanced tab of the Boundary Hatch dialogue box, alter the island detection style to Ignore, and add hatching to the third square and circle – fig. (e).

4 *Note:* it is usual to leave the style at 'Normal' and the user controls the hatch area by picking the relevant points within the area to be hatched.

5 Save if required, but we will not use this drawing again.

Release 2000's predefined hatch patterns

R2000 has several stored hatch patterns which can be accessed using the command line HATCH entry or from the Boundary Hatch dialogue box, which is slightly easier. With predefined hatch patterns, the user specifies:
a) the scale of the patterns
b) the angle of the pattern.

1 Open your standard sheet, refer to Fig. 25.6(A) and:
  a) draw a 50 unit square
  b) multiple copy the square to eleven other places on the screen
  c) add other lines and circles as displayed.

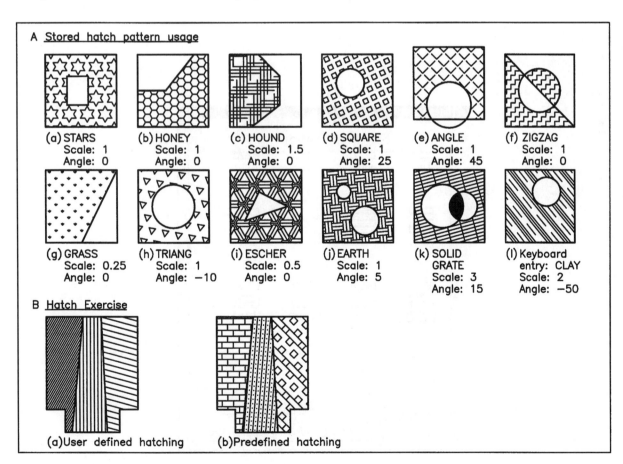

Figure 25.6 Using predefined (stored) hatch patterns.

2 Select the HATCH icon and:

 prompt Boundary Hatch dialogue box

 respond 1) with Advanced tab, set Island detection style: Normal

     2) pick Quick tab

     3) pick Type: Pattern

     4) pick **...** at pattern

 prompt Hatch Pattern Palette dialogue box with four tab selections:

     ANSI, ISO, Other Predefined, Custom

 respond 1) ensure Other Predefined tab active

     2) scroll until PLAST to ZIGZAG displayed – Fig. 25.7

     3) pick STARS then OK

 prompt Boundary Hatch dialogue box

 with   1) Pattern: STARS

     2) Swatch: display of stars hatch pattern

 respond 1) Angle: 0

     2) Scale: 1 – dialogue box as Fig. 25.8

     3) pick Pick Points

     4) select any internal point in first square

     5) right-click and Enter

     6) Preview-right click-OK

 and   Hatching added as fig. (a).

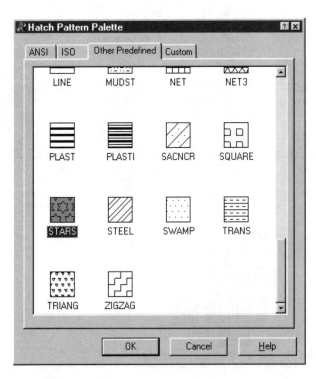

Figure 25.7 Hatch Palette dialogue box.

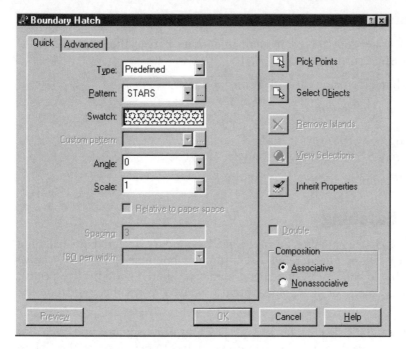

Figure 25.8 Boundary Hatch (Predefined) dialogue box.

3 Repeat the HATCH icon selection and using the following hatch pattern names, scales and angles, add hatching to the other squares using the pick points option:

fig.	pattern	scale	angle
b	HONEY	1	0
c	HOUND	1.5	0
d	SQUARE	1	25
e	ANGLE	1	45
f	ZIGZAG	1	0
g	GRASS	0.25	0
h	TRIANG	1	−10
i	ESCHER	0.5	0
j	EARTH	1	5
k	SOLID		
	GRATE	3	15

4 Finally enter **HATCH <R>** and the command line and:

prompt   Enter a pattern name or [?/Solid/...

enter   **CLAY <R>**

prompt   Specify a scale for the pattern and enter: **2 <R>**

prompt   Specify an angle for the pattern and enter: -50 <R>

prompt   Select objects

respond   pick lines and circle then right-click – fig. (l).

5 Exercise is complete, so save if required.

Hatch exercise

1 Open the A:USEREX and copy the component to another part of the screen. Refer to Fig. 25.6(B). Layer SECT current.

2 Add the following hatching using the Pick Points option:

User-defined	*Predefined*
1) angle: 60, spacing: 2	1) BRICK, scale: 1, angle: 0
2) angle: 90, spacing: 4	2) SACNCR, scale: 2, angle: 40
3) angle: −15, spacing: 6	3) BOX, scale: 1, angle: 45.

3 Save this exercise if required, but not as A:USEREX.

Associative hatching

Release 2000 has associative hatching, i.e. of the hatch boundary is altered, the hatching within the boundary will be 'regenerated' to fill the new boundary limits. Associative hatching is applicable to both user-defined and predefined hatch patterns, irrespective of whether the select objects or pick points option was used. We will demonstrate the effect by example so:

1 Open A:A3PAPER standard sheet, refer to Fig. 25.9 and draw squares and circles as displayed. Note that I have drawn two sets of each squares to demonstrate the 'before and after' effect.

2 Make layer SECT current.

3 With the HATCH icon:
   a) Type: User defined; angle: 45; spacing: 5
   b) Composition: Associative ON, i.e. tick in box
   c) Pick Points and hatch the first square.

4 Select the MOVE icon and:
   a) pick the circle in the first square
   b) move it to another position in the square
   c) hatching 'changes' – fig. (a), i.e. it is associative

5 Figure 25.9 displays some associative hatching effects, which you should try for yourself. The effects are:
   b) scaling the circle
   c) rotating two trimmed circles
   d) two circle moves
   e) moving the line
   f) mirror the triangle and deleting old objects
   g) scaling the circle with two hatch areas
   h) scaling the circle
   i) moving the circle.

6 Associative hatch 'quirks'. Associative hatching does not occur with every modify operation as is displayed in Fig. 25.9 with:
   j) filleting two corners of the square
   k) multiple copy of the circle
   l) moving the line – compare with fig. (e) – why?

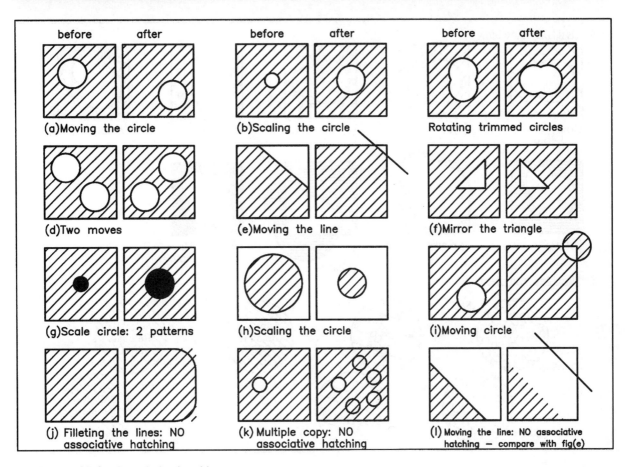

(a)Moving the circle (b)Scaling the circle Rotating trimmed circles

(d)Two moves (e)Moving the line (f)Mirror the triangle

(g)Scale circle: 2 patterns (h)Scaling the circle (i)Moving circle

(j) Filleting the lines: NO associative hatching (k) Multiple copy: NO associative hatching (l) Moving the line: NO associative hatching — compare with fig(e)

Figure 25.9 Associative hatching.

Modifying hatching

Hatching which has been added to an object can be modified, i.e. the angle, spacing or scale can be altered, or the actual pattern changed.

1 Open A:A3PAPER and refer to Fig. 25.10(A). Display the MODIFY II toolbar.

2 Draw a square with two trimmed circles inside it – any size.

3 *a*) Use the HATCH icon to add hatching to the square with:
   User defined pattern; angle: 45; spacing: 8 – fig. (a)
   b) ensure that Associative hatching is on.

4 Menu bar with **Modify–Object–Hatch** and:
   prompt Select associative hatch object
   respond **pick the added hatching**
   prompt Hatch Edit dialogue box
   respond 1) alter angle to –45
          2) alter spacing to 4
          3) pick OK – fig. (b).

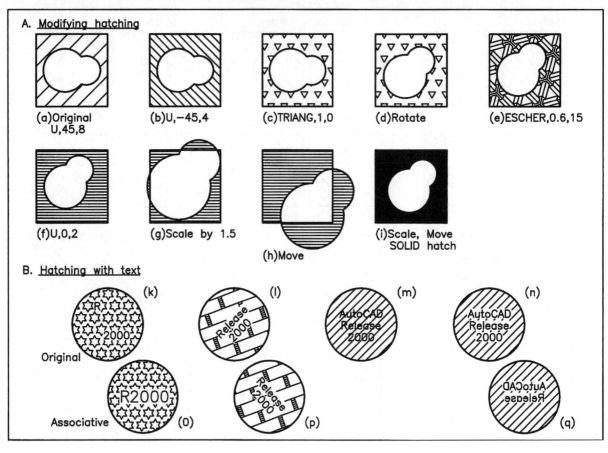

Figure 25.10 Modifying hatching and hatching with text.

5   Select the EDIT HATCH icon from the Modify II toolbar and:

prompt   Select associative hatch object
respond   **pick the altered hatching**
prompt   Hatch Edit dialogue box
respond   1) Type: Predefined
           2) Pattern: pick ...
           3) scroll and pick TRIANG then OK
           4) scale: 1 and angle: 0
           5) pick OK – fig. (c).

6   Rotate the trimmed circles by 45 degrees – fig. (d).

7   Using the Edit Hatch icon:
    a) Type: Predefined ESCHER
    b) scale: 0.6 and angle: 15 – fig. (e).

8   Edit the hatching to User-defined, angle: 0, spacing: 2 – fig. (f).

9   Scale the circles by 1.5 – fig. (g). Zoom needed to pick?

10 Move the circles – fig. (h).

11 Finally: *a*) scale the circles by 0.667
              b) move the circles into the square
              c) change hatch pattern to SOLID
              d) fig. (i).

Text and hatching

Text which is placed in an area to be hatched can be displayed with a 'clear border' around it.

1 Refer to Fig. 25.10(B) and draw four 50 diameter circles.

2 Add any suitable text as shown. This text can have any height, rotation angle, position, etc.

3 With the HATCH icon:
   a) Type: Predefined STARS with scale: 0.75 and angle: 0
   b) Pick Points and pick any point in first circle
   c) Preview–right click–OK and result as fig. (k).

4 Use the HATCH icon with:
   a) Type: Predefined BRSTONE, scale: 1, angle: 20
   b) Pick Points and pick any point inside second circle
   c) Preview–right click–OK and result as fig. (l).

5 HATCH icon using:
   a) User defined at 45 with 4 spacing
   b) Select Objects and pick third circle only
   c) Preview, etc. – fig. (m).

6 Final HATCH with:
   a) User defined, angle: 45, spacing: 4
   b) Select Objects and pick fourth circle **and** text items
   c) Preview, etc. – fig. (n).

7 Associative hatching works with text items:

   fig. (o): moving and scaling the two items of text
   fig. (p): rotating the text item
   fig. (q): mirroring the text item, then erase part of it.

8 Save if required – the exercise is complete.

Summary

1 Hatching is a draw command, activated:
   a) from the menu bar
   b) by icon selection
   c) with keyboard entry – HATCH or BHATCH.

2 AutoCAD has three types of hatch pattern:
   a) user-defined: this is line only hatching. The user specifies the angle for the hatch lines, the spacing between these lines and whether the hatching is to be single or double, i.e. cross-hatching.
   b) predefined: these are stored hatch patterns. The user specifies the pattern scale and angle
   c) custom: are patterns designed by the user, but are outside the scope of this book.

3 The hatch boundary can be determines by:
   a) selecting the objects which make the boundary
   b) picking an internal point within the hatch area.

4 Hatching is a single object and can be exploded.

5 Release 2000 has associative hatching which allows the added hatching to change when the hatch boundary changes.

6 Added hatching can be edited.

Assignments

Some AutoCAD users may not use the hatching in their draughting work, but they should still be familiar with the process. The pick points option makes hatching fairly easy and for this reason I have included five interesting exercises for you to attempt. These should test all your existing CAD draughting skills.

1 Activity 16: three different types of component to be drawn and hatched:
   a) a small engineering component. The hatching is user defined and use your own angle and spacing values
   b) a pie chart. The text is to have a height of 8 and the hatch names and variables are given
   c) a model airport runway system.

2 Activity 17: cover plate. A relatively simple drawing to complete. The MIRROR command is useful and the hatching should give no problems. Add text and the dimensions.

3 Activity 18: protected bearing housing. Four views to complete, two with hatching. A fairly easy drawing to complete.

4 Activity 19: steam expansion box. This activity has proved very popular in my previous books and is easier to complete than it would appear. Create the outline from lines and circles, trimming the circles as required. The complete component uses many commands, e.g. offset, fillet, mirror, etc. The hatching should not be mirrored – why?

5 Activity 20: gasket cover. An interesting exercise to complete. Draw the 'left view' which consists only of circles – layers correctly. The right view can be completed using offset, trim and mirror. Do not dimension.

Chapter 26

Point, polygon and solid

These are three useful draw commands which will be demonstrated by example, so:

1   Open A:A3PAPER standard sheet with layer OUT current.
2   Activate the Draw, Modify and Object Snap toolbars.
3   Refer to Fig. 26.1.

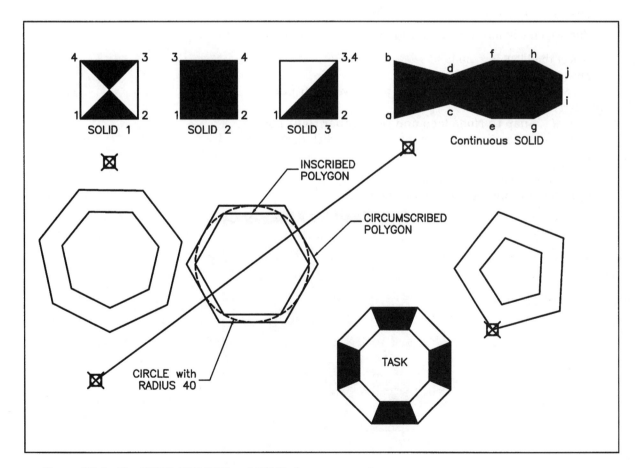

Figure 26.1   The POINT, POLYGON and SOLID draw commands.

Point

A point is an object whose size and appearance is controlled by the user.

1   From the Draw toolbar select the POINT icon and:
    prompt   Current point modes: PDMODE=0 PDSIZE=0.00
             Specify a point
    enter   **50,50 <R>**
    prompt   Specify a point and enter: **60,200 <R>**
    prompt   Specify a point and **ESC** to end the command.

2   Two point objects will be displayed in red on the screen. You may have to toggle the grid off to 'see' these points

3   From the menu bar select **Format–Point Style** and:
    prompt   Point Style dialogue box as Fig. 26.2
    respond 1) pick point style indicated
             2) set Point Size to 5%
             3) check: Set Size Relative to Screen is active
             4) pick OK.

4   The screen will be displayed with the two points regenerated to this new point style.

5   Menu bar with **Draw–Point–Multiple Point** and:
    prompt   Specify a point and enter: **330,85 <R>**
    prompt   Specify a point and enter: **270,210 <R>**
    prompt   Specify a point and **ESC**.

6   The screen will now display two additional points in the selected style.

7   Select the LINE icon and:
    prompt   Specify first point
    respond **Snap to Node icon and pick lower left point**
    prompt   Specify next point
    respond **Snap to Node icon and pick upper right point**
    prompt   Specify next point and right-click then Enter.

8   *Task.*
    a) set a new point style and size
    b) restore the previous point style and size.

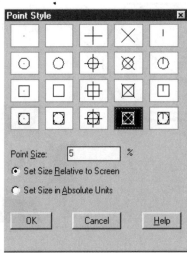

Figure 26.2   Point Style dialogue box.

Polygon

A polygon is a multi-sided figure, each side having the same length and can be drawn by the user specifying:
a) a centre point and an inscribed/circumscribed radius
b) the endpoints of an edge of the polygon.

A polygon is a POLYLINE type object and has the 'properties' of polylines – next chapter.

1 Select the POLYGON icon from the Draw toolbar and:
   prompt   Enter number of sides<4> and enter: **6 <R>**
   prompt   Specify center of polygon or [Edge]
   respond **Snap to Midpoint icon and pick the line**
   prompt   Enter an option [Inscribed in circle/Circumscribed about
            circle]<I>
   enter   **I <R>** – the inscribed (default) option
   prompt   Specify radius of circle and enter: **40 <R>**.

2 Repeat the POLYGON icon selection and:
   prompt   Enter number of sides<6> and enter: **6 <R>**
   prompt   Specify center of polygon or...
   respond **Snap to Midpoint icon and pick the line**
   prompt   Enter an option [Inscribed/Circumscribed...
   enter   **C <R>** – the circumscribed option
   prompt   Specify radius of circle and enter: **40 <R>**.

3 The screen will display an inscribed and circumscribed circle drawn relative to a 40 radius circle as shown in Fig. 26.1. These hexagonal polygons can be considered as equivalent to:
   a) inscribed: ACROSS CORNERS (A/C)
   b) circumscribed: ACROSS FLATS (A/F).

4 From the menu bar select **Draw–Polygon** and:
   prompt   Enter number of sides<6> and enter: **5 <R>**
   prompt   Specify center of polygon or [Edge]
   enter   **E <R>** – the edge option
   prompt   Specify first endpoint of edge
   respond **Snap to Node icon and pick lower right point**
   prompt   Specify second endpoint of edge
   enter   **@50<15 <R>**.

5 At the command line enter **POLYGON <R>** and:
   a) Number of sides: 7
   b) Edge/Center: E
   c) First point: 60,100
   d) Second point: @30<25.

6 Using the OFFSET icon, set an offset distance of 15 and:
   a) offset the 5 sided polygon 'inwards'
   b) offset the 7 sided polygon 'outwards'.

Solid (or more correctly 2D Solid)

A command which 'fills-in' lined shapes, the appearance of the final shape being determined by the pick point order.

1 With the snap on, draw three squares of side 40, towards the top part of the screen – Fig. 26.1.

2 Menu bar with **Draw–Surfaces–2D Solid** and:
prompt   Specify first point and pick point 1 of SOLID 1
prompt   Specify second point and pick point 2
prompt   Specify third point and pick point 3
prompt   Specify fourth point and pick point 4
prompt   Specify third point and right-click to end command.

3 At the command line enter **SOLID <R>** and:
prompt   Specify first point and pick point 1 of SOLID 2
prompt   Specify second point and pick point 2
prompt   and pick points 3 and 4 in order displayed.

4 Activate the SOLID command and with SOLID 3 pick points 1–4 in the order given, i.e. 3 and 4 are the same points.

5 The three squares demonstrate how three- and four-sided shapes can be solid filled.

6 Using the SOLID command enter the following:
First point: with SNAP ON, pick a point a
Second point: pick a point b
Third point: pick point c
Fourth point: pick point d
Third point: pick point e
Fourth point: pick point f
Third point: pick point g
Fourth point: pick point h
Third point: .pick point i
Fourth point: pick point j
Third point: right-click.

7 These last entries demonstrate how continuous filled 2D shapes can be created.

8 *Task.*
    1) *a*) Draw an 8 sided polygon, centre at 260,60 and circumscribed in a 40 radius circle
        b) offset the polygon inwards by a distance of 15
        c) use the SOLID command to produce the effect in Fig. 26.1.
        d) a running object snap to Endpoint will help.

    2) What are the minimum and maximum number of sides allowed with the POLYGON command?

    3) *a*) at the command line enter **FILL <R>** and:
        prompt   Enter mode [ON/OFF]<ON>
        enter   **OFF <R>**
        b) at command line enter REGEN <R>
        c) the solid fill effect is not displayed
        d) turn FILL back on then REGEN the screen.

9 The exercise is complete and can be saved if required.

Assignment

Activity 21 requires a backgammon board to be drawn. This is a nice simple drawing to complete. The filled triangles can be created with the 2D SOLID command or by hatching with the predefined SOLID pattern. The multiple copy and mirror commands are useful.

Summary

1 A point is an object whose appearance depends on the selection made from the Point Style dialogue box.

2 Only **one** point style can be displayed on the screen at any time.

3 The Snap to Node icon is used with points.

4 A polygon is a multi-sided figure having equal sides.

5 A polygon is a polyline type object.

6 Line shapes can be 'solid filled', the appearance of the solid fill being dependent on the order of the pick points.

7 Only three- and four-sided shapes can be solid filled.

Chapter 27

Polylines and splines

A polyline is a single object which can consist of line and arc segments and can be drawn with varying widths. It has its own editing facility and can be activated by icon selection, from the menu bar or by keyboard entry.

A polyline is a very useful and powerful object yet it is probably one of the most underused draw commands. The demonstration which follows is quite long and several keyboard options are required.

1 Open the A:A3PAPER standard sheet with layer OUT current. Refer to Fig. 27.1 and display the Draw, Modify, Object Snap and Modify II toolbars.

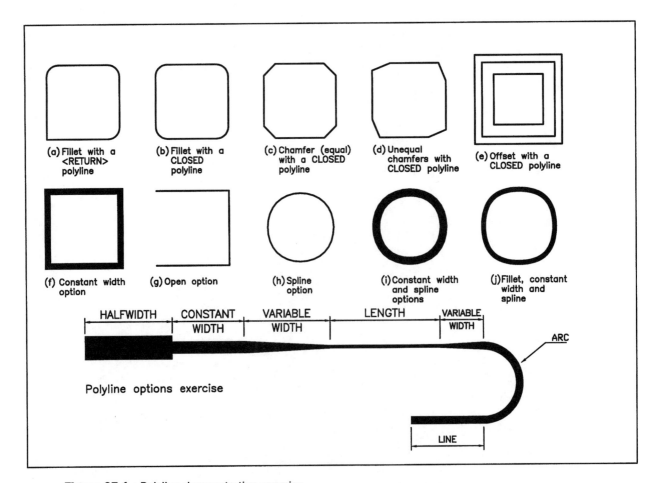

Figure 27.1 Polyline demonstration exercise.

2 Select the POLYLINE icon from the Draw toolbar and:
- *prompt*   Specify start point and enter: **15,220 <R>**
- *prompt*   Specify next point or [Arc/Close/Halfwidth... and enter: **@50,0 <R>**
- *prompt*   Specify next point and enter: **@0,50 <R>**
- *prompt*   Specify next point and enter: **@–50,0 <R>**
- *prompt*   Specify next point and enter: **@0,–50 <R>**
- *prompt*   Specify next point and right-click.

3 From menu bar select **Draw–Polyline** and:
- *prompt*   Specify start point and enter: **85,220 <R>**
- *prompt*   Specify next point and enter: **@50<0 <R>** – polar
- *prompt*   Specify next point and enter: **135,270 <R>** – absolute
- *prompt*   Specify next point and enter: **@–50,0 <R>** – relative
- *prompt*   Specify next point and enter: **C <R>** – close option.

4 Select the COPY icon and:
- *prompt*   Select objects
- *respond*   **pick any point on SECOND square**
- *and*   all four lines are highlighted with one pick
- *then*   right-click
- *prompt*   Specify base point
- *and*   multiple copy the square to eight other parts of the screen.

5 Selecting the appropriate icon:
- *a*) set the fillet radius to 8
- *b*) set chamfer distances to 8.

6 Select the FILLET icon and:
- *prompt*   Select first object or [Polyline/Radius/Trim]
- *enter*   **P <R>** – polyline option
- *prompt*   Select 2D polyline
- *respond*   **pick any point on first square**
- *prompt*   3 lines were filleted – fig. (a).

7 Repeat the fillet icon selection and:
- *a*) enter **P <R>**
- *b*) pick any point on second square
- *c*) prompt: *4 lines were filleted* – fig. (b).

8 *Note*:
- *a*) the difference between the two fillet operations is:
  - fig. (a): not a 'closed' polyline, so only three corners filleted
  - fig. (b): a 'closed' polyline, so all four corners filleted
- *b*) the corner 'not filleted' in fig. (a) is the start point.

9 Select the CHAMFER icon and:
- *a*) enter **P <R>**
- *b*) pick any point on third square
- *c*) prompt: *4 lines were chamfered* – fig. (c).

10 *Task:* set chamfer distances to 12 and 5 then CHAMFER the fourth square remembering to enter **P <R>** to activate the polyline option. The result is fig. (d). Note the orientation of the 12 and 5 chamfer distances.

11 *a*) Set the offset distance to 5 and offset the fifth square 'outwards'
- *b*) set the offset distance to 8 and offset the fifth square 'inwards'
- *c*) the complete square is offset with a single pick – fig. (e).

12 Select the EDIT POLYLINE icon from the Modify II toolbar and:
prompt   Select polyline
respond **pick the sixth square**
prompt   Enter an option [Open/Join/Width...
enter   **W <R>** – the width option
prompt   Specify new width for all segments
enter   **4 <R>**
prompt   Enter an option [Open/Join/Width...
respond right-click and Enter to end command – fig. (f).

13 Menu bar with **Modify–Object–Polyline** and:
prompt   Select polyline
respond **pick the seventh square**
prompt   Enter an option [Open/Join/Width...
enter   **O <R>** – the open option
prompt   Enter an option [Open/Join/Width...
enter   right-click and Enter
and   square displayed with 'last segment' removed – fig. (g).

14 At the command line enter **PEDIT <R>** and:
prompt   Select polyline and pick the eighth square
prompt   options and enter: S <R> – the spline option
prompt   options and enter: **X <R>** – exit command
and   square displayed as a splined curve, in this case a circle – fig. (h).

15 Activate the polyline edit command, pick the ninth square then:
a) enter **W <R>** then **5 <R>**
b) enter **S <R>**
c) enter **X <R>** – fig. (i).

16 *a*) Set the fillet radius to 12
b) fillet the tenth square – remember P
c) use the polyline edit command with options: (*i*) width of 3, (*ii*) spline and (*iii*) exit – fig. (j).

Polyline options

The polyline command has several options displayed at the prompt line when the start point has been selected. These options can be activated by entering the letter corresponding to the option. The options are:

Arc: draws an arc segment
Close: closes a polyline shape to the start point
Halfwidth: user enters start and end halfwidths
Length: length of line segment entered
Undo: undoes the last option entered
Width: user enters the start and end widths

To demonstrate these options, at the command line enter **PLINE** <R> and:

prompt   Start point and enter: **40,80 <R>** – or pick a suitable point
prompt   Next point/options and enter: **H <R>** – the halfwidth option
prompt   Starting half-width<0.00> and enter: **8 <R>**
prompt   Ending half-width<8.00> and enter: **8 <R>**
prompt   Next point/options and enter **@60,0 <R>** – segment endpoint
prompt   Next point/options and enter: **W <R>** – the width option
prompt   Starting width<16.00> and enter **8 <R>**
prompt   Ending width<8.00> and enter **8 <R>**
prompt   Next point/options and enter: **@50,0 <R>** – segment endpoint
prompt   Next point/options and enter: **W <R>**
prompt   Starting width<8.00> and enter: **8 <R>**
prompt   Ending width<8.00> and enter: **2 <R>**
prompt   Next point/options and enter: **@60,0 <R>** – segment endpoint
prompt   Next point/options and enter: **L <R>** – the length option
prompt   Length of line and enter: **75 <R>**
prompt   Next point/options and enter: **W <R>**
prompt   Starting width<2.00> and enter: **2 <R>**
prompt   Ending width<2.00> and enter: **5 <R>**
prompt   Next point/options and enter: **@30,0 <R>** – segment endpoint
prompt   Next point/options and enter: A <R> – the arc option
prompt   Arc options and enter: **@0,–50 <R>** – arc endpoint
prompt   Arc options and enter: **L <R>** – back to line option
prompt   Next point/options and enter: **@–50,0 <R>** – segment endpoint
prompt   Next point/options, right-click and Enter.

Task

Before leaving this exercise:

1 MOVE the complete polyline shape with a single pick from its start point by **@25,25**.

2 With FILL <R> at the command line, toggle fill off.

3 REGEN the screen.

4 Turn FILL on then REGEN the screen.

5 This exercise is now complete. Save if required, but it will not be used again.

Line and arc segments

A continuous polyline object can be created from a series of line and arc segments of varying width. In the demonstration which follows we will use several of the options and the final shape will be used in the next chapter. The exercise is given as a rather **long** list of options and entries, but persevere with it.

1 Open A:A3PAPER, layer OUT current, toolbars to suit.

2 Refer to Fig. 27.2, select the polyline icon and:

Prompt	Enter	Ref
Start point	50,50	pt 1
next pt/options	L	
Length of line	45	pt 2
next pt/options	W	
Starting width	0	
Ending width	10	
next pt/options	@120,0	pt 3
next pt/options	A	
arc end/options	@50,50	pt 4
arc end/options	L	
next pt/options	W	
Starting width	10	
Ending width	0	
next pt/options	@0,100	pt 5
next pt/options	220,220	pt 6
next pt/options	W	
Starting width	0	
Ending width	5	
next pt/options	@30<−90	pt 7
next pt/options	A	
arc end/options	@−40,0	pt 8
arc end/options	@−50,30	pt 9
arc end/options	L	
next pt/options	W	
Starting width	5	
Ending width	0	
next pt/options	50,180	pt 10
next pt/options	C	pt 1 again.

3 If your entries are correct the polyshape will be the same as that displayed in Fig. 27.2. Mistakes with polylines can be rectified as each segment is being constructed with the **U** (undo) option. Both the line and arc segments have their own option entries.

4 Repeat the polyline icon selection and:

Prompt	*Enter*	*Ref*
Start point	80,120	pt a
next pt/options	A	
arc end/options	W	
Starting width	0	
Ending width	5	
arc end/options	@60<0	pt b
arc end/options	W	
Starting width	5	
Ending width	15	
arc end/options	@20,20	pt c
arc end/options	L	
next pt/options	right-click and Enter.	

5 Save the two polyshapes as **A:POLYEX** for the next chapter.

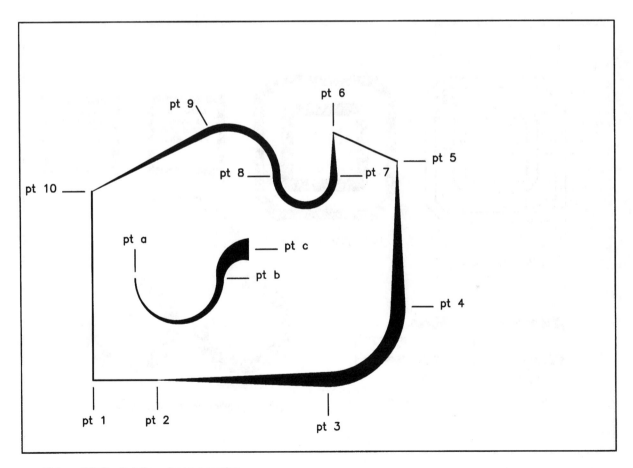

Figure 27.2 Polyline shape exercise.

Polyline tasks

Polyline shapes can be used with the modify commands. To demonstrate their use, open your A:A3PAPER standard sheet and refer to Fig. 27.3.

1 Draw a 100 closed polyline square and use the sizes given to complete the component in fig. (a). It is easier than you may think. Commands are OFFSET, CHAMFER, FILLET.

2 Draw a 100 closed polyline square of width 7. Use the sizes from the first exercise to complete a solid filled component – fig. (b).

3 Draw two 50 sided polyline squares each of width 5 but:
   a) first square to be drawn as four lines and ended with <RETURN>
   b) second square to be closed with close option.

   Note the difference at the polyline start point – fig. (c).

4 Polylines can be trimmed and extended. Try these operations with an 'arrowhead' type polyline with starting width 10 and ending width 0 – fig. (d).

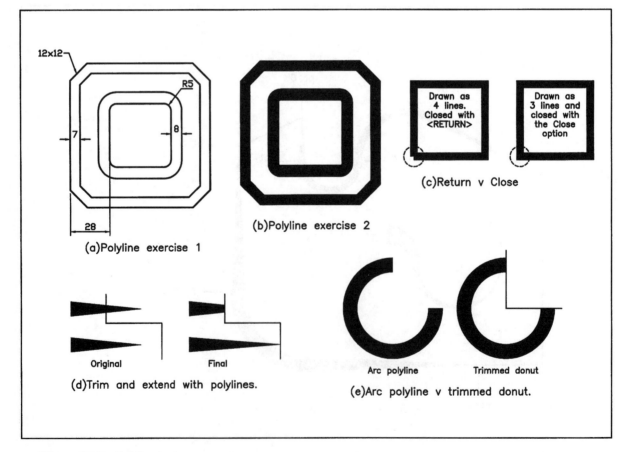

Figure 27.3 Polyline tasks.

5 *a*) Draw a polyline arc with following entries:

Prompt	*Enter*
Start point	pick to suit
next pt/options	A
arc end/options	W
Starting width	5
Ending width	5
arc end/options	CE
Center point	@0,–30
options	A
arc end/included angle	270
arc end/options	<RETURN>

   b) draw a donut with:
   Inside diameter: 50
   Outside diameter: 70
   Centre: pick to suit
   c) draw two lines and trim the donut to these lines
   d) decide which method is easier – fig. (e).

6 No need to save these tasks.

Splines

A spline is a smooth curve which passes through a given set of points. These points can be picked, entered as coordinates or referenced to existing objects. The spline is drawn as a non-uniform rational B-spline or **NURBS**. Splines have uses in many CAD areas, e.g. car body design, contour mapping, etc. At our level we will only investigate the 2D spline curve.

1 Open your standard sheet or clear all objects from the screen.

2 Refer to Fig. 27.4 and with layer CL current, draw two circles:
   a) centre: 80,150 with radius: 50
   b) centre: 280,150 with radius: 25.

3 Layer OUT current and select the SPLINE icon from the Draw toolbar and:

prompt	Specify first point or [Object]
respond	**Snap to Center icon and pick larger circle**
prompt	Specify next point and enter: **90,220 <R>**
prompt	Specify next point or [Close/Fit tolerance] and enter: **110,80 <R>**
prompt	Specify next point and enter: **130,220 <R>**
prompt	Specify next point and enter: **150,80 <R>**
prompt	Specify next point and enter: **170,220 <R>**
prompt	Specify next point and enter: **190,80 <R>**
prompt	Specify next point and enter: **210,220 <R>**
prompt	Specify next point and enter: **230,80 <R>**
prompt	Specify next point and enter: **250,220 <R>**
prompt	Specify next point and enter: **270,80 <R>**
prompt	Specify next point and **Center icon and pick smaller circle**
prompt	Specify next point and right-click and Enter
prompt	Specify start tangent and enter: **80,150 <R>**
prompt	Specify end tangent and enter: **280,150 <R>**.

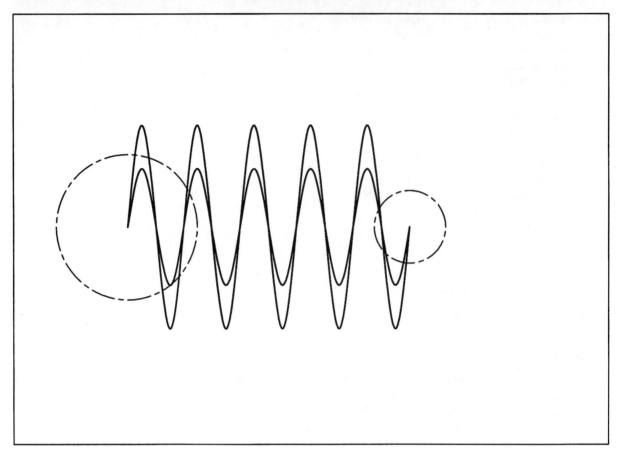

Figure 27.4 Spline curve exercise.

4 Menu bar with **Draw–Spline** and:

prompt	Specify first point or [Object]
respond	**Snap to center of larger circle**
prompt	Specify next point and enter: **90,190 <R>**
prompt	Specify next point and enter: **110,110 <R>**
prompt	Specify next point
respond	enter following coordinate pairs: 130,190 150,110 170,190 190,110 210,190 230,110 250,190 270,110 280,150
then	right-click and Enter
prompt	Enter start tangent and snap to center of larger circle
prompt	Enter end tangent and snap to center of small circle.

5 At this stage save drawing as **A:SPLINEX** for next chapter.

6 The spline options have not been considered at this introductory level, although close should be obvious?

Summary

1 A polyline is a single object which can consist of line and arc segments of varying width.

2 A polyshape which is to be closed should be completed with the Close option.

3 Polyline shapes can be chamfered, filleted, trimmed, extended, etc.

4 Polylines have their own edit command – next chapter.

5 A spline is **not** a polyline but a NURBS curve with specific properties.

Assignments

Two activities of varying difficulty have been included for you to test your polyline ability.

1 Activity 22: shapes. Some basic polyline shapes created from line and arc segments. All relevant sizes are given for you. Snap on helps.

2 Activity 23: printed circuit board. An interesting application of the polyline command. It is harder to complete than you may think, especially with the dimensions being given in ordinate form. Can you add the dimensions given? All the relevant sizes are given on the drawing. Use your discretion when positioning the 'lines'.

Chapter 28

Modifying polylines and splines

Polylines have their own special editing facility which gives the user access to several extra options in addition to the existing modify commands.

1 Open the polyline exercise A:POLYEX and refer to Fig. 28.1.

2 Select the EDIT POLYLINE icon from the Modify II toolbar and:

prompt   Select polyline
respond **pick any point on outer polyline shape**
prompt   Enter an option [Open/Join/Width/Edit vertex/Fit/Spline/
           Decurve...

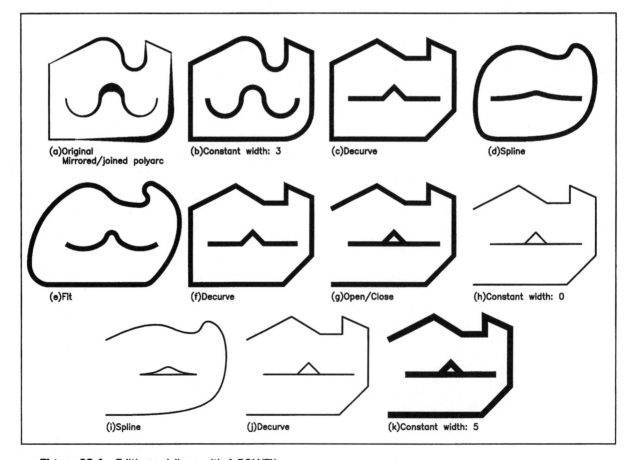

Figure 28.1   Editing polylines with A:POLYEX.

Prompt	*Enter*	*Ref*	*Options*
respond enter the following in respond to the prompt:			
Open/Join...	W		constant width
new width	3	fig. (b)	
options	D	fig. (c)	decurve
options	S	fig. (d)	spline
options	F	fig. (e)	fit
options	D	fig. (f)	
options	O	fig. (g)	open
options	W		constant width
new width	0	fig. (h)	
options	S	fig. (i)	
options	D	fig. (j)	
options	W		constant width
new width	5	fig. (k)	
options	ESC		end command.

The join option

This is a very useful option as it allows several individual polylines to be 'joined' into a single polyline object. Refer to Fig. 28.1 and:

1 Use the MIRROR command to mirror the polyarc shape about a vertical line through the right end of the object – ortho on may help, but remember to toggle it off.

2 At the command line enter **PEDIT <R>** and:
   prompt   `Select polyline`
   respond **pick any point on original polylarc**
   prompt   `Enter an option [Close/Join/Width/Edit...`
   enter   **J <R>**
   prompt   `Select objects`
   respond **pick the two polyarcs then right-click**
   prompt   `2 segments added to polyline`
   then   `Enter an option [Close/Join/Width`
   enter   **X <R>** to end command.

3 The two arc segments will now be one polyline object.

4 Menu bar with **Modify–Polyline** and:
   a) pick the mirrored joined polyshape
   b) enter the same options as step 2 of the first part of the exercise, **except** enter C(lose) instead of O(pen).

5 *Note:* when the Edit Polyline command is activated and a polyline selected, the prompt is:
   a) `Open/Join/Width` etc if the selected polyshape is 'closed'
   b) `Close/Join/Width` etc if the selected polyshape is 'opened'.

Edit vertex option

The options available with the Edit Polyline command usually 'redraws' the selected polyshape after each entry, e.g. if **S** is entered at the options prompt, the polyshape will be redrawn as a splined curve. Using the Edit vertex option is slightly different from this. When **E** is entered as an option, the user has another set of options. Refer to Fig. 28.2 and:

1 Erase all objects from the screen or open A:A3PAPER.

2 Draw an 80 sided **closed** square polyshape and multiple copy it to three other areas of the screen.

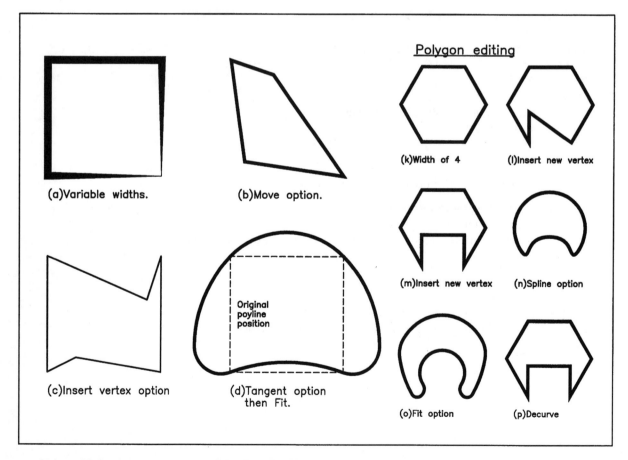

Figure 28.2   Edit vertex option of the Edit Polyline command.

3 *Variable widths.* Menu bar with **Modify–Polyline** and:

prompt	`Select polyline`
respond	**pick the first square**
prompt	`Enter an option [Open/Join/Width...`
enter	**W <R>** and then: **5 <R>**
prompt	`Enter an option [Open/Join/Width...`
enter	**E <R>** – the edit vertex option
prompt	`Enter a vertex editing option`
	`[Next/Previous/Break/Insert/...`
and	an X is placed at the start vertex (lower left for me)
enter	**W <R>**
prompt	`Specify starting width for next segment` and enter: **5 <R>**
prompt	`Specify ending width for next segment<5>` and enter: **0 <R>**
prompt	`Enter a vertex editing option [Next/Previous/Break...`
enter	**N <R>** and X moves to next vertex (lower right for me)
prompt	`Enter a vertex editing option [Next/Previous/Break...`
enter	**W <R>**
prompt	`Specify starting width for next segment` and enter: **0 <R>**
prompt	`Specify ending width for next segment` and enter: **5 <R>**
prompt	`Enter a vertex editing option [Next/Previous/Break...`
enter	**X <R>** – to exit the edit vertex option
then	**X <R>** – to exit the edit polyline command – fig. (a).

4 *Moving a vertex.* Select the Edit Polyline icon and:

a) pick the second square
b) enter a constant width of 2
c) enter **E <R>** – the edit vertex option

prompt	`Enter a vertex editing option [Next/Previous/Break`
enter	**N <R>** until X at lower left vertex – probably is?
then	**M <R>** – the move option
prompt	`Specify new location for marked vertex`
enter	**@10,10 <R>**
prompt	`Enter a vertex editing option [Next/Previous/Break..`
enter	**N <R>** until X at diagonally opposite vertex
then	**M <R>**
prompt	`Specify new location for marked vertex` and enter: **@–50,–10 <R>**
prompt	`Enter a vertex editing option [Next/Previous/Break`
enter	**X <R>** then **X <R>** – fig. (b).

5 *Inserting a new vertex.* At the command line enter **PEDIT <R>** and:

a) pick the third square
b) enter a constant width of 1
c) pick the edit vertex option
d) enter N <R> until X at lower left vertex then:

prompt	`Enter a vertex editing option[Next/Previous/Break..`
enter	**I <R>** – the insert new vertex option
prompt	`Specify location of new vertex`
enter	**@20,10 <R>**
prompt	`Enter a vertex editing option [Next/Previous/Break...`
prompt	**N <R>** until X at opposite corner then **I <R>**
prompt	`Specify location of new vertex`
enter	**@–10,–30 <R>**
then	**X <R>** and **X <R>** – fig. (c).

6 *Tangent–Fit Options.* Activate the edit polyline command, set a constant width of 2, select the edit vertex option with the X at lower left vertex and:

prompt	`Enter a vertex editing option [Next/Previous/Break...`
enter	**T <R>** – the tangent option
prompt	`Specify direction of vertex tangent`
enter	**20 <R>**
and	note arrowed line direction
prompt	`Enter a vertex editing option [Next/Previous/Break...`
enter	**N <R>** until X at lower right vertex
then	**T <R>**
prompt	`Specify direction of vertex tangent`
enter	**–20 <R>** – note arrowed line direction
prompt	`Enter a vertex editing option [Next/Previous/Break...`
enter	X <R> – to end the edit vertex options
prompt	`Enter an option [Open/Join...`
enter	**F <R>** – the fit option
then	**X <R>** – to end command and give fig. (d).

Note: the final fit shape 'passes through' the vertices of the original polyline square.

Editing a polygon

A polygon is a polyline and can therefore be edited with the Edit Polyline command. To demonstrate the effect:

1 Draw a 6 sided polygon inscribed in a 40 radius circle towards the right of the screen.

2 Activate the Edit Polyline command, pick the polygon then enter the following option sequence:

a) W then 4 – fig. (k)
b) E
c) N until X at lower left vertex
d) I
e) @0,30 – fig. (l)
f) I
g) @40,0 – fig. (m)
h) X
i) S – fig. (n)
j) F – fig. (o)
k) D – fig. (p)
l) X.

Editing a spline curve

Spline curves can be edited in a similar manner to polylines, so open drawing A:SPLINEX and refer to Fig. 28.3.

1 Select the EDIT SPLINE icon from the Modify II toolbar and:

prompt	Select spline
respond	**pick the larger spline curve**
and	blue grip type boxes appear
prompt	Enter an option [Fit Data/Close/Move vertex...
enter	**F <R>** – the fit data option
and	boxes at each entered vertex of curve
prompt	Enter a fit data option [Add/Close/Delete...
enter	**M <R>** – the move option
prompt	Specify new location or [Next/Previous...
and	red box at left end of spline
enter	**N <R>** until red box at second from left lower vertex
then	**@0,–50 <R>**
prompt	Specify new location or [Next/Previous...
enter	**N <R>** until red box at third from left lower vertex
then	**@0,–50 <R>**
prompt	Specify new location or [Next/Previous...
enter	**X <R>** – to end the move option
prompt	Enter a fit data option [Add/Close/Delete...
enter	**D <R>** the delete option
prompt	Specify control point
respond	**pick the sixth from left vertex then right-click**
prompt	Enter a fit data option [Add/Close... and enter: **X <R>**
prompt	Enter an option [Fit Data... and enter: **X <R>**.

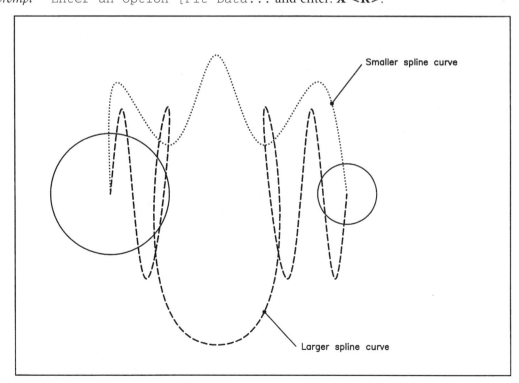

Figure 28.3 Editing the spline curves from A:SPLINEX.

2 Menu bar with **Modify–Spline** and:

prompt	Select spline
respond	**pick the smaller spline**
prompt	Enter an option [Fit Data/Close... and enter: **F <R>**
and	blue boxes at entered vertices
prompt	Enter a fit data option [Add/Close/Delete... and enter: **D <R>**
prompt	Specify control point and pick third vertex from left
prompt	Specify control point and pick fourth vertex from left
prompt	Specify control point and pick fifth vertex from left
prompt	Specify control point and pick sixth vertex from left
prompt	Specify control point and pick seventh vertex from left
prompt	Specify control point and right-click
prompt	Enter a fit data option [Add/Close/Delete...
enter	**M <R>** – the move option
prompt	Specify new location or [Next/Previous...
enter	**N <R>** until second left vertex is red
then	**@0,50 <R>**
then	**N <R>** until fourth left vertex is red
then	**@0,75 <R>**
then	**N <R>** until sixth left vertex is red
then	**@0,50 <R>**
then	**X <R>** and **X <R>** and **X <R>**.

3 The two spline curves will be displayed as edited.

4 Save this modified drawing if required.

Summary

1 Polylines and splines can be modified using their own commands.

2 Each edit command has several options.

This chapter has been a brief introduction to the edit commands.

Chapter 29

Divide, measure and break

These are three useful modify commands which will be demonstrated by example, so:

1 Open your standard sheet with later OUT current.

2 Activate the Draw, Modify, Dimension and Object Snap toolbars.

3 Refer to Fig. 29.1 and set the point style and size indicated (Format–Point Style).

4 Draw the following objects:
   a) LINE: from: 20,250 to: @65<15
   b) CIRCLE: centre: 125,250 with radius: 25
   c) POLYLINE: from: 170,270 to: @50,0 arc to: @0,−50 line to: @−30,0
   d) SPLINE: draw any spline to suit.

5 Copy the four objects below the originals.

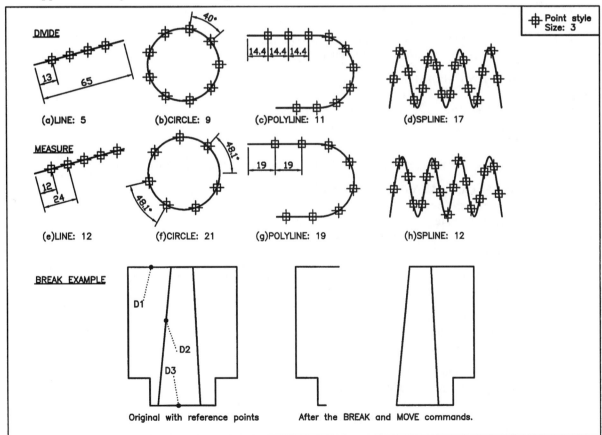

Figure 29.1   The DIVIDE, MEASURE and BREAK commands.

Divide

A selected object is 'divided' into an equal number of segments, the user specifying this number. The current point style is 'placed' at the division points.

1 Menu bar with **Draw–Point–Divide** and:
prompt   Select object to divide
respond   **pick the line**
prompt   Enter the number of segments or [Block]
enter   **5 <R>**.

The line will be divided into five equal parts, and a point is placed at the end of each segment length – fig. (a).

2 At the command line enter **DIVIDE <R>** and:
prompt   Select object to divide
respond   **pick the circle**
prompt   Enter the number of segments or [Block]
enter   **9 <R>**.

The circle will be divided into nine equal arc lengths and nine points placed on the circle circumference – fig. (b).

3 Use the DIVIDE command with:
a) POLYLINE: 11 segments – fig. (c)
b) SPLINE: 17 segments – fig. (d).

Measure

A selected object is 'divided' into a number of user-specified equal lengths and the current point style is placed at each measured length.

1 Menu bar with **Draw–Point–Measure** and:
prompt   Select object to measure
respond   **pick the line** – the copied one of course!
prompt   Specify length of segment or [Block]
enter   **12 <R>**.

The line is divided into measured lengths of 12 units from the line start point – fig. (e).

2 At command line enter **MEASURE <R>** and:
prompt   Select object to measure
respond   **pick the circle**
prompt   Specify length of segment or [Block]
enter   **21 <R>**.

The circle circumference will display points every 21 units from the start point, which is where? – fig. (f).

3 Use the MEASURE command with:
a) POLYLINE: segment length of 19 – fig. (g)
b) SPLINE: segment length of 19 – fig. (h).

4 *Task*: with menu bar **Dimension–Style**:
a) select Modify then the Primary Units tab
b) set Linear and Angular Dimensions Precision to 0.0 then OK
c) pick Close from Dimension Style Manager dialogue box
d) add the dimension shown – Snap to Node for points.

5 This completes the exercise – no need to save.

Break

This command allows a selected object to be broken at a specified point – similar to trim, but no erase effect.

1 Open A:USEREX and refer to Fig. 29.1. We want to split the component into two parts and will use the Break command to achieve the desired effect.

2 Select the BREAK icon from the Modify toolbar and:
prompt   Select object
respond **pick line D1**
prompt   Specify second point or [First point]
enter   **F <R>** – the first point option
prompt   Specify first break point
respond **Snap to Endpoint of 'top' of line D2**
prompt   Specify second break point
enter   **@ <R>**.

3 At command line enter **BREAK <R>** and:
prompt   Select object and: **pick line D3**
prompt   Specify second point or [First point]
enter   **F <R>**
prompt   Specify first break point
respond **Snap to Endpoint of 'lower' end of line D2**
prompt   Specify second break point
enter   **@ <R>**.

4 Now move line D2 and the other lines to the right of D2 (seven lines) from any suitable point **by @50,0**.

5 *Note:* the **@ entry** at the second point prompt, ensures that the first and second points are the same.

Summary

1 Objects can be 'divided' into:
   a) an equal number of parts – DIVIDE
   b) equal segment lengths – MEASURE.

2 The BREAK command allows objects to be 'broken' at specified points.

3 The three commands can be used on line, circle, arc, polyline and spline objects.

Chapter 30

Lengthen, align and stretch

Three useful modify commands which will greatly increase drawing efficiency. To demonstrate the commands, open the A:A3PAPER standard sheet and refer to Fig. 30.1.

Lengthen

This command will alter the length of objects (including arcs) but cannot be used with CLOSED objects.

1 Draw a horizontal line of length 80 – fig. (a) – and multiple copy it below four times.

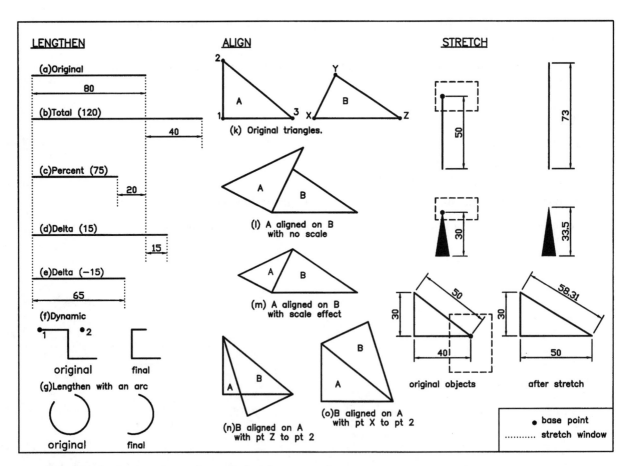

Figure 30.1 The lengthen, align and stretch commands.

2 Select the LENGTHEN icon from the Modify toolbar and:
prompt `Select an object or [Delta/Percent/Total/Dynamic]`
enter **T <R>** – the total option
prompt `Specify total length or [Angle]<1.00>`
enter **120 <R>**
prompt `Select an object to change or [Undo]`
respond **pick the second line**
then right click and Enter – fig. (b).

3 Menu bar with **Modify–Lengthen** and:
prompt `Select an object or [Delta/Percent...`
enter **P <R>** – the percent option
prompt `Enter percentage length<100.00>`
enter **75 <R>**
prompt `Select an object to change or [Undo]`
respond **pick the next line**
then right click and Enter – fig. (c).

4 At the command line enter **LENGTHEN <R>** and:
enter DE <R> – the delta option
enter 15 <R> – the delta length
respond pick the next line – fig. (d).

5 Activate the LENGTHEN command and:
prompt `Select an object or...`
respond **pick the fifth line**
prompt `Current length: 80.00`
then `Select an object or...`
enter DE <R>
prompt `Enter delta length or [Angle]`
enter **–15 <R>**
prompt `Select an object to change or...`
respond **pick the fifth line** – fig. (e).

6 *a*) Draw a Z shape as fig. (f)
  b) activate the lengthen command and:
    1) enter DY <R> – the dynamic option
    2) pick point 1 on the line as indicated
    3) move the cursor and pick a point 2
    4) the original shape will be altered as shown.

7 *a*) Draw a three point arc as fig. (g)
  b) activate the lengthen command and:
    prompt `Select an object or...`
    respond **pick the arc**
    prompt `Current length: 70.87, included angle: 291.0`
           (these values depend on the arc you have drawn)
    prompt `Select an object or...`
    enter **T <R>** – the total option
    prompt `Specify total length or [Angle]`
    enter **A <R>** – the angle option
    prompt `Specify total angle`
    enter **180 <R>**
    prompt `Select an object to change or...`
    respond **pick the arc.**

8 *Note:*
   a) an object is 'lengthened' at the end of the line selected
   b) if an object is picked before an option is entered, the length of the object is displayed. With arcs, the arc length and included angle is displayed
   c) when the angle option is used with arcs, the entered total angle is relative to the arc start point.

9 *Task.* Dimension the five lines to check the command has been performed correctly.

Align

A very powerful command which combines the move and rotate commands into one operation. The command is mainly used with 3D objects, but can also be used in 2D.

1 Draw any two triangles in the orientation shown – fig. (k). Copy these two triangles to four other areas of the screen – the snap ON will help.

2 We want to align:
   a) side 13 of triangle A onto side XY of triangle B
   b) side XZ of triangle B onto side 23 of triangle A.

3 Menu bar with **Modify–3D Operation–Align** and:
   prompt Select objects
   respond **pick the three lines of triangle A** then right-click
   prompt Specify first source point and **pick point 1**
   prompt Specify first destination point and **pick point X**
   prompt Specify second source point and **pick point 3**
   prompt Specify second destination point and **pick point Y**
   prompt Specify third source point and right-click
   prompt Scale objects based on alignment points? [Yes/No]<N>
   enter   **N <R>**.

4 Triangle A is moved and rotated onto triangle B with sides 13 and XY in alignment – fig. (l).

5 Repeat the Align selection and:
   a) pick the three lines of the next triangle A then right-click
   b) pick the same source and destination points as step 3
   c) enter **Y <R>** at the Scale prompt
   d) triangle A will be aligned onto triangle B and side 13 scaled to side XY – fig. (m).

6 At the command line enter **ALIGN <R>** and:
   prompt Select objects
   respond **pick three lines of a triangle B** then right-click
   prompt Specify first source point
   respond **Snap to Midpoint icon and pick line XZ**
   prompt Specify first destination point
   respond **Snap to Midpoint icon and pick line 23**
   prompt Specify second source point and **pick point Z**
   prompt Specify second destination point and **pick point 2**
   prompt Specify third source point and right-click
   prompt Scale objects based on alignment points
   enter   **Y <R>**.

7 The selected triangle B will be aligned onto triangle A as fig. (n).

8   Repeat the align command and:
    a) pick three lines of a triangle B then right-click
    b) Midpoint of side XZ as first source point
    c) Midpoint of side 23 as first destination point
    d) point X as second source point
    e) point 2 as second destination point
    f) right click at third source point prompt
    h) Y to scale option – fig. (o).

9   The orientation of the aligned object is thus dependent on the order of selection of the
    source and destination points.

Stretch

This command does what it says – it 'stretches' objects. If hatching and dimensions have
been added to the object to be stretched, they will both be affected by the command –
remember that hatch and dimensions are associative.

1   Select a clear area of the drawing screen and draw:
    a) a vertical dimensioned line
    b) a dimensioned variable width polyline
    c) a dimensioned triangle.

2   Select the STRETCH icon from the Modify toolbar and:
prompt	`Select object to stretch by crossing-window or crossing-polygon`
then	`Select objects`
enter	**C <R>** – the crossing option
prompt	`Specify first corner`
respond	**window the top of vertical line and dimension**
prompt	`2 found`
then	`Select objects`
respond	**right-click**
prompt	`Specify base point or displacement`
respond	**pick top end of line** (endpoint)
prompt	`Specify second point of displacement`
enter	**@0,23 <R>**.

3   The line and dimension will be stretched by the entered value.

4   Menu bar with **Modify–Stretch** and:
prompt	`Select objects`
enter	**C <R>** – crossing option
prompt	`First corner`
respond	**window the top of polyline and dimension**
then	right-click
prompt	`Specify base point` and **pick top end of polyline**
prompt	`Specify second point` and enter: **@0,3.5 <R>**.

5   The polyline and dimension are stretched by the entered value.

6   At the command line enter **STRETCH <R>** and:
    a) enter C <R> for the crossing option
    b) window the vertex of triangle indicated then right-click
    c) pick indicated vertex as the base point
    d) enter @10,0 as the displacement.

7   The triangle is stretched as are the appropriate dimensions.

Stretch example

1 Open your A:WORKDRG and refer to Fig. 30.2.

2 *a*) Erase the centre lines
   b) add hatching – own selection
   c) dimension the two lines as shown.

3 Activate the STRETCH command and:
   a) enter C <R> – crossing option
   b) first corner: pick a point P1
   c) opposite corner: pick a point P2 then right-click
   d) base point: pick any suitable point
   e) second point: enter @15,0 <R>.

4 Repeat the STRETCH command and:
   a) activate the crossing option
   b) pick a point P3 for the first corner
   c) pick a point P4 for the opposite corner
   d) pick a suitable base point
   e) enter @0,–15 as the second point.

5 The component and dimensions will be stretched with the entered values.

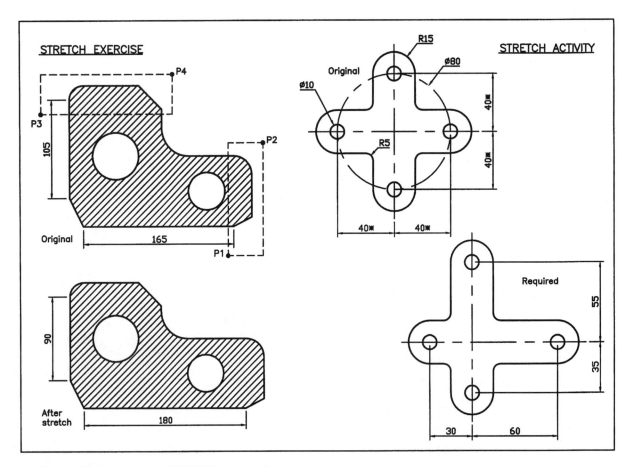

Figure 30.2 Using the STRETCH command.

Stretch activity

Refer to Fig. 30.2 and:

1 Draw the original component as shown adding the four * dimensions.

2 Using the STRETCH command only, produce the modified component. The stretch command will need to be used ? times.

3 There is no need to save this activity.

Summary

1 Lengthen will increase/decrease the length of lines, arcs and polylines. There are several options available.

2 Dimensions are not lengthened with the command.

3 Align is a powerful command which combines move and rotate into one operation. The order of selecting points is important.

4 Stretch can be used with lines, polylines and arcs. It does not affect circles.

5 Dimensions and hatching are stretched due to association.

Chapter 31

Interrogating a drawing

Drawings contain information which may be useful to the user, e.g. coordinate data, distances between points, area of shapes, etc. We will investigate how this information can be obtained, so:

1 Open A:USEREX and refer to Fig. 31.1.

2 Draw a circle, centre at: 190,140 and radius: 30.

3 Activate the Inquiry toolbar.

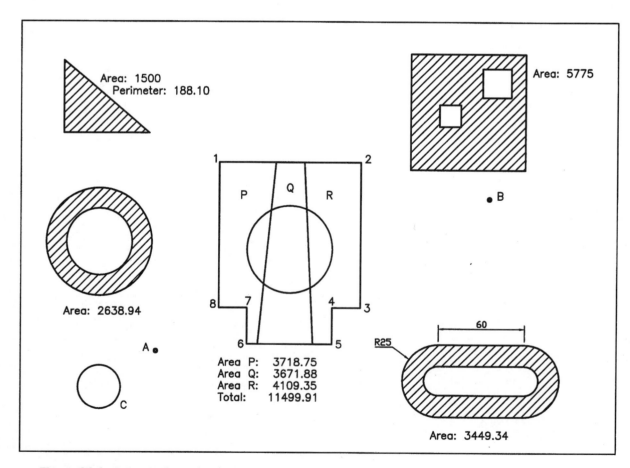

Figure 31.1 Interrogating a drawing.

Point identification

This command displays the coordinates of a selected point.

1   Select the LOCATE POINT icon from the Inquiry toolbar and:
    prompt   Specify point
    respond **Snap to Midpoint icon and pick line 23**
               The command line area displays:
               X = 240.00   Y = 150.00   Z = 0.00.

2   Menu bar with **Tools–Inquiry–ID Point** and:
    prompt   Specify point
    respond **Snap to Center icon and pick the circle**
    display X = 190.00   Y = 140.00   Z = 0.00.

3   The command can be activated with **ID <R>** at the command line.

Distance

Returns information about a line between two selected points including the distance and the angle to the horizontal.

1   Select the DISTANCE icon from the Inquiry toolbar and:
    prompt   Specify first point
    respond **pick point 8** (snap to endpoint or intersection)
    prompt   Specify second point
    respond pick point 2

    The command prompt area will display:

    Distance=141.42, Angle in XY plane=45.0, Angle from XY plane=0.0
    Delta X=100.00, Delta Y=100.00, Delta Z=0.00.

2   Menu bar with **Tools–Inquiry–Distance** and:
    prompt   Specify first point
    respond **snap to centre of circle**
    prompt   Specify second point
    respond pick midpoint of line 23

    The information displayed will be:

    Distance=50.99, Angle in XY plane=11.3, Angle from XY plane=0.0.
    Delta X=50.00, Delta Y=10.00, Delta Z=0.00.

3   Using the DISTANCE command, select point 2 as the first point and point 8 as the second point. Is the displayed information any different from step 1?

4   Entering **DIST <R>** at the command line will activate the command.

List

A command which gives useful information about a selected object.

1 Select the LIST icon from the Inquiry toolbar and:

   prompt   `Select objects`
   respond **pick the circle** then right-click
   prompt   AutoCAD Text Window with information about the circle.
   respond F2 to flip back to drawing screen.

2 Menu bar with **Tools–Inquiry–List** and:

   prompt   `Select objects`
   respond pick line 12 then right-click
   prompt   AutoCAD text window
   either   *a*) F2 to flip back to drawing screen
   or   *b*) cancel icon from text window title bar.

3 Figure 31.2 is a screen dump of the AutoCAD Text window display for the two selected objects.

4 LIST <R> is the command line entry.

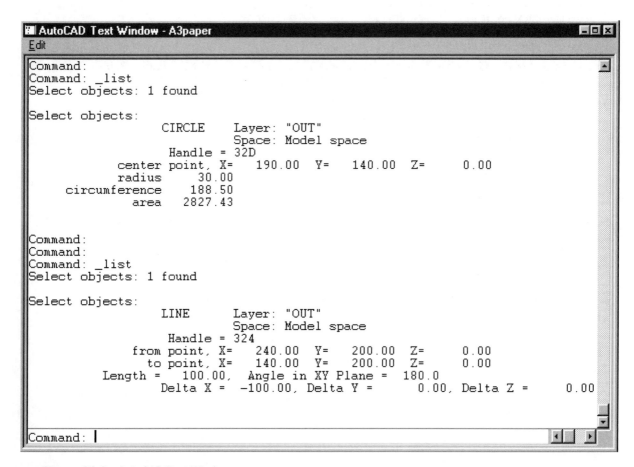

Figure 31.2 AutoCAD Text Window.

Area

This command will return the area and perimeter for selected shapes or polyline shapes. It has the facility to allow composite shapes to be selected.

1 Select the AREA icon from the Inquiry toolbar and:

prompt   Specify first corner point or [Object/Add/Subtract]
enter   **O <R>** – the object option
prompt   Select objects
respond   **pick the circle**

The command prompt area will display:

Area=2827.43, Circumference=188.50 – same values as the LIST command?

2 Menu bar with **Tools–Inquiry–Area** and:
prompt   Specify first corner point or [Object/Add/Subtract]
respond   **Snap to endpoint and pick point 1**
prompt   Specify next corner point or press ENTER for total
respond   **Snap to endpoint and pick point 2**
prompt   Specify next corner point or...
respond   Snap to endpoint and pick points 3,4,5,6,7,8
prompt   Specify next corner point or press ENTER for total
respond   **press <RETURN>**
prompt   Area=11500.00, Perimeter=450.00.

Are these figures correct for the shape?

3 At the command line enter **AREA <R>** and:
prompt   Specify first corner point or [Object/Add/Subtract]
enter   **A <R>** – the add option
prompt   Specify first corner point or [Object/Subtract]
respond   **Endpoint icon and pick point 1**
prompt   Specify next corner point or press ENTER for total
            (ADD mode)
respond   **Endpoint icon and pick point 2**
prompt   Specify next corner point or press ENTER for total
            (ADD mode)
respond   **Endpoint icon and pick points 3,4,5,6,7,8**
prompt   Specify next corner point or press ENTER for total
            (ADD mode)
respond   **press <RETURN>**
prompt   Area=11500.00, Perimeter: 450.00
            Total area=11500.00
then   Specify first corner point or [Object/Subtract]
enter   **S <R>** – the subtract option
prompt   Specify first corner point or [Object/Add]
enter   **O <R>** – the object option
prompt   (SUBTRACT mode) Select objects
respond   **pick the circle**
prompt   Area: 2827.43, Circumference: 188.50
            Total area=8672.57
then   (SUBTRACT mode) Select objects
respond   **ESC** to end command.

4 Is the area value of 8672.57 correct for the outline area minus the circle area?

Time

1 Gives information about the current drawing:
   a) when it was originally created
   b) when it was last updated
   c) the length of time worked on it.

2 The command can be activated from the menu bar with **Tools–Inquiry–Time** or by entering **TIME <R>** at the command line.

3 The command has options of Display, On, Off and Reset.

4 A useful command for your boss?

Status

This command gives additional information about the current drawing as well as disk space information. Select the sequence **Tools–Inquiry–Status** to 'see' the status display in the AutoCAD text window.

Calculator

1 AutoCAD R2000 has a built-in calculator which can be used:
   a) to evaluate mathematical expressions
   b) to assist on the calculation of coordinate point data.

2 The mathematical operations obey the usual order of preference with brackets, powers, etc.

3 At the command line enter **CAL <R>** and:
   prompt   Initializing...>> Expression:
   enter   **12.6*(8.2+5.1) <R>**
   prompt   167.58 – is it correct?

4 Enter CAL <R> and:
   prompt   >>Expression:
   enter   **(5*(7–4))^3.5 <R>**
   prompt   13071.3.

5 What is the answer to $((7 - 4) + (2 \times (8 + 1)))$ – a key question?

Transparent calculator

A transparent command is one which can be used 'while in another command' and is activated from the command line by entering the ' symbol. The calculator command has this transparent ability.

1 Activate the DONUT command and set diameters of 0 and 3, then:
   prompt   Specify center of donut
   enter   **'CAL <R>** – the transparent calculator command
   prompt   >>Expression:
   enter   **CEN/2 <R>**
   prompt   >>Select entity for CEN snap
   respond **pick the circle**
   prompt   (95.0 70.0 0.0)
   and   donut at position A
   prompt   Specify center of donut

enter	**'CAL <R>**
prompt	>>Expression:
enter	**(MID+INT) <R>**
prompt	>>Select entity for MID snap and: **pick line 65**
prompt	>>Select entity for INT snap and: **pick point 8**
prompt	(330.0 175.0 0.0)
and	donut at position B
prompt	Specify center of donut and right-click.

2 Activate the circle command and:

prompt	Specify center point for circle and enter: **55,45 <R>**
prompt	Specify radius of circle
enter	**'CAL <R>**
prompt	>>Expression:
enter	**rad/2 <R>**
prompt	>>Select circle, arc or polyline segment for RAD function
respond	**pick the circle**
and	circle at position C.

3 Check the donut centre points with the ID command. They should be *a*) 95,70 and *b*) 330,175. These values were given at the prompt line. How are these coordinate values obtained?

Task

1 Refer to Fig. 31.1 and create the following (anywhere on the screen, but use SNAP ON to help):
a) triangle: vertical side 50; horizontal side 60
b) square: side 80, with two other squares, side 15 and 20 inside
c) circles: radii 23 and 37 – concentric
d) polyshape: to size given, offset 15 'inwards'.

2 Find the shaded areas using the AREA command.

3 Obtain the areas of the three 'vertical strips' of the original USEREX, i.e. without the circle.

Summary

1 Drawings can be 'interrogated' to obtain information about:
a) coordinate details
b) distance between points
c) area and perimeter of composite shapes
d) the status of objects.

2 AutoCAD has a built-in calculator which can be used transparently.

Chapter 32

Text fonts and styles

Text has been added to previous drawings without any discussion about the 'appearance' of the text items. In this chapter we will investigate:
a) text fonts and text styles
b) text control codes.

The words 'font' and 'style' are extensively used with text and they can be explained as:

Font: defines the pattern which is used to draw characters, i.e. it is basically an alphabet 'appearance'. AutoCAD R2000 has over 90 fonts available to the user, and Fig. 32.1 displays the text item 'AutoCAD R2000' using 30 of these fonts.

Style: defines the parameters used to draw the actual text characters, i.e. the width of the characters, the obliquing angle, whether the text is upside-down, backwards, etc.

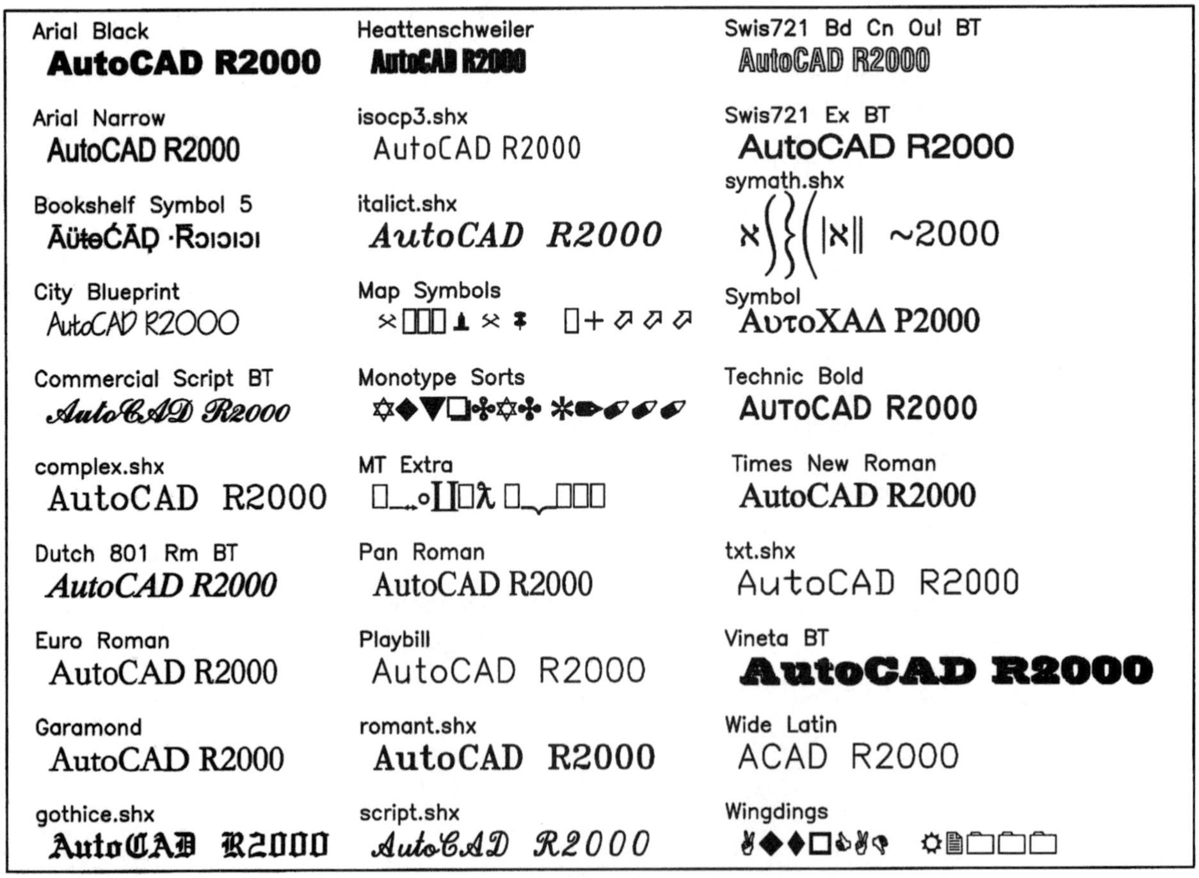

Figure 32.1 Some of AutoCAD Release 2000's text fonts, all at height 8.

Notes

1 Text fonts are 'part of' the AutoCAD package.

2 Text styles are created by the user.

3 Any text font can be used for many different styles.

4 A text style uses only one font.

5 If text fonts are to be used in a drawing, a text style **must be created**.

6 New text fonts can be created by the user, but this is outside the scope of this book.

7 Text styles can be created *a*) by keyboard entry or *b*) via a dialogue box.

Getting started

1 Open A:A3PAPER with layer TEXT current.

2 At the command line enter **-STYLE <R>** and:
   prompt   Enter name of text style or [?]<Standard>
   enter   **? <R>** – the 'query' option
   prompt   Enter text style(s) to list<*>
   enter   **<R>**
   prompt   AutoCAD Text Window
   with   Style name: "Standard" Font files: txt
             Height: 0.00 Width Factor: 1.00 Obliquing angle: 0.0
             Generation: Normal.

3 This is R2000's 'default' text style with the name *STANDARD*. The text font used is *txt* – this may be different on your system?

4 Cancel the text window.

5 With the Single Line Text command, add the text item **AutoCAD R2000** at 110,275 with height 8 and rotation angle 0.

Creating a text style from the keyboard

1 At the command line enter **-STYLE <R>** and:
   prompt   Enter name of text style or [?]
   enter   **ST1 <R>** – the style name
   prompt   Specify full font name or font filename (TTF or SHX)
   enter   **romans.shx <R>**
   prompt   Specify height of text and enter: **0 <R>**
   prompt   Specify width factor and enter: **1 <R>**
   prompt   Specify obliquing angle and enter: **0 <R>**
   prompt   Display text backwards? and enter: **N <R>**
   prompt   Display text upside-down? and enter: **N <R>**
   prompt   Vertical? and enter: **N <R>**
   prompt   "st1" is now the current style.

2 The above entries of height, width factor, etc. are the parameters which must be defined for every text style created.

Creating a text style from a dialogue box

1 From the menu bar select **Format–Text Style** and:

prompt	Text Style dialogue box
with	1) st1 as the Style Name
	2) romans.shx as the Font Name
	3) Height: 0.0
respond	**pick New** and:
prompt	New Text Style dialogue box
respond	1) alter Style Name to **ST2**
	2) pick OK
prompt	Text Style dialogue box
with	ST2 as the Style Name
respond	1) pick the scroll arrow at right of romans.shx
	2) scroll and pick **italicc.shx**
	3) ensure that: Height: 0.00, Width Factor: 1.00, Oblique Angle: 0.0
	4) note the Preview box
	5) dialogue box as Fig. 32.2
	6) pick **Apply** then **Close**.

2 With the menu bar selection Format–Text Style, use the Text Style dialogue box as step 1 to create the following text styles:

Style name	Font name	Ht	Width factor	Obl'g angle	Back-wards	Upside down	Vert'l
					Effects		
ST3	gothice.shx	12	1	0	OFF	OFF	OFF
ST4	Arial Black	10	1	0	OFF	OFF	OFF
ST5	italict.shx	5	1	30	OFF	OFF	OFF
ST6	Romantic	10	1	0	OFF	ON	—
ST7	scriptc.shx	5	1	−30	OFF	OFF	OFF
ST8	monotxt.shx	6	1	0	OFF	OFF	ON
ST9	Swis721BdOulBT	12	1	0	OFF	OFF	
ST10	complex.shx	5	1	0	ON	OFF	OFF
ST11	isoct.shx	5	1	0	ON	ON	—
ST12	romand.shx	5	1	0	ON	ON	ON

3 *Note*: when using the Text Style dialogue box, a TICK in a box means that the effect is on, a blank box means that the effect is off.

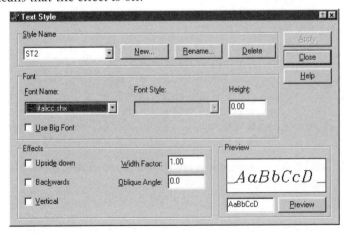

Figure 32.2 Text Style dialogue box.

Using created text styles

1 Menu bar with **Draw–Single Line Text** and:

prompt	`Specify start point of text or [Justify/Style]`
enter	**S <R>** – the style option
prompt	`Enter style name (or ?)<ST12>` – should be?
enter	**ST1 <R>**
prompt	`Specify start point of text or [Justify/Style]`
enter	**20,240 <R>**
prompt	`Specify height` and enter: **8 <R>**
prompt	`Specify rotation angle of text` and enter: **0 <R>**
prompt	`Enter text` and enter: **AutoCAD R2000 <R>**.

2 Using the single line text command, add the text item AutoCAD R2000 using the following information:

Style	Start pt	Ht	Rot
ST1	20,260	8	0 – already entered
ST2	225,265	8	0
ST3	15,145	NA	0
ST4	250,240	NA	0
ST5	25,175	NA	30
ST6	100,220	NA	0
ST7	145,195	NA	−30
ST8	215,235	NA	270 (default angle)
ST9	235,195	NA	0
ST10	365,165	NA	0
ST11	325,145	NA	0
ST12	400,140	NA	270 (default angle).

3 When completed, the screen should display 13 different text styles – the 12 created and the STANDARD default as Fig. 32.3.

4 There is no need to save this drawing but:
   a) erase all the text from the screen
   b) save the 'blank' screen as **A:STYLEX** – you are really saving the created text styles for future use.

Notes

Text styles and fonts can be confusing to new AutoCAD users due to the terminology, and by referring to Fig. 32.3, the following may be of assistance:

1 *Effects*: three text style effects which can be 'set' are upside-down, vertical and backwards. These effects should be obvious to the user, and several styles had these effects toggled on.

2 *Width factor*: a parameter which 'stretches' the text characters and fig. (a) displays an item of text with six width factors. The default value is 1.

3 *Obliquing angle*: this parameter 'slopes' the text characters as is apparent in fig. (b). The default is 0.

4 *Height*: when the text command was used with the created text styles, only two styles prompted for a height – ST1 and ST2. The other text styles had a height value entered when the style was created – hence no height prompt. This also means that these text styles cannot be used at varying height values. The effect of differing height values is displayed in fig. (c).

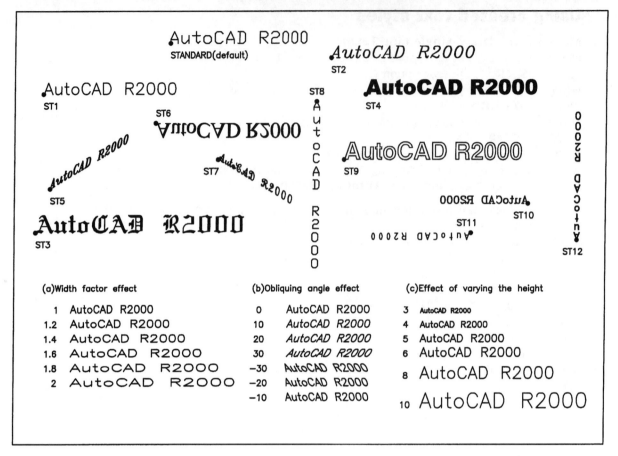

Figure 32.3 Using the created text styles.

5 *Recommendation*: I would strongly recommend that if text styles are being created, the height be left at 0. This will allow you to enter any text height at the prompt when the text command is used.

6 The text items displayed using styles ST5 and ST7 are interesting, these items having:
ST5   30 obliquing   30 rotation
ST7   −30 obliquing   −30 rotation.

These styles give an 'isometric text' appearance.

Text control codes

When text is being added to a drawing, it may be necessary to underline the text item, or add a diameter/degree symbol. AutoCAD has several control codes which when used with text will allow underscoring, overscoring and symbol insertion. The available control codes are:

%%O   toggles the OVERSCORE on/off
%%U   toggles the UNDERSCORE on/off
%%D   draws the DEGREE symbol for angle or temperature (°)
%%C   draws the DIAMETER symbol (Ø)
%%P   draws the PLUS/MINUS symbol (±)
%%%   draws the PERCENTAGE symbol (%).

1 Open A:STYLEX with the 12 created text styles.

2 Refer to Fig. 32.4, select **Draw–Text–Single Line Text** and:
   prompt Specify start point of text or [Justify/Style]
   enter   **S <R>**
   prompt Enter style name...
   enter   **ST1 <R>**
   prompt Specify start point of text and enter: **25,250 <R>**
   prompt Specify height and enter: **10 <R>**
   prompt Specify rotation angle of text and enter: –5 <R>
   prompt Enter text and enter: **%%UAutoCAD R2000%%U <R>**
   prompt Enter text and enter: **<R>**.

3 At the command line enter **DTEXT <R>** and:
   a) style: ST3
   b) start point: 175,255
   c) angle: 0
   d) text: 123.45%%DF.

4 Activate the single line text command and:
   a) style: ST4
   b) start point: 35,175
   c) angle: 0
   d) text: %%UUNDERSCORE%%U and %%OOVERSCORE%%O.

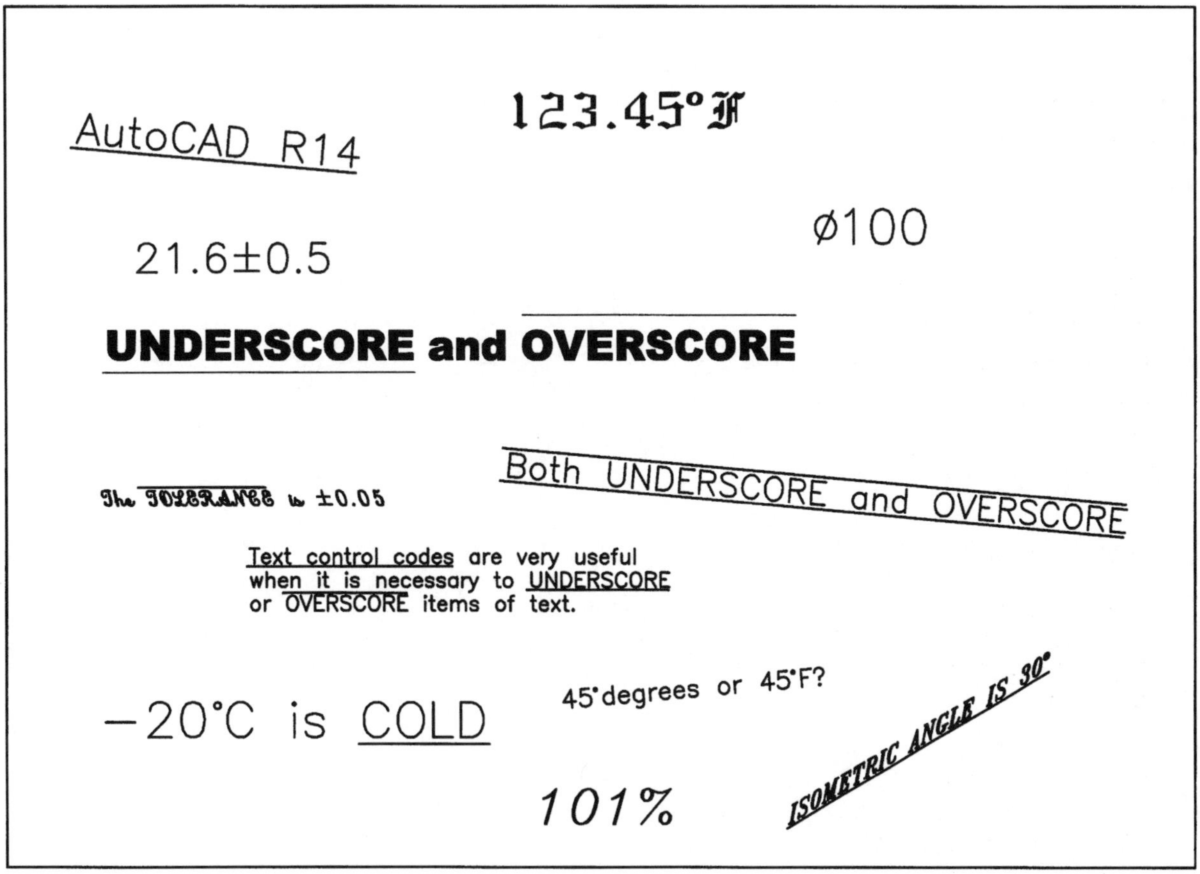

Figure 32.4 Text control codes.

5 With the single line text command:
   a) style: ST9
   b) start point: 285,215
   c) angle: 0
   d) text: %%C100.

6 Refer to Fig. 32.4 and add the other text items – or text items of your choice. The text style used is at your discretion.

7 Save if required, but we will not use this drawing again.

Summary

1 Fonts define the pattern of characters.

2 Styles define the parameters for drawing characters.

3 Text styles must be created by the user.

4 A font can be used for several text styles.

5 Every text style must use a text font.

6 The AutoCAD R2000 default text style is called STANDARD.

7 Text control codes allow under/overscoring and symbols to be added to text items.

Chapter 33

Multiline text

Multiline text is often called paragraph text. It is a useful draughting tool as it allows large amounts of text to be added to a pre-determined area on the screen. The added text can also be edited.

1 Open the A:STYLEX with the created text styles.

2 With layer TEXT current, select the TEXT icon from the Draw toolbar and:

prompt	Specify first corner
enter	**10,275 <R>**
prompt	Specify opposite corner or [Height...
enter	**S <R>** then **ST1 <R>** – the style option
prompt	Specify opposite corner or [Height...
enter	**H <R>** then **5 <R>** – the height option
prompt	Specify opposite corner or...
enter	**125,190 <R>**
prompt	Multiline Text Editor dialogue box
with	flashing cursor in the 'window area'
respond	1) enter the following text including typing errors which have been underlined
	2) **do not press the return key**
enter	CAD is a draughting <u>tol</u> with many benefits when compared to conventional draughting <u>techniches</u>. Some of these <u>benefitds</u> include <u>incresed</u> productivity, shorter lead <u>tines</u>, standardisation, <u>acuracy</u> <u>amd</u> rapid <u>resonse</u> to change.
and	dialogue box as Fig. 33.1
respond	pick OK.

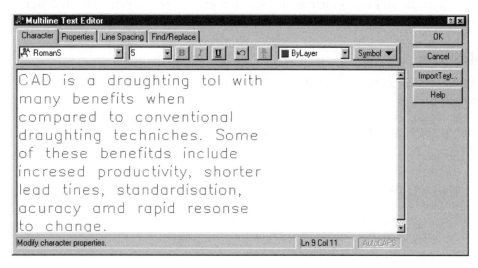

Figure 33.1 Multiline Text Editor dialogue box.

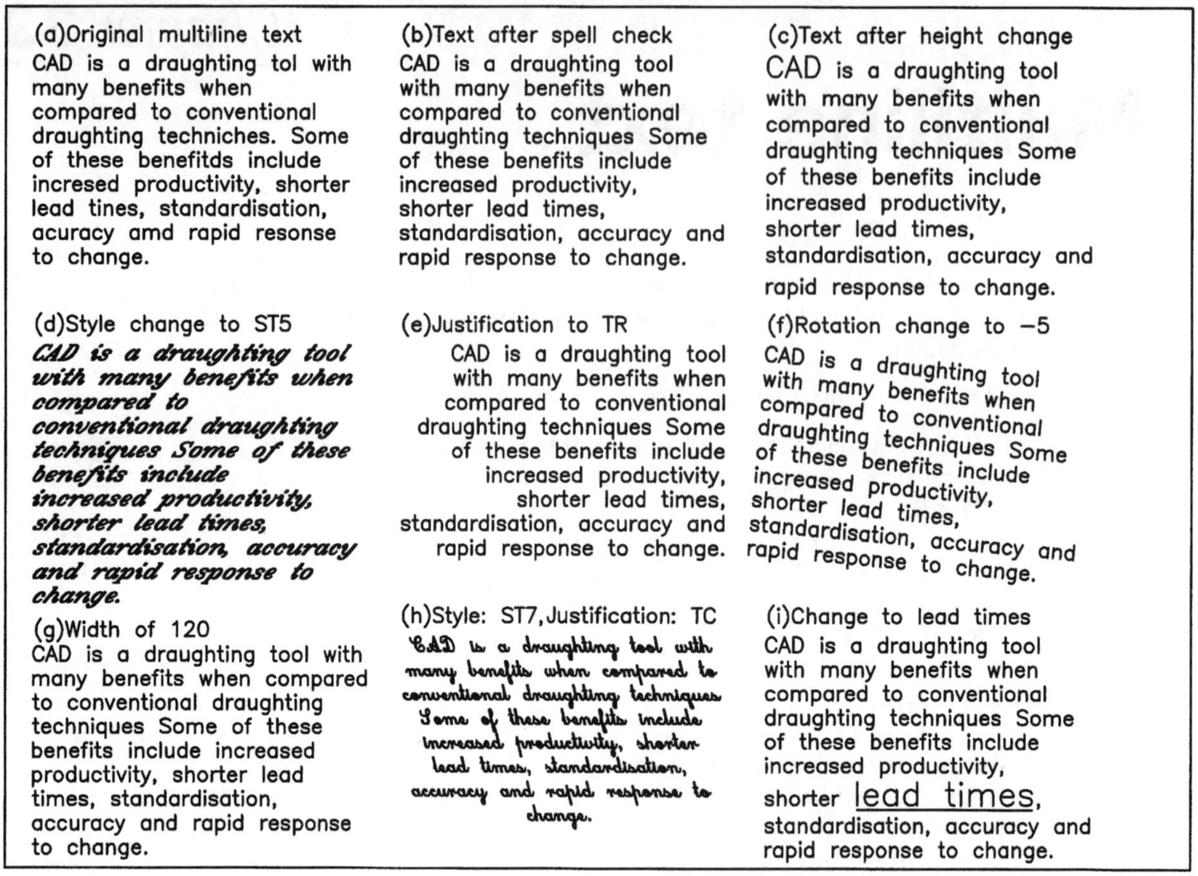

(a)Original multiline text
CAD is a draughting tol with many benefits when compared to conventional draughting techniches. Some of these benefitds include incresed productivity, shorter lead tines, standardisation, acuracy amd rapid resonse to change.

(b)Text after spell check
CAD is a draughting tool with many benefits when compared to conventional draughting techniques Some of these benefits include increased productivity, shorter lead times, standardisation, accuracy and rapid response to change.

(c)Text after height change
CAD is a draughting tool with many benefits when compared to conventional draughting techniques Some of these benefits include increased productivity, shorter lead times, standardisation, accuracy and rapid response to change.

(d)Style change to ST5
CAD is a draughting tool with many benefits when compared to conventional draughting techniques Some of these benefits include increased productivity, shorter lead times, standardisation, accuracy and rapid response to change.

(e)Justification to TR
CAD is a draughting tool with many benefits when compared to conventional draughting techniques Some of these benefits include increased productivity, shorter lead times, standardisation, accuracy and rapid response to change.

(f)Rotation change to −5
CAD is a draughting tool with many benefits when compared to conventional draughting techniques Some of these benefits include increased productivity, shorter lead times, standardisation, accuracy and rapid response to change.

(g)Width of 120
CAD is a draughting tool with many benefits when compared to conventional draughting techniques Some of these benefits include increased productivity, shorter lead times, standardisation, accuracy and rapid response to change.

(h)Style: ST7,Justification: TC
CAD is a draughting tool with many benefits when compared to conventional draughting techniques Some of these benefits include increased productivity, shorter lead times, standardisation, accuracy and rapid response to change.

(i)Change to lead times
CAD is a draughting tool with many benefits when compared to conventional draughting techniques Some of these benefits include increased productivity, shorter lead times, standardisation, accuracy and rapid response to change.

Figure 33.2 Multiline text exercise.

3 The entered text is displayed as Fig. 33.2(a).

4 *Notes:*
   a) the text 'wraps around' the Text Editor window as it is entered from the keyboard
   b) the text is fitted into the **width** of the selected area of the screen – not the full rectangular area.

Spellcheck

AutoCAD R2000 has a built-in spellchecker which has been used in an earlier chapter. It can be activated:
a) from the menu bar with Tools–Spelling
b) by entering **SPELL <R>** at the command line.

1 Activate the spell check command and:
   prompt   Select objects
   respond   **pick any part of the entered text then right-click**
   prompt   Check Spelling dialogue box
   with   1) current dictionary: American English or similar
               2) current word: probably *draughting*
               3) suggestions: probably draughtiness
               4) context: *CAD is a draughting tol ...*

respond	1) pick Change Dictionaries
	2) scroll at Main dictionary
	3) pick British English (ise)
	4) pick Apply and Close – Check Spelling dialogue box
	5) pick **Ignore All** – for the word: draughting
prompt with	Check Spelling dialogue box
	1) current word: *tol*
	2) suggestions: toll, tool, to...
respond	1) pick **tool** – becomes highlighted
	2) tool added to Suggestion box
	3) dialogue box as Fig. 33.3
	4) pick **Change**
prompt with	Check Spelling dialogue box
	1) current word: *techniches*
	2) suggestions: tech
respond	1) alter *techniches* to techniques
	2) pick **Change**
prompt	Check Spelling dialogue box
respond	change the following as they appear:

benefitds	→	benefits
incresed	→	increased
acuracy	→	accuracy
amd	→	and (manual change required)
resonse	→	response

then	AutoCAD Message
	Spelling check complete
respond	pick OK.

2 The paragraph text will be displayed with the correct spelling as Fig. 33.2(b).

3 One of the original spelling mistakes was '**tines**' (times) and this was not highlighted with the spellcheck. This means that the word 'tines' is a 'real word' as far as the dictionary used is concerned although it is wrong to us. This can be a major problem with spellchecks.

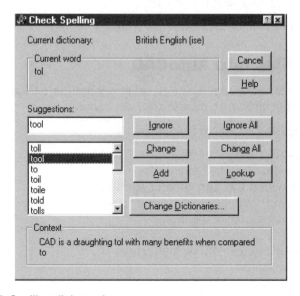

Figure 33.3 The Check Spelling dialogue box.

4 Enter **DDEDIT <R>** at the command line and:
a) pick any part of the text
b) the Multiline Text Editor dialogue box will be displayed and the word *tines* can be altered to **times**
c) when the alteration is complete, pick OK.

5 Multiple copy the corrected text to seven other places on the screen and refer to Fig. 33.2.

Editing multiline text

1 Select the EDIT TEXT icon from the Modify II toolbar and:
prompt   Select an annotation object or [Undo]
respond   **pick a paragraph text item**
prompt   Multiline Text Editor dialogue box
with   text displayed
respond   1) left-click and drag mouse over CAD
            2) pick height of 7 then OK
            3) right-click and Enter to end command
            4) text displayed as fig. (c).

2 Menu bar with **Modify–Text** and:
prompt   Select an annotation object
respond   **pick a text item**
prompt   Multiline Text Editor dialogue box
respond   1) pick Properties tab
            2) scroll at Style then pick ST5
            3) pick OK then right-click and Enter – fig. (d).

3 Using the Edit Text command alter the other paragraph text items using the following information:
a) Properties: Justification to Top Right – fig. (e)
b) Properties: Rotation to -5 – fig. (f)
c) Properties: Width to 120 – fig. (g)
d) Properties: Style to ST7
   Justification to Top Centre – fig. (h)
e) underline lead times and alter height to 8 – fig. (i).

4 This exercise is now complete and can be saved if required.

Importing text files into AutoCAD

Text files can be imported into AutoCAD from other application packages using the Multiline Text Editor dialogue box. To demonstrate the concept:

1 Ensure that the drawing has been saved if required.

2 Menu bar with **Modify–Text** and:
prompt   Select an annotation text object
respond   **pick the text which has the correct spelling**
prompt   Multiline Text Editor dialogue box
respond   in the text space, right-click the mouse
prompt   pop-up menu
respond   1) pick Select All and text will be highlighted
            2) right-click the mouse
            3) pick Copy
            4) cancel the dialogue box, then right click and Enter.

3 Menu bar with File–Close then File–Open and select your A3PAPER drawing file.

4 Select **Start** from the Windows taskbar, then select **Programs–Applications–Notepad** and:

   prompt   Blank Notepad screen displayed

   respond 1) menu bar with **Edit-Paste** and the multiline text is pasted into Notepad as a 'long character string'

           2) move the cursor along the character string line and press <RETURN> **before** the following words:

              with; compared; draughting; Some; include; shorter; accuracy; then after the final .

           3) menu bar with **File–Save As** and:

   prompt   Save As dialogue box

   respond 1) ensure A: as save in

           2) alter file name to **TEST.txt**

           3) Pick Save

           4) cancel Notepad to return to AutoCAD.

5 Make layer TEXT current.

6 Activate the Multiline Text command with the first corner at the point 70,260 and the opposite corner at 360,20 and:

   prompt   Multiline Text Editor dialogue box

   respond 1) enter: **THIS IS A TEST ITEM OF TEXT <R>**

           2) scroll at Symbol and pick **Plus/Minus**

           3) enter: **123.45** then a space

           4) scroll at Symbol and pick **Diameter**

           5) enter: **150 <R>**

           6) pick **Import Text** and:

   prompt   Open dialogue box

   respond 1) scroll and pick A:

           2) pick TEST

           3) pick Open

   prompt   Multiline Text Editor dialogue box

   with   imported text file displayed

   respond pick OK.

7 The text will be displayed as Fig. 33.4 and can be saved.

```
THIS IS A TEST ITEM OF TEXT
±123.45 ø150
CAD is a draughting tool
with many benefits when
compared to conventional
draughting techniques
Some of these benefits
include increased productivity,
shorter lead times, standardisation,
accuracy and rapid response to change.
```

Figure 33.4 Importing a text file into AutoCAD.

Summary

1 Multiline text is also called paragraph text.

2 The text is entered using the Multiline Text Editor dialogue box.

3 The command can be activated by icon, from the menu bar or by entering **MTEXT** at the command line.

4 Multiline text has powerful editing facilities.

5 Text files can be imported into AutoCAD from other application packages with the Multiline Text Editor.

Chapter 34

The array command

Array is a command which allows multiple copying of objects in either a rectangular or circular (polar) pattern. It is one of the most powerful and useful of the commands available, yet is one of the easiest to use. To demonstrate the command:

1 Open the A:A3PAPER standard sheet with layer OUT current and the toolbars Draw, Modify and Object snap.

2 Refer to Fig. 34.1 and draw the rectangular shape using the given sizes. Do **not add** the dimensions.

3 Multiple copy the rectangular shape from the mid-point indicated to the points A(25,175); B(290,235); C(205,110) and D(35,130). The donuts are for reference only.

4 Draw two circle, centre at 290,190 with radius 30 and centre at 205,65 with radius 15.

5 Move the original shape to a 'safe place' on the screen.

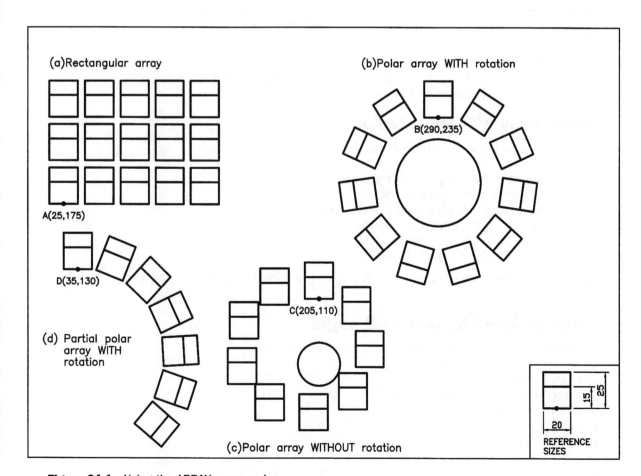

Figure 34.1 Using the ARRAY command.

Rectangular array

1 Select the ARRAY icon from the Draw toolbar and:
   prompt Select objects
   respond **window the shape at A then right-click**
   prompt Enter the type of array [Rectangular or Polar]<R>
   enter   **R <R>** – the rectangular option
   prompt Enter the number of rows(--)<1> and enter: **3 <R>**
   prompt Enter the number of columns(||||)<1> and enter: **5 <R>**
   prompt Enter the distance between rows or specify unit cell (---)
   enter   **30 <R>**
   prompt Specify the distance between columns(||||)
   enter   **25 <R>**.

2 The shape at A will be copied 14 times into a three row and five column matrix pattern
   – fig. (a).

Polar array with rotation

1 Menu bar with **Modify–Array** and
   prompt Select objects
   respond **window the shape at B then right-click**
   prompt Enter the type of array [Rectangular or Polar] and enter: **P <R>**
   prompt Specify center point of array
   respond **Snap to Center icon and pick large circle**
   prompt Enter the number of items in the array and enter: **11 <R>**
   prompt Specify the angle to fill... and enter: **360 <R>**
   prompt Rotate arrayed objects? [Yes/No]<Y>
   enter   **Y <R>**.

2 The shape at B is copied in a circular pattern about the selected centre point. The objects
   are 'rotated' about this point as they are copied – fig. (b).

Polar array without rotation

1 At the command line enter **ARRAY <R>** and:
   prompt Select objects
   respond **window the shape at C, right-click** and:
          a) type of array: enter: **P <R>**
          b) center point: **pick small circle centre**
          c) number of items: enter: **9 <R>**
          d) angle to fill: enter: **360 <R>**
          e) rotate objects: enter: **N <R>**.

2 The original shape is copied about the selected centre point but is not 'rotated' as it is
   copied – fig. (c).

Polar array with partial fill angle

1 Activate the array command and:
   a) objects: window the shape at D
   b) type of array: P
   c) center point: enter the point 35,70
   d) number of items: 7
   e) angle to fill: –130
   f) rotate objects: Y.

2 The result is fig. (d).
   Your drawing should resemble Fig. 34.1 and can be saved if required.

Array exercise
Polar array

The polar array command is very useful and will be further demonstrated so:

1 Erase the arrays from the screen (but not the original shape) and refer to Fig. 34.2.
2 Draw three concentric circles:
   a) on layer OUT with radii 40 and 10
   b) on layer CL with radius 25.

3 Multiple copy these three circles to three other areas of the screen using Fig. 34.2 for positioning.

4 Draw a line (on layer CL) and a circle (on layer OUT) using the reference sizes given, then multiple copy the two objects to the centre of each circle. Use the Snap to Endpoint and Snap to Centre icons.

5 With the polar option of the array command, array the centre line and circle using the following information:
   a) 6 items, fill angle 360
   b) 7 items, fill angle 360
   c) 8 items, fill angle 240
   d) 10 items, fill angle −240.

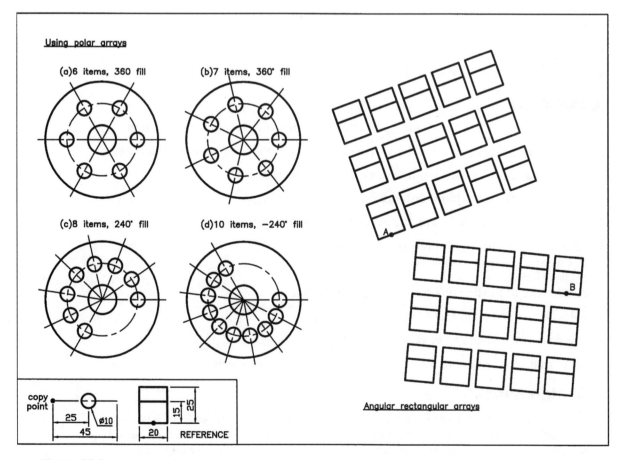

Figure 34.2 Array exercise.

Angular rectangular array

A rectangular array can be created at an angle using the **Snap Angle** variable, so:

1 Multiple copy the original rectangular shape from the point indicated to the points A(265,145) and B(390,105).

2 Rotate the shape at A by 20 and the shape at B by −5.

3 Menu bar with **Tools–Drafting Settings** and:
    prompt   Drafting Settings dialogue box
    respond   1) pick the Snap and Grid tab
                 2) alter Angle to 20
                 3) pick OK.

4 Note that the grid and cursor are rotated by 20.

5 Use the array command and:
    a) window the shape at A
    b) enter the rectangular option
    c) enter 3 rows and 5 columns
    d) enter a row distance of 35 and column distance of 25.

6 At the command line enter **SNAPANG <R>** and:
    prompt   Enter new value for SNAPANG<20.0>
    enter   **−5 <R>**

7 Rectangular array the shape at B with:
    a) 3 rows and 5 columns
    b) row distance: −35 and column distance: −25.

8 Set the snap angle value to 0.

9 The exercise is now complete (Fig. 34.2) and can be saved.

Summary

1 The ARRAY command allows multiple copying in a rectangular or circular pattern.

2 The command can be activated by keyboard entry, from the menu bar or in icon form.

3 Rectangular arrays must have at least one row and one column.

4 The rectangular row/column distance can be positive or negative.

5 Altering the snap angle will produce angular rectangular arrays.

6 Circular (polar) arrays require a centre point which:
    a) can be entered as coordinates
    b) picked on the screen
    c) reference to existing objects, e.g. Snap to Center icon.

7 Polar arrays can be full (360) or partial.

8 The polar angle to fill can be positive or negative.

9 Polar array objects can be rotated/not rotated about the centre point.

Assignments

It has been some time since any activities have been attempted and six have been included at this stage. All involve using the array command as well as hatching, adding text, etc. I have tried to make these activities varied and interesting so I hope you enjoy attempting them. As with all activities:

a) start with your A:A3PAPER standard sheet
b) use layers correctly for outlines, text, hatching, etc.
c) when complete, save as A:ACT_?? or similar
d) use your discretion for any sizes which have been omitted.

1 Activity 24: ratchet and saw tip blade. Two typical examples of how the array command is used. The ratchet tooth shape is fairly straightforward and the saw blade tooth is more difficult than you would think. Or is it? Draw each tooth in a clear area of the screen, then copy them to the appropriate circle points. The trim command is extensively used.

2 Activity 25: fish design. Refer to Fig. 34.3 and create the fish design using the sizes given. Save this drawing as A:FISH for future work. When the drawing has been completed and saved, create the following array patterns:
   a) a 5 × 3 angular rectangular array at 10 degrees with a 0.2 scale. The distances between the rows and columns are at your discretion
   b) three polar arrays with:
      1) scale 0.25 with radius of 90 and 9 items
      2) scale 0.2 with radius of 70 and 7 items
      3) scale 0.15 with radius of 35 and 7 items.

3 Activity 26: the light bulb. This was one of my first array exercises and has proved very popular in previous AutoCAD books. It is harder than you would think, especially the R10 arc. The basic bulb is copied and scaled three times. The polar array centre is at your discretion. The position of the smaller polar bulb is relative to the larger polar array, but how is it positioned? – your problem. No hints are given on how to draw the basic bulb.

4 Activity 27: bracket and gauge. The bracket is fairly easy, the hexagonal rectangular array to be positioned to suit yourself. The gauge drawing requires some thought with the polar arrays. I drew a vertical line and arrayed 26 items twice, the fill angles being +150 and −150 – think about this! The other gauge fill angles are +140 and −140. What about the longer line in the gauge? The pointer position is at your discretion. Another method is to array lines and trim to circles?

5 Activity 28: pinion gear wheel. Another typical engineering application of the array command. The design details are given for you and the basic tooth shape is not too difficult. Copy and rotate the second gear wheel – but at what angle? Think about the number of teeth. I realize that the gears are not 'touching' – that's another problem for you to think about.

6 Activity 29: propeller blade. Draw the outline of the blade using the sizes given. Trimmed circles are useful. When the blade has been drawn, use the COPY, SCALE and polar ARRAY commands to produce the following propeller designs:
   a) 2-bladed at a scale of 0.75
   b) 3-bladed at a scale of 0.65
   c) 4-bladed at a scale of 0.5
   d) 5-bladed at a scale of 0.35.

Note that the 4- and 5-bladed designs require some 'tidying up'.

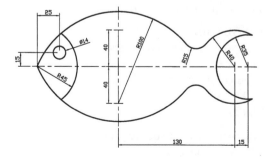

Figure 34.3 Information for Activity 25.

Chapter 35

Changing properties

All objects have properties, e.g. linetype, colour, layer, position, etc. Text has also properties such as height, style, width factor, obliquing angle, etc. This chapter will demonstrate how an object's properties can be changed, and this will be achieved by a series of simple exercises.

1 Open A:A3PAPER with layer OUT current, toolbars to suit and refer to Fig. 35.1.

2 Draw a 40 unit square and copy it to six other places on the screen.

3 *a*) at the command line enter **LTSCALE <R>** and:
   prompt   Enter new linetype scale factor and enter: **0.6 <R>**
   b) at the command line enter **LWDISPLAY <R>** and:
   prompt   Enter new value for LWDISPLAY and enter: **ON <R>**.

Command line CHANGE

1 At the command line enter **CHANGE <R>** and:
   prompt   Select objects
   respond **window the second square then right-click**
   prompt   Specify change point or [Properties]
   enter   **P <R>** – the properties option
   prompt   Enter property to change [Color/Elev/LAyer/LType/ ltScale/LWeight/Thickness]
   enter   **LA <R>** – the layer option
   prompt   Enter new layer name<OUT>
   enter   **HID <R>**
   prompt   Enter property to change
   respond right-click and Enter – fig. (b).

2 The square will be displayed as yellow hidden lines.

3 Repeat the CHANGE command line entry and:
   a) objects: window the third square then right-click
   b) change point or properties: enter P <R> for properties
   c) options: enter LT <R> for linetype
   d) new linetype: enter CENTER <R> for center linetypes
   e) options: right-click/Enter to end command – fig. (c).

4 Use the command line CHANGE with:
   a) objects: window the fourth square then right-click
   b) change point or properties: enter P <R>
   c) options: enter C <R> – the color option
   d) new color: enter BLUE <R>
   e) options: press <R> – fig. (d).

5 Use the CHANGE command with the fifth square and:
   a) enter P <R> then LA <R> – the layer option
   b) new layer: DIMS <R>

c) options: enter LT <R>
d) new linetype: CENTER <R>
e) options: enter: C <R>
f) new color: enter GREEN <R>
g) options: right-click/Enter – fig. (e).

6　With the command entry CHANGE:
　　a) objects: window the sixth square and right-click
　　b) change point or properties: activate properties
　　c) options: enter LW <R> – the lineweight option
　　d) new lineweight: enter 0.5 <R>
　　e) options: press <R> – fig. (f).

7　CHANGE <R> at the command line and:
　　a) objects: window the seventh square and right-click
　　b) activate properties
　　c) options: enter LT <R> then CENTER <R>, i.e. centre linetype
　　d) options: enter S <R> – the linetype scale option
　　e) new linetype scale: enter 0.5 <R>
　　f) options: press <R> – fig. (g).

8　Compare the center linetype appearance of fig. (c) and fig. (g).

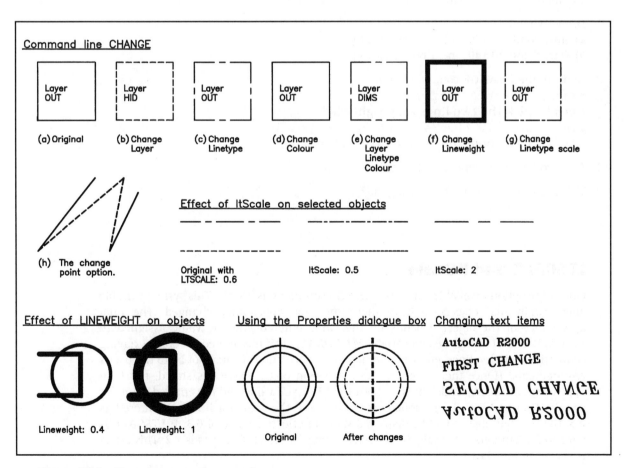

Figure 35.1 Changing properties exercise.

9 Menu bar with **Format–Layer** and:
   a) make layer 0 current
   b) freeze layer OUT then OK
   c) only a yellow hidden line square and a green centre line square displayed?
   d) thaw layer OUT and make it current.

10 *Note:*
   a) this exercise with the CHANGE command has resulted in:

fig.	square appearance	layer
(a)	red continuous lines	OUT
(b)	yellow hidden lines	HID
(c)	red center lines	OUT
(d)	blue continuous lines	OUT
(e)	green center lines	DIMS

   b) I would suggest to you that only figs (a) and (b) are 'ideally' correct, i.e. the correct colour and linetype for the layer being used. The other squares demonstrate that it is possible to have different colours and linetypes on named layers. This can become confusing.

The change point option

The above exercise has only used the Properties option of the command line CHANGE command, the there is another option – change point.

1 Draw two lines:
   a) start point: 20,140   next point: 60,190
   b) start point: 70,140   next point: 90,180.

2 Activate the CHANGE command and:
   prompt   Select objects
   respond **pick the two lines then right-click**
   prompt   Specify change point or [Properties]
   respond **pick about the point 80,190 on the screen**.

3 The two lines are redrawn to this point – fig. (h).

4 This could be a very useful drawing aid?

LTSCALE and ltScale

One of the options available with the CHANGE command is ltScale. This system variable allows individual objects to have their line type appearance changed. The final appearance of the object depends on the value entered and the value assigned to LTSCALE. The LTSCALE system variable is *GLOBAL*, i.e. if it is altered, all objects having center lines, hidden lines, etc. will alter in appearance and this may not be to the user's requirements. Hence the use of the ltScale option of CHANGE. As stated, the final appearance of the object depends on both the LTSCALE value and the entered value for ltScale. Thus, if LTSCALE is globally set to 0.6, and the value for ltScale is entered as 0.5, the selected objects will be displayed with an effective value of 0.3. If LTSCALE is 0.6 and 2 is entered for ltScale, the effective value for selected objects is 1.2. This effect is shown in Fig. 35.1.

Lineweight

LINEWEIGHT allows selected objects to be displayed at varying width. Although this may seem to be similar to the polyline-width type of object, it is not. Objects can be drawn directly with varying lineweight or the LWeight option of the CHANGE command can be used. It is necessary to toggle the LWDISPLAY system variable to ON before lineweight can be used. This was achieved at the start of the chapter.

1 Right-click on **LWT** in the Status bar, pick (left-click) Settings and:
   prompt   Lineweight Settings dialogue box
   respond 1) ensure Millimeters active
             2) scroll at Lineweights and pick 0.4mm
             3) dialogue box as Fig. 35.2
             4) note the default and pick OK.

2 Now draw some lines and circles.

3 Menu bar with **Format–Lineweight** to display the Lineweight Settings dialogue box. Set the lineweight to 1 and pick OK. Now draw some other lines and circles.

4 Finally set the lineweight back to the default value – 0.25?

5 Figure 35.2 displays some objects at the set lineweights.

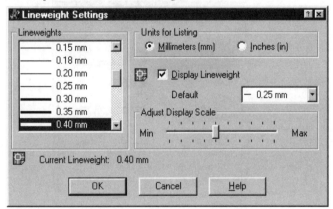

Figure 35.2 Lineweight Settings dialogue box.

Pickfirst

When objects require to be modified, the normal procedure is to activate the command then select the objects. This procedure can be reversed with the **PICKFIRST** system variable. To demonstrate how this is achieved:

1 Draw a line and circle anywhere on the screen.

2 Menu bar with Modify–Erase and select the two objects then <R>.

3 The objects are erased.

4 Draw another line and circle.

5 At the command line enter **PICKFIRST <R>** and:
   prompt   Enter new value for PICKFIRST<0>
   enter   **1 <R>**.

6 A pickbox will be displayed on the cursor cross-hairs. Do not confuse this pickbox with the grips box. They are different.

7   Pick the line and circle with the pickbox, then menu bar with Modify–Erase. The objects are erased from the screen.

8   Thus PICKFIRST allows the user to alter the selection process and:
    PICKFIRST: 0 – activate the command then select the objects
    PICKFIRST: 1 – select the objects then activate the command.

9   We will use PICKFIRST set to 1 to activate the Properties dialogue box.

Changing properties using dialogue boxes

1   With layer Out current, draw:
    a) two concentric circles
    b) two lines to represent centre lines.

2   Ensure PICKFIRST is set to 1.

3   With the pick box, select the horizontal line then the PROPERTIES icon from the Standard toolbar and:
    prompt   Properties dialogue box as Fig. 35.3
    with   two tab selections: *a*) alphabetical and *b*) categorized.

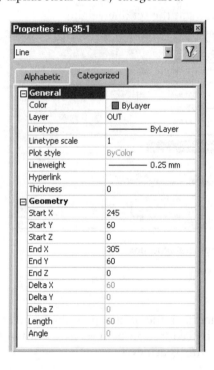

Figure 35.3   Properties dialogue box.

4   This dialogue box gives two types of detail:
    a) General: layer, colour, linetype, etc.
    b) Geometry: start and end point of line, etc.

5   Respond to the dialogue box by:
    a) pick Layer line and scroll arrow appears
    b) scroll and pick layer CL
    c) alter linetype scale value to 0.5
    d) cancel the dialogue box – top right X box
    e) press ESC.

6 The selected line will be displayed as a green centre line.

7 Pick the vertical line then the Properties icon and from the Properties dialogue box alter:
   a) colour: Magenta
   b) linetype: Hidden
   c) lineweight: 0.5
   d) cancel dialogue box then ESC.

8 Finally pick the smaller circle then the Properties icon and alter:
   a) layer: HID
   b) linetype scale: 0.75
   c) cancel and ESC.

9 Figure 35.1 displays the before and after effects of using the Properties dialogue box to change objects.

10 *Note:*
   a) the Properties dialogue box gives useful information about the objects which are selected:
      1) lines: start and end point; delta values; length; angle
      2) circles: centre point; radius; diameter; area; circumference
   b) these values can be alter in the dialogue box, and the object will be altered accordingly. You can try this for yourself.

Changing text

Text has several properties which other objects do not, e.g. style, height, width factor, etc. as well as layer, linetype and colour. These properties can be altered with the properties command. To demonstrate how text can be modified:

1 Create the following text styles:

name	STA	STB
font	romant	italict
height	0	8
width	1	1
oblique	0	0
backwards	N	N
upside-down	N	Y
vertical	N	N.

2 With layer TEXT current and STA the current style, enter the text item AutoCAD R2000 at height 5 and rotation 0 at a suitable part of the screen.

3 Multiple copy this item of text to three other places.

4 At the command line enter **CHANGE <R>** and:
   prompt   Select objects
   respond   **pick the second text item then right-click**
   prompt   Specify change point or [Properties]
   respond   **<RETURN>**
   prompt   Specify new text insertion point <no change>
   respond   **<RETURN>** – no change for text start point
   prompt   Enter new text style <STA>
   respond   **<RETURN>** – no change to text style
   prompt   Specify new height and enter: **6 <R>**
   prompt   Specify new rotation angle and enter: **5 <R>**
   prompt   Enter new text <AutoCAD R2000>
   enter   **FIRST CHANGE <R>**.

5 With CHANGE <R> at the command line, pick the third item of text and:
   a) change point: <R>
   b) new text insertion point: <R>
   c) new text style: enter STB <R>
   d) new rotation angle: 0
   e) new text: enter SECOND CHANGE
   f) question: why no height prompt?

6 With PICKFIRST on (i.e. set to 1) pick the fourth item of text then the Properties icon:
   a) the Properties dialogue box will display the following details for the text item: General; Text; Geometry and Misc.
   b) using the Properties dialogue box, alter the text style to STB, then cancel the dialogue box then ESC.

7 Figure 35.1 displays these text changes.

8 This exercise is now complete and can be saved if required.

Combining ARRAY and CHANGE

Combining the array command with the properties command can give interesting results. To demonstrate the effect:

1 Open your standard A:A3PAPER sheet and refer to Fig. 35.4.

2 Draw the two arc segments as trimmed circles using the information given in fig. (a).

3 Draw the polyline and 0 text item using the reference data.

4 With the ARRAY command, polar array (twice) the polyline and text item using an arc centre as the array centre point:
   a) for 4 items, angle to fill +30° with rotation
   b) for 7 items, angle to fill −60° with rotation – fig. (b).

5 Using *a*) the command line CHANGE or *b*) the Properties icon, pick each text item and alter:
   a) the text values to 10, 20, 30 to 90
   b) the text height to 8.

6 The final result should be as fig. (c).

7 Save if required as the exercise is complete.

Note

The first exercise demonstrated that it was possible to change the properties of objects independent of the current layer. This means that if layer OUT (red, continuous) is current, objects can be created on this layer as green centre lines, blue hidden lines, etc. This is a practice I **would not recommend** until you are proficient at using the AutoCAD draughting package. If green centre lines have to be created, use the correct layer, or make a new layer if required. Try not to 'mix' different types of linetype and different colours on the one layer. Remember that this is only a recommendation – the choice is always left to the user.

Summary

1 Objects have properties such as colour, layer. Linetype, etc.

2 An objects properties can be changed with:
   a) the command line CHANGE
   b) the Properties icon.

3 The icon method gives the Properties dialogue box.

4 To use the Properties dialogue box, the PICKFIRST variable must be set ON, i.e. value 1.

5 With PICKFIRST:
   value 0: select the command then the objects
   value 1: select the objects then the command.

6 The properties command is very useful when text items are arrayed.

7 Individual objects can have specific linetype scale factors.

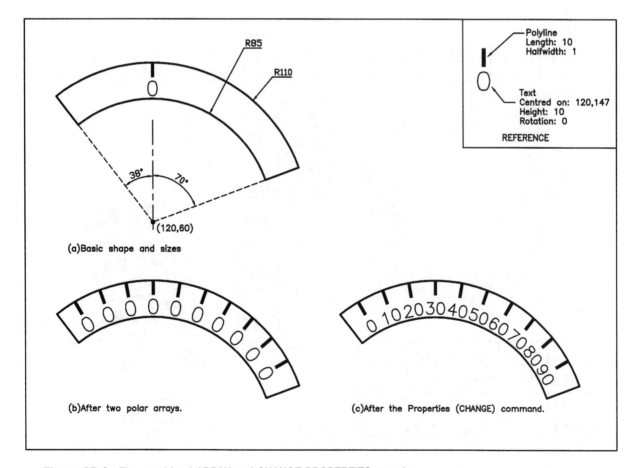

Figure 35.4 The combined ARRAY and CHANGE PROPERTIES exercise.

Chapter 36

User exercise 3

This exercise will involve creating different arrays with already created text styles.

1 Open A:STYLEX to display a blank screen but with 12 created and saved text styles (ST1–ST12) from Chapter 32 – I hope?

2 Refer to Fig. 36.1.

3 With layer OUT current, draw a 30 unit square at A(10,10).

4 Read the note (9) before the next operation.

5 Multiple copy the square from point A to the points B(85,220), C(200,70), D(280,15) and E(20,255).

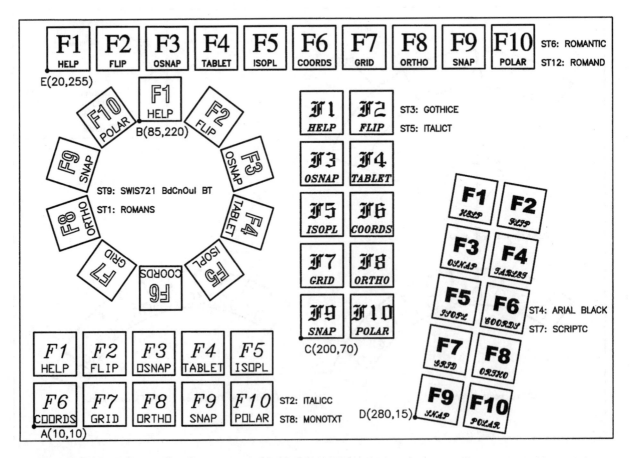

Figure 36.1 User exercise 3.

6 Array the squares using the following information:

A: rectangular with 2 rows and 5 columns, both distances 35

B: polar for 10 items, full circle with rotation, the centre point of the array being 100,170

C: rectangular with 5 rows and 2 columns and 35 distances

D: angular rectangular (snap angle of –10) with 5 rows and 2 columns, the distances both 35. Remember to rotate?

E: rectangular for 1 row and 10 columns, the distance 35.

7 Add the text items using the style names listed.

8 Save the completed layout as A:UEREX3.

9 *Note:*

a) text can be added after the squares are arrayed, or before the first square is multiple copied

b) after array: the text items are added using single line text, then the style, rotation angle and start point being entered by the user. This is fairly straightforward with the exception of the polar and angular arrays – what are the rotation angles?

c) before the multiple copy: two text items are added to the original square and it is then multiple copied and arrayed. The added text items can then be altered with the change properties command

d) it is the user's preference as to which method is used – I used the change properties method.

Assignments

Two activities have been added which require the array and change properties commands to be used. Hopefully these activities will give you some relaxation?

1 Activity 27: telephone dials. The 'old-fashioned' type has circles arrayed for a fill angle of ?? Is the text arrayed or just added to the drawing as text? You have to decide! The modern type has a polyline 'button' with middled text. The array distances are at your discretion as is the outline shape.

2 Activity 28: flow gauge and dartboard.

a) Flow gauge: a nice simple drawing to complete, but it takes some time! The text is added during the array.

b) Dartboard: draw the circles then array the 'spokes'. The filled sections are trimmed donuts. The text is middled, height 10 and ROMANT. Array then change properties?

Chapter 37

Dimension styles 2

In Chapter 20 we investigated how dimensions could be customized to user requirements by setting and saving a dimension style. The dimension style A3DIM was created and saved with our A:A3PAPER standard sheet.

In this chapter we will:
a) create and use several new dimension styles
b) add tolerance dimensions
c) investigate geometric tolerance.

The process for creating new dimension styles involves altering the values for specific variables which control how the dimensions are displayed on the screen.

Getting started

1 Open your A:A3PAPER standard sheet.

2 Create the following text styles, all with height and rotation 0:

name	font
ST1	romans.shx
ST2	scriptc.shx
ST3	italict.shx
ST4	Arial Black.

3 Menu bar with **File–Save** to update the A:A3PAPER standard sheet with the four created text styles. These are then available for future use if required.

4 Now continue with the exercise.

Creating the new dimension styles

1 A:A3PAPER standard sheet on the screen?

2 Menu bar with **Dimension–Style** and:
   prompt   Dimension Style Manager dialogue box with style A3DIM
   respond   **pick New**
   prompt   Create New Dimension Style dialogue box
   with   1) New Style Name: Copy of A3DIM
               2) Start with: A3DIM
               3) Use for: All dimensions
   respond   1) alter New Style Name to **DIMST1**
               2) pick Continue
   prompt   New Dimension Style: DIMST1 dialogue box with tab selections
   respond   pick OK at present
   prompt   Dimension Style Manager dialogue box
   with   Styles: A3DIM and DIMST1
   respond   **pick A3DIM then NEW**   (A)
   prompt   Create New Dimension Style dialogue box as before   (B)
   respond   1) alter New Style Name to **DIMST2**   (C)
               2) pick Continue   (D)
   prompt   New Dimension Style: DIMST1 dialogue box   (E)
   respond   pick OK at present   (F)
   prompt   Dimension Style Manager dialogue box
   with   Styles: A3DIM, DIMST1 and DIMST2
   respond   using steps A,B,C,D,E and F, pick A3DIM then New and create new dimension
               styles DIMST3, DIMST4, DIMST5 and DIMST6
   then   when DIMST6 has been created
   prompt   Dimension Style Manager dialogue box
   with   Styles: A3DIM, DIMST1–DIMST6
   respond   1) pick A3DIM then Set Current
               2) pick Close.

3 We have now created six new dimension styles (DIMST1–DIMST6) and these all have the same 'settings' as the A3DIM dimension style.

4 These six new dimension styles have now to be individually modified to meet our requirements.

Modifying the new styles

In the exercise which follows, we will only alter certain dimension variables. The rest of the dimension variables will have the same 'settings' as A3DIM. We will start with DIMST1, so:

1 Menu bar with **Dimension–Style** and:
   prompt   `Dimension Style Manager dialogue box`
   respond 1) pick DIMST1
              2) pick Modify
   prompt   `Modify Dimension Style: DIMST1 dialogue box` with tab selections
   respond 1) pick the Text tab
              2) Draw frame around text active, i.e. tick
              3) Text Placement: Vertical: Centered; Horizontal: Centered
              4) Text Alignment: Align with dimension line
              5) Text Appearance: Text style: ST1 with height: 4
              6) pick OK
   prompt   `Dimension Style Manager dialogue box`
   respond pick Close.

2 The above process is the basic procedure for 'customizing' dimension styles, the steps being:
   a) pick Dimension–Style (or the Dimension Style icon)
   b) pick required style name, e.g. DIMST1
   c) pick Modify
   d) pick required tab and alter as required
   e) pick OK then Close.

3 Using the procedure described, alter the named dimension styles to include the following:

Style	Tab	Alteration
DIMST2	Lines and Arrows	Arrowheads: both Box filled
		Arrow size: 4
		Center Mark Type: Line
		Size: 3
	Text	Appearance Style: ST1 with height: 4
		Alignment: Aligned with dimension line
	Primary Units	Zero suppression
		Trailing off: linear and angular
DIMST3	Lines and Arrows	Arrowheads: both Oblique, size: 4
		Center Mark Type: Mark with size: 4
	Text	Appearance Style: ST2 with height: 4
	Alternative Units	Display alternative units active
		Unit format: Decimal
		Precision: 0.00
		Multiplier: 0
		Round distances to: 0
DIMST4	Lines and Arrows	Arrowheads: both Dot Small, height: 8
	Text	Appearance Style: ST1, height: 4
		Alignment: Horizontal
	Primary Units	Measurement scale factor: 2
DIMST5	Text	Appearance Style: ST3 with height: 5
		Offset from dimension line: 0
DIMST6	Text	Appearance Style: ST4 with height: 6
		Offset from dimension line: 3.

4   When the six dimension styles have been altered, return to the Dimension Style Manager dialogue box, pick **A3DIM–Set Current** then Close.

Using the created dimension styles

1   Using Fig. 37.1 for reference, draw seven horizontal and vertical lines, seven circles and seven angled lines – the sizes are not of any significance but try and 'fit' all the objects into your drawing 'frame'.

2   Dimension one set of objects, i.e. a horizontal and vertical line, a circle with diameter and an angled line. The dimensions added will be with the A3DIM style as fig. (a).

3   Menu bar with **Dimension–Style** and:
prompt   Dimension Style Manager dialogue box
respond   1) pick DIMST1
              2) pick Set Current
              3) pick Close.

4   Using the set dimension style (DIMST1) dimension another set of four objects.

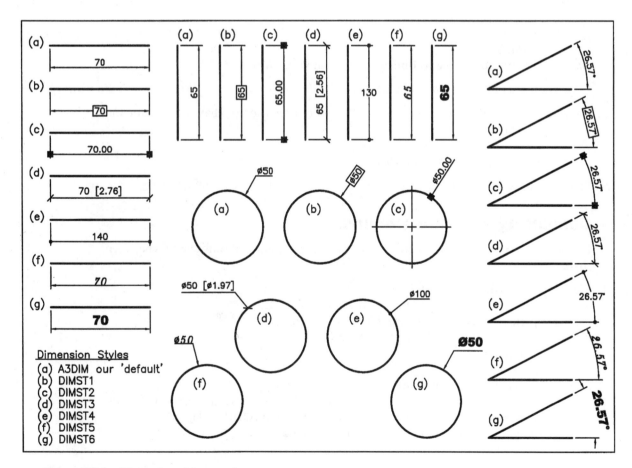

Figure 37.1   Dimension style exercise.

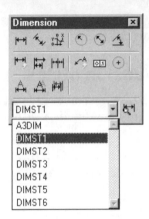

Figure 37.2 Dimension toolbar with created types.

5 Display the dimension toolbar (View–Toolbars) and note that DIMST1 is displayed, i.e. it is the current dimension style:
   a) pick the scroll arrow to display the other styles – Fig. 37.2
   b) pick DIMST2 to make it current
   c) dimension a set of objects with the DIMST2 style.

6 At the command line enter **-DIMSTYLE <R>** and:
   prompt   Current dimension style: DIMST2
   then   Enter a dimension style option [Save/Restore...
   enter   **R <R>** – the restore option
   prompt   Enter a dimension style name, [?] or <select dimension>
   enter   **DIMST3 <R>**
   and   DIMST3 displayed in Dimension toolbar (it is current).

7 Dimension a set of objects with the DIMST3 style.

8 Using the menu bar selection Dimension–Style, the Dimension toolbar or the command line -DIMSTYLE entry:
   a) make each created dimension style current
   b) dimension a set of objects with each style.

9 Figure 37.1 displays the result of the exercise which can be saved if required.

Comparing dimension styles

It is possible to compare dimension styles with each other and note any changes between them.

1 Menu bar with **Dimension Style** and:
   prompt   Dimension Style Manager dialogue box
   respond **pick DIMST4 then Compare**
   prompt   Compare Dimension Styles dialogue box
   with   Compare: DIMST4
   with   DIMST4
   respond scroll and alter With name to A3DIM
   prompt   Compare Dimension Styles dialogue box with a comparison between the different dimension variables of DIMST4 and A3DIM – Fig. 37.3
   respond note the differences then Close both dialogue boxes.

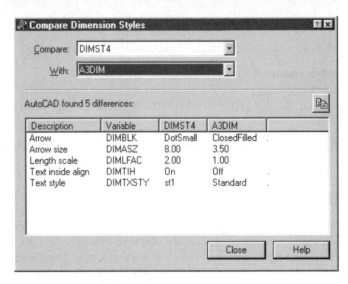

Figure 37.3 Compare Dimension Styles dialogue box.

Dimension variables

The above comparison between the two dimension styles displays some of the AutoCAD dimension variables. Some readers may remember using dimension variables before Dimension Styles were introduced. All dimension variables (dimvars) can still be altered by keyboard entry, although the Dimension Style dialogue box has tended to 'supersede' this method of altering dimension styles. To demonstrate how dimension variables can be entered from the keyboard:

1 Make DIMST1 the current dimension style and note the dimensions which used this style – the second set of dimensioned objects.

2 At the command line enter **DIMASZ <R>** and:
prompt   Enter new value for DIMASZ <3.50>
enter   **8 <R>**.

3 Pick the Dimension Style icon from the Dimension toolbar and:
prompt   Dimension Style Manager dialogue box
with   1) Current Style: DIMST1
           2) DIMST1
              └────────── <style overrides>
           3) Description: DIMST1+Arrow size=8.00 (i.e. DIMST1 has been altered)
respond 1) move pointer over <style overrides>
           2) right-click the mouse
prompt   Shortcut menu displayed
respond 1) pick Save to current style
           2) pick Close.

4 The dimensions which used the DIMST1 dimension style will be displayed with an arrow size of 8.

5 Now change the DIMASZ variable for DIMST1 back to 3.5.

6 This exercise is now complete and can be saved if required.

Task

1 Open your A:A3PAPER standard sheet with the four saved text styles ST1–ST4.

2 Using the Dimension Style Manager dialogue box:
   a) check current style is A3DIM
   b) with Modify–Text tab, set the text style to ST1 with height 4
   c) close the dialogue box.

3 **File–Save** to update the A:A3PAPER standard sheet with the modified A3DIM dimension style.

Tolerance dimensions

Dimensions can be displayed with tolerances and limits, the 'types' available being symmetrical, deviation, limits and basic. These are displayed in Fig. 37.4(a) with the standard default dimension type, i.e. no tolerances displayed. To use tolerance dimensions correctly, a dimension style should be created for each 'type' which is to be used in the drawing. As usual we will investigate the topic with an exercise so:

1 Open your A:A3PAPER standard sheet and refer to Fig. 37.4.

2 Draw a line, circle and angled line and copy them to four other areas of the screen.

3 Dimension one set of objects with your standard A3DIM dimension style setting – fig. (p).

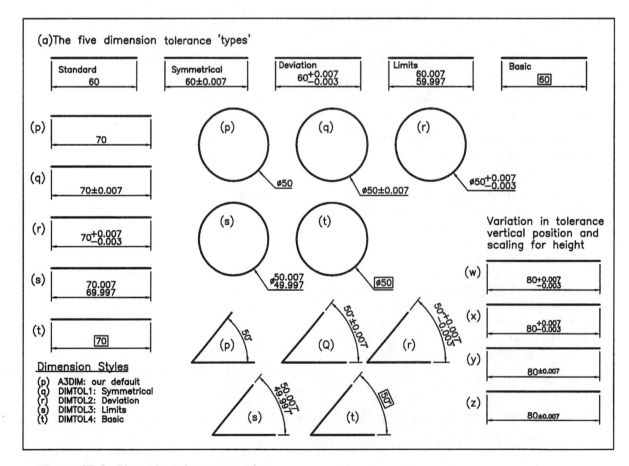

Figure 37.4 Dimension tolerance exercise.

Creating the tolerance dimension styles

1 Using the Dimension Style Manager dialogue box, create four new named dimension styles, all starting with A3DIM. The four new style names are DIMTOL1, DIMTOL2, DIMTOL3 and DIMTOL4.

2 With the Dimension Style Manager dialogue box:
   a) pick each new dimension style
   b) pick Modify then:
       1) Primary Units tab and alter both the Linear and Angular precision to 0.000
       2) Tolerances tab and alter as follows:

	DIMTOL1	*DIMTOL2*	*DIMTOL3*	*DIMTOL4*
Method	Symmetrical	Deviation	Limits	Basic
Precision	0.000	0.000	0.000	—
Upper value	0.007	0.007	0.007	—
Lower value	—	0.003	0.003	—
Scaling for height	1	1	1	—
Vertical position	Middle	Middle	Middle	—

3 Making each new dimension style current, dimension a set of three objects. The effect is displayed in Fig. 37.4 with:

    fig. (q): style DIMTOL1   fig. (r): style DIMTOL2
    fig. (s): style DIMTOL3   fig. (t): style DINTOL4.

4 *Task*. Investigate the vertical position and the scaling for height options available in the Tolerances tab dialogue box. Figure 37.4 displays the following:

    fig. (w): deviation top, height 0.8
    fig. (x): deviation bottom, height 0.8
    fig. (y): symmetrical top, height 0.7
    fig. (z): symmetrical bottom, height 0.7.

Geometric tolerancing

AutoCAD R2000 has geometric tolerancing facilities and to demonstrate this feature:

1 Open your A:A3PAPER standard sheet.

2 Menu bar with **Dimension–Tolerance** and:
   prompt   Geometric Tolerance dialogue box
   with   Feature Control Frames
   respond   move pointer to box under Sym and right-click
   prompt   Symbol dialogue box as Fig. 37.5
   respond   1) press ESC to cancel the Symbol dialogue box
              2) study the layout of the Geometric Tolerance dialogue box
              3) pick Cancel at present.

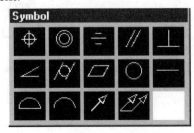

Figure 37.5 Symbol dialogue box.

Feature control frames

Geometric tolerances define the variations which are permitted to the form or profile of a component, its orientation and location as well as the allowable runout from the exact geometry of a feature. Geometric tolerances are added by the user in **feature control frames**, these being displayed in the Geometric Tolerances dialogue box. A feature control frame consists of two/three sections or compartments. These are displayed in Fig. 37.6(a) and are:

1 The geometric characteristic symbol – a symbol for the tolerance which is to be applied. These geometric symbols can represent location, orientation, form, profile and runout. The symbols include symmetry, flatness, straightness, angularity, concentricity, etc.

2 The tolerance section (1 and 2) which creates the tolerance value in the Feature Control Frame. The tolerance indicates the amount by which the geometric tolerance characteristic can deviate from a perfect form. It consist of three boxes:

- First box: inserts an optional diameter symbol
- Second box: the actual tolerance value
- Third box: displays the material code which can be:
  a) M: at maximum material condition
  b) L: at least material condition
  c) S: regardless of feature size.

3 The primary, secondary and tertiary datum information which can consist of the reference latter and the material code.

4 Typical types of geometric tolerance 'values' are displayed in Fig. 37.6(b).

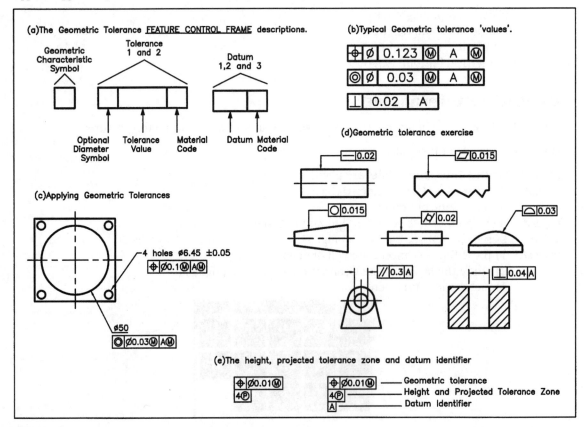

Figure 37.6 Geometric tolerance terminology and usage.

5 *Note:*

   a) feature control frames are added to a dimension by the user

   b) a feature control frame contains all the tolerance information for a single dimension. The tolerance information must be entered by the user

   c) feature control frames can be copied, moved, erased, stretched, scaled and rotated once 'inserted' into a drawing

   d) feature control frames can be modified with DDEDIT.

Geometric tolerance example

1 Refer to Fig. 37.6(c) and create a square with circles as shown. The size and layout is of no importance.

2 Diameter dimension the larger circle using the A3DIM dimension style (should be current) and the DIMS layer.

3 Select the TOLERANCE icon from the Dimension toolbar and:

   prompt   Geometric Tolerance dialogue box
   respond **pick top box under Sym**
   prompt   Symbol dialogue box
   respond **pick Concentricity symbol then OK** (2nd top left)
   prompt   Geometric Tolerance dialogue box
   with   Concentricity symbol displayed
   respond 1) at Tolerance 1, pick left box
              2) at Tolerance 1, enter 0.03
              3) at Tolerance 1, pick MC box and:
   prompt   Material Condition dialogue box
   respond **pick M then OK**
              4) at Datum 1, enter A
              5) at Datum 1, pick MC box, pick M then OK
              6) Geometric Tolerance dialogue box as Fig. 37.7
   then   **pick OK**
   prompt   Enter tolerance location
   respond **pick 'under' the diameter dimension.**

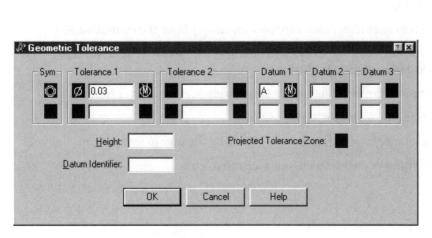

Figure 37.7   Geometric Tolerance dialogue box.

4   Menu bar with **Dimension–Tolerance** and:
    prompt   `Geometric Tolerance dialogue box`
    respond   pick top Sym box
    prompt   `Symbol dialogue box`
    respond   **pick Position symbol** (top left)
    prompt   `Geometric Tolerance dialogue box`
    respond   1) at Tolerance 1 pick left box (for diameter symbol)
                2) at Tolerance 1 enter value of 0.1
                3) at Tolerance 1 pick MC box and pick M
                4) at Datum 1 enter datum A
                5) at Datum 1 pick MC box and pick M
                6) pick OK
    prompt   `Enter tolerance location`
    respond   **pick to suit** – refer to Fig. 37.7(c).

5   Select the LEADER icon from the Dimension toolbar and:
    prompt   `Specify first leader point` and pick a smaller circle
    prompt   `Specify next point` and pick a point to suit
    prompt   `Specify text width` and enter: 0 <R>
    prompt   `Enter first line of annotation text` and: **right-click**
    prompt   `Multiline Text Editor dialogue box`
    enter   4 holes $\varnothing$ 6.45 ± 0.05 (use symbols)
    then   pick OK.

Geometric tolerance exercise

1   Refer to Fig. 37.7(d) and create 'shapes' as shown – size is not important.

2   Add the geometric tolerance information.

3   Investigate the height, projected tolerance zone and datum identifier options from the Geometric Tolerance dialogue box as fig. (e).

Summary

1   Dimension styles are created by the user and 'customized' for company/customer requirements.

2   Dimension styles are created with the Dimension Style Manager dialogue box using several tab selections.

3   It is still possible to alter dimension variables (dimvars) from the command line.

4   Tolerance dimensions can be created as dimension styles. The four 'types' are symmetrical, deviation, limits and basic.

5   Geometric tolerances can be added to drawings using feature control frames.

6   There are 14 geometric tolerance 'types' available.

7   All geometric tolerance information must be added by the user in feature control frames.

8   Feature control frames can be copied, moved, scaled, etc.

Assignments

Two assignments on dimension styles, tolerance dimensions and geometric tolerancing. Adding dimensions to a drawing is generally a tedious process and if dimension styles and geometric tolerancing are required, the process does not get any easier.

1 Activity 32: tolerance dimensions. The drawings are easy to complete. Adding the dimensions requires four created styles, all from the A3DIM default. The dimension styles use the symmetrical, limits, deviation and basic tolerance methods. You have the enter the upper and lower values.

2 Activity 33: geometric tolerances. A slightly more complex drawing to complete. Several dimension styles have to be created and two geometric tolerances have to be added.

Chapter 38

Drawing to different sizes

Two of the most common questions from new AutoCAD users are:

1 Can I draw with imperial units?

2 Can you set a scale at the start of a drawing?

The answer to the both these questions is yes:
a) you can draw in feet and inches
b) you can set a scale at the start of a drawing, but remember that all drawing work should be completed full-size. This is a concept that some CAD users find difficult to accept.

In this chapter we will investigate both these topics with three exercises – a component drawn and dimensioned in inches, a large scale drawing and a small scale drawing. Each exercise will involve modifying the existing A:A3PAPER standard sheet.

Drawing in inches

To draw in inches we require a new standard sheet which could be created:
a) from scratch
b) using the Wizard facility
c) altering the existing A:A3PAPER standard sheet which is set to metric sizes.

We will alter our existing standard sheet, the only reason being that it has already been 'customized' to our requirements, i.e. it has layers, a text style and a dimension style. This may save us some time? The conversion from a metric standard sheet to one which will allow us to draw in inches is relatively straightforward. We have to alter several parameters, e.g. units, limits, drawing aids and the dimension style variables.

1 Open your A:A3PAPER standard sheet and erase the black border as it is the wrong size for drawing in inches.

2 *Units:* menu bar with **Format–Units** and using the Drawing Units dialogue box set:
   a) *Length:* Type: Engineering; Precision: 0'-0.00"
   b) *Angle:* Type: Decimal Degrees; Precision: 0.00
   c) *Insert blocks:* Scale to inches
   d) pick OK.

3 *Limits*: menu bar with **Format–Drawing Limits** and:
   prompt   Specify lower left corner and enter: **0,0 <R>**
   prompt   Specify upper right corner and enter: **16",12" <R>**. Note: shift 2 for the inches (").

4 *Drawing area:*
   a) with layer 0 current, draw a rectangular border from 0,0 to 15.5",11.75"
   b) menu bar with View–Zoom–All

5 *Drawing Aids:*
   a) set grid spacing to 0.5
   b) set snap spacing to 0.25
   c) set global LTSCALE value to 0.025.

6 *Dimension Style:*
   Menu bar with **Dimension–Style** and using the Dimension Style Manager dialogue box
   create a new dimension style:
   a) New Style Name: STDIMP
   b) Start with: A3DIM
   c) Tab alterations:

	Lines and Arrows	Baseline spacing: 0.75″
		Extend beyond dim line: 0.175″
		Offset from origin: 0.175″
		Arrowheads: Closed Filled, Size: 0.175″
		Centre: None
		Scale factor: 1
	Text	Style: ST1 with height: 0.18″
		Offset from dim line: 0.08″
		Text alignment: Align with dimension line
	Primary Units	Unit Format: Engineering
		Precision: 0′-0.00″
		Degrees: Decimal
		Precision: 0.00
		Zero suppression: both ON, i.e. tick.

7 *a*) Make layer OUT current
   b) save the drawing as **A:STDIMP** – it may be useful to you.

8 Refer to Fig. 38.1 and draw the component as shown. Add all text and dimensions. You
   should have no problems in completing the drawing or adding the dimensions. What
   should be the value for text height? Use the grid spacing as a guide.

9 When complete, save the drawing – plot?

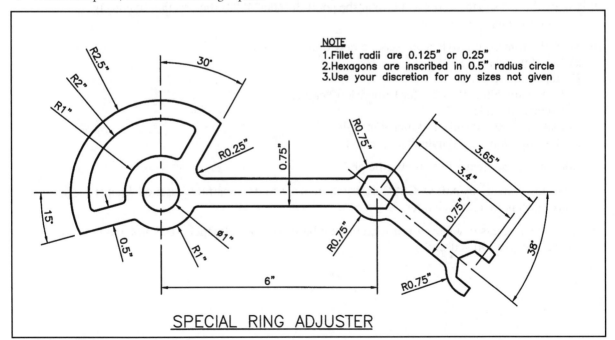

Figure 38.1 Drawing in inches.

Large-scale drawing

This exercise will require the A:A3PAPER standard sheet to be modified to allow a very large drawing to be drawn (full-size) on A3 paper.

1   Open A:A3PAPER standard sheet and erase the black border – it is too small for the limits to be used.

2   Make layer 0 current.

3   At the command line enter **MVSETUP <R>** and:

prompt	`Enable paper space? (No/Yes)`
enter	**N <R>**
prompt	`Enter units type [Scientific/Decimal...`
enter	**M <R>** – for metric units
prompt	AutoCAD Text Window with Metric scales
and	`Enter the scale factor`
enter	**50 <R>**, i.e. scale of 1:50
prompt	`Enter the paper width` and enter: **420 <R>**
prompt	`Enter the paper height` and enter: **297 <R>**.

4   A polyline black border will be displayed. This is our drawing area.

5   Pan the drawing to suit the screen.

6   With the menu bar **Tools–Inquiry–ID Point**, obtain the coordinates of the lower left and upper right corners of the black border. These should be:
    lower left: X=0.00   Y=0.00   Z=0.00
    upper right: X=21000.00   Y=14850.00   Z=0.00.

7   Set the grid to 40 and the snap to 20.

8   With layer OUT current refer to Fig. 38.2 and complete the factory plan layout using the sizes as given, the start point being at A(2000,2000). The wall thickness is 250.

9   Create the 300 square section column at the point B(16000,4500) then rectangular array it using the information given.

10 With the Dimension Style icon create a new dimension style
    a) New Style Name: STD50
    b) start with: A3DIM
    c) Fit tab and alter the Scale for Dimension Features
        Use overall scale of: 50
    d) make STD50 the current dimension style
    e) close the Dimension Style dialogue box.

11 Add appropriate text – but at what height?

12 Save this drawing as **A:LARGESC** as it will be used to demonstrate the model/paper space concept in a later chapter.

13 If you have access to a plotter/printer, obtain a hard copy on A3 paper – the problem is the plot figures (50 is useful!).

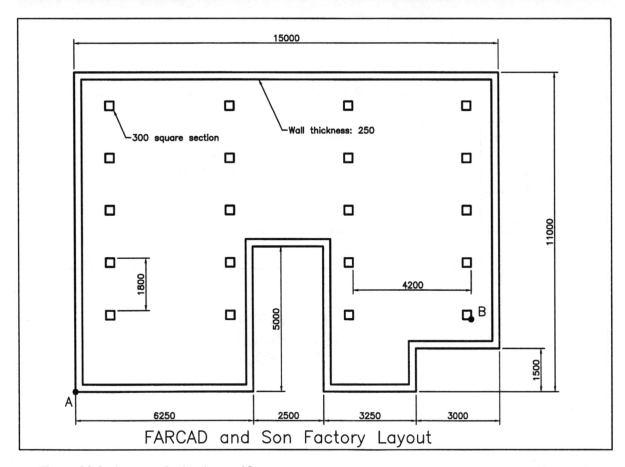

Figure 38.2 Large-scale drawing on A3 paper.

Small-scale drawing

This exercise requires the A3 standard sheet to be modified to suit a very small-scale drawing, which (as always) will be drawn full size.

1 Open A:A3PAPER standard sheet and erase the border.

2 Make layer 0 current, enter **MVSETUP <R>** and:
prompt Enable paper space? and enter: **N <R>**
prompt Enter units type and enter: **M <R>** – metric
prompt Enter the scale factor and enter: **0.001 <R>**
prompt Enter the paper width and enter: **420 <R>**
prompt Enter the paper height and enter: **297 <R>**.

3 A black border is displayed on the screen – the drawing area.

4 Set UNITS to four decimal places, then ID the lower left and upper right corners
lower left: X=0.0000   Y=0.0000   Z=0.0000
upper right: X=0.4200   Y=0.2970   Z=0.0000.

5 Set the grid to 0.01 and the snap to 0.005.

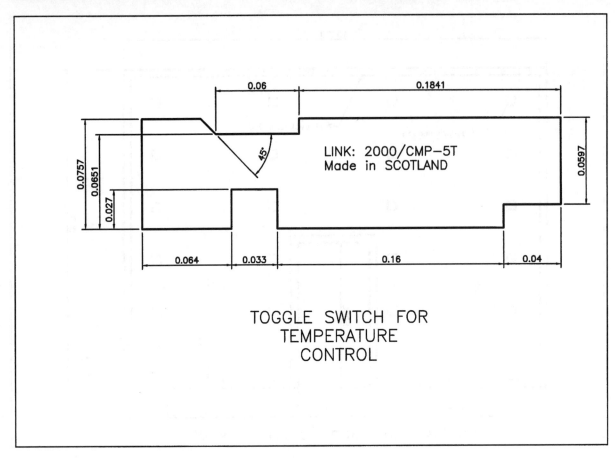

LINK: 2000/CMP—5T
Made in SCOTLAND

TOGGLE SWITCH FOR
TEMPERATURE
CONTROL

Figure 38.3   Small-scale drawing on A3 paper.

6   With layer OUT current, refer to Fig. 38.3 and draw the toggle switch (full size) using the sizes given.

7   Add all dimensions after altering the A3DIM dimension style with:
Fit tab: overall scale: 0.001
Primary units tab: Linear precision: 0.0000.

8   Add text, but you have to decide on the height.

Summary

1   Scale drawings require the MVSETUP command to be used.

2   Large- and small-scale drawings can be 'fitted' onto any size of paper.

3   Dimensions with scaled drawings are controlled with the Overall scale factor in the Dimension Styles dialogue box – Fit tab. This is equivalent to altering the dimension variable **DIMSCALE**.

4   Text is scaled according to the overall scale factor.

Chapter 39

Multilines, complex lines and groups

Layers have allowed us to display continuous, centre and hidden linetypes, but AutoCAD has the facility to display multilines and complex lines, these being defined as:

Multiline: parallel lines which can consist of several line elements of differing linetype. They must be created by the user.

Complex: lines which can be displayed containing text items and shapes. They can be created by the user, although AutoCAD has several 'stored' complex linetypes.

In this chapter we will only investigate a two element multiline and only use the stored AutoCAD complex linetypes. Creating both multilines with several different elements and complex linetypes is outside the scope of this book.

Multilines

Multilines have their own terminology, the basic terms being displayed in Fig. 39.1(a). To investigate how to use multilines:

1   Open your A:A3PAPER standard sheet with layer OUT current and refer to Fig. 39.1.

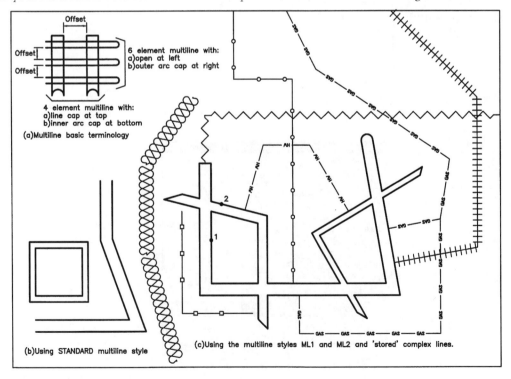

Figure 39.1   Multiline and complex line exercise.

2 Select the MULTILINE icon from the Draw toolbar and:

prompt   Justification=Top,Scale=??,Style=STANDARD
then   Specify start point or [Justification/Scale/STyle]
enter   **S <R>** – the scale option
prompt   Enter mline scale<??>
enter   **10 <R>**
prompt   Specify start point and enter: **20,40 <R>**
prompt   Specify next point and enter: **@80,0 <R>**
prompt   Specify next point and enter: **@70<110 <R>**
prompt   Specify next point and enter: **@0,50 <R>**
prompt   Specify next point and right-click/Enter.

3 Menu bar with **Draw–Multiline** and:

   a) set scale to 5
   b) draw a square of side 40 from the point 20,60 using the close option – fig. (b).

4 From the menu bar select **Format–Multiline Style** and:

prompt   Multiline Styles dialogue box
respond   1) alter Name to: **ML1**
          2) enter description as: **first attempt**
          3) pick Element Properties.
prompt   Element Properties dialogue box
respond   note layout then pick OK
prompt   Multiline Styles dialogue box
respond   pick Multiline Properties
prompt   Multiline Properties dialogue box
respond   1) pick **Line-Start**
          2) pick **Outer arc-End** – Fig. 39.2
          3) pick OK
prompt   Multiline Styles dialogue box – Fig. 39.3
respond   1) pick Add
          2) pick OK.

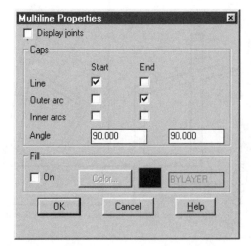

Figure 39.2   Multiline Properties dialogue box.

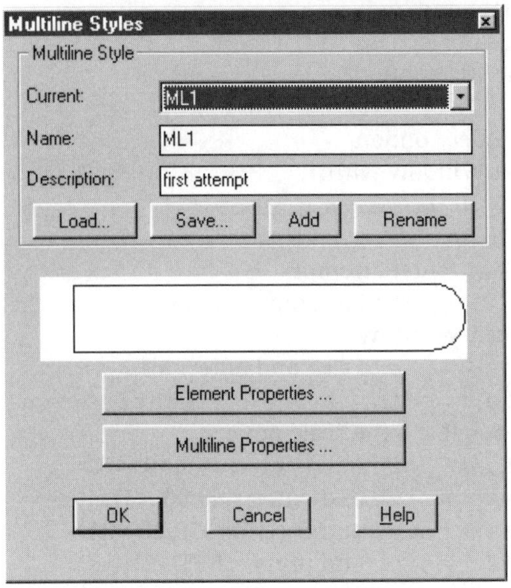

Figure 39.3 Multiline Styles dialogue box.

5 At the command line enter **MLINE <R>** and:

prompt	Specify start point or [Justification/Scale/STyle]
enter	**ST <R>** – the style option
prompt	Enter mline style name and enter: **ML1 <R>**
prompt	Specify start point or [Justification/Scale/Style]
enter	**S <R>** – the scale option
prompt	Enter mline scale and enter: **10 <R>**
prompt	Specify start point and enter: **170,170 <R>**
prompt	Specify next point and enter: **@0,–100 <R>**
prompt	Specify next point and enter: **@150,0 <R>**
prompt	Specify next point and enter: **@120<100 <R>**
prompt	Specify next point and right-click/Enter.

6 Menu bar with **Format–Multiline Style** and:

prompt	Multiline Styles dialogue box
respond	1) alter name to: ML2
	2) enter description as: second attempt
	3) pick Multiline Elements
prompt	Element Properties dialogue box
respond	note layout then pick OK
prompt	Multiline Styles dialogue box
respond	pick Multiline Properties
prompt	Multiline Properties dialogue box
respond	1) cancel any existing end caps
	2) pick Line-Start
	3) pick Line-End
	4) alter angles to 45 and 30
	5) pick OK
	6) Multiline Styles dialogue returned
	7) pick Add the OK.

7 Activate the MLINE command and:

prompt	Specify start point or [Justification/Scale/STyle]
enter	ST <R> – the style option
prompt	Enter mline style name (or ?)
enter	**? <R>** – the query option
prompt	AutoCAD Text Window with:

                  Name   *Description*

                  STANDARD

                  ML1   first attempt

                  ML2   second attempt

respond	**cancel the text window**
prompt	Enter mline style name and enter: ML2 <R>
prompt	Specify start point or [Justification/Scale/STyle
enter	**S <R>** then **8 <R>** – the scale option
prompt	Specify start point and enter: **210,40 <R>**
prompt	Specify next point and enter: **@0,80 <R>**
prompt	Specify next point and enter: **@-80,20 <R>**
prompt	Specify next point and press <RETURN>.

8 Repeat the MLINE command and:

   a) set the scale to 5

   b) ensure ML2 is current style

   c) draw from: 350,160 to: @100<–150 to: @80<–60 to: <RETURN>.

9 Menu bar with Modify–Multiline and:

prompt	Multiline Edit Tools dialogue box – Fig. 39.4
respond	**pick Open Cross then OK** (middle row left)
prompt	Select first mline and pick multiline 1
prompt	Select second mline and pick multiline 2
prompt	Select first mline
respond	pick as required until all the 'crossed' multilines are opened – fig. (c).

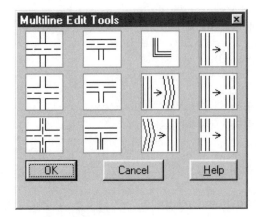

Figure 39.4 Multiline Edit Tools dialogue box.

Complex linetypes

1 Continue with the exercise on the screen.

2 Menu bar with **Format–Layer** create a new layer:
   a) Name: L1
   b) Colour: to suit
   c) Linetype: pick 'Continuous' in L1 layer line and:
prompt	Select Linetype dialogue box
respond	pick Load
prompt	Load or Reload Linetypes dialogue box
respond	scroll and pick GAS_LINE then OK
prompt	Select Linetype dialogue box
with	GAS_LINE displayed
respond	pick GAS_LINE then OK
prompt	Layer Properties Manager dialogue box
with	layer L1 displayed with GAS_LINE linetype
respond	pick OK.

3 Using step 2 as a guide, create another six layers using the following information:

Name	Colour	Linetype
L2	to suit	BATTING
L3	to suit	FENCELINE1
L4	to suit	FENCELINE2
L5	to suit	HOT_WATER_SUPPLY
L6	to suit	TRACKS
L7	to suit	ZIGZAG.

4 With each layer current, refer to fig. (c) and draw lines with each loaded linetype.

5 *Task*. Using the CHANGE PROPERTIES command (command line CHANGE or icon) use the ltScale option to optimise the appearance of the new added linetypes.

6 The exercise is now complete and can be saved if required.

Groups

A group is a named collection of objects. Groups are stored with a saved drawing and group definitions can be externally referenced. To demonstrate how groups are created and used:

1 Open your standard sheet, layer OUT current and refer to Fig. 39.5.

2 Draw the reference shape using your discretion for any sizes not given. Ensure the lowest vertex is at the point 210,120.

3 At the command line enter **GROUP <R>** and:

prompt	Object Grouping dialogue box
respond	1) at Group Name enter: **GR1**
	2) at Description enter: **first group**
	3) ensure Selectable is ON, i.e. tick in box
	4) pick Create Group: **New<**
prompt	Select objects
respond	pick the two inclined lines and the large circle then right-click
prompt	Object Grouping dialogue box
with	Group Name Selectable
	GR1 Yes
respond	pick OK.

4 At the command line enter **GROUP <R>** and:

prompt	Object Grouping dialogue box
respond	1) at Group Name enter: **GR2**
	2) at Description enter: **second group**
	3) Selectable ON – should be
	4) pick Create Group: ·**New<**
prompt	Select objects
respond	pick the text and the top three small circles then right-click
prompt	Object Grouping dialogue box with GR2 listed?
respond	pick OK.

5 Repeat the GROUP command and:
   a) Name: GR3
   b) Description: third group
   c) Create Group: New<
   d) Objects: pick the two vertical and the horizontal lines
   e) Dialogue box as Fig. 39.6
   f) pick OK.

6 Activate the ARRAY command and:

prompt	Select objects
enter	**GROUP <R>**
prompt	Enter group name and enter: **GR1 <R>**
prompt	3 found, then Select objects and right-click
prompt	Enter type of array and enter: **P <R>**
prompt	Specify center point of array and enter: 210,100 <R>
prompt	Enter the number of items and enter: **4 <R>**
prompt	Specify the angle to fill and enter: **360 <R>**
prompt	Rotate arrayed objects and enter: **Y <R>**.

7 The named group (GR1) will be displayed as fig. (a).

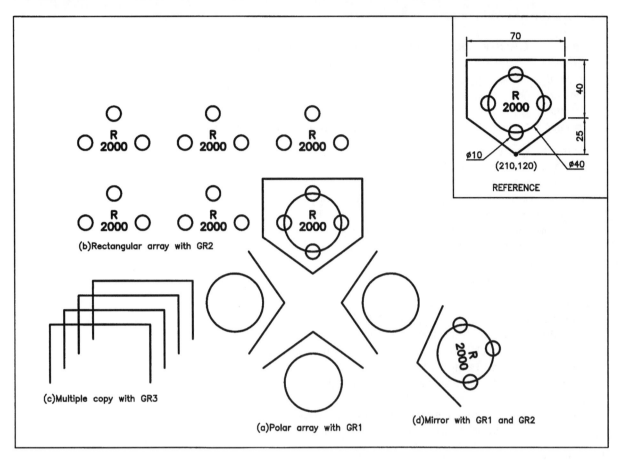

Figure 39.5 Group exercise.

Figure 39.6 Object Grouping dialogue box.

8 With the ARRAY command:
   prompt Select objects
   enter   **GROUP <R>** then **GR2 <R><R>** – why two returns?
   prompt Type of array and enter: **R <R>**
   prompt Enter the number of rows and enter: **2 <R>**
   prompt Enter the number of columns and enter: **3 <R>**
   prompt Enter the row distance and enter: **55 <R>**
   prompt Enter the column distance and enter: **–70 <R>** – fig. (b).

9 With the COPY command:
   a) objects and enter: GROUP <R>
   b) group name and enter: GR3 <R><R>
   c) base point and enter: M <R> – multiple copy option
   d) base point and enter: 175,145 <R> – why these coordinates?
   e) second point and enter: @–150,–100 <R>
   f) second point and enter: @–140,–90 <R>
   g) second point and enter: @–130,–80 <R>
   h) second point and enter: @–120,–70 <R><R> – fig. (c).

10 Select the MIRROR icon and:
   a) select objects and enter: GROUP <R>
   b) group name and enter: GR1 <R>
   c) 3 found then select objects and enter: GROUP <R>
   d) group name and enter: GR2 <R>
   e) 5 found, 8 total then select objects and right-click
   f) first point of mirror line – Center icon and pick bottom circle
   g) second point – Intersection icon and pick top right of border
   h) delete source objects and enter: N <R> – fig. (d).

11 Did your text item mirror? Why didn't mine?

12 The exercise is complete and can be saved if required.

13 Do not quit the drawing.

Task

1 Erase the original text item – complete group (GR2) erased?

2 Undo this effect with the UNDO icon.

3 Select the explode icon and select any group object and: '? were not able to be exploded' displayed at prompt line.

4 At the command line enter GROUP <R> from the dialogue box:
   a) pick GR2 line
   b) pick Explode
   c) pick OK.

5 Now erase the text item.

Summary

1 Multilines can be created by the user with different linetypes and can have several elements in their definition – not considered in this book.

2 Multilines have line or arc end caps.

3 Multilines have their own editing facility.

4 Complex linetypes can be have text or shape items in their definition and can be created by the user – not considered in this book.

5 Groups are collections of objects defined by the user.

7 Once created, a group must be exploded from the Object Grouping dialogue box.

8 The GROUP command can only be entered from the keyboard.

Chapter 40

Blocks

A block is part of a drawing which is 'stored away' for future recall **within the drawing in which it was created**. The block may be a nut, a diode, a tree, a house or any part of a drawing. Blocks are used when repetitive copying of objects is required, but they have another important feature – text can be attached to them. This text addition to blocks is called **attributes** and will be considered in a later chapter.

Getting started

1 Open the A:A3PAPER standard sheet and refer to Fig. 40.1.

2 Draw the house shape using the reference sizes given with:
   a) the outline on layer OUT
   b) the circular windows on layer OUT but green (CHANGE)
   c) a text item on layer TEXT
   d) four dimensions on layer DIMS
   e) use your discretion for any size not given.

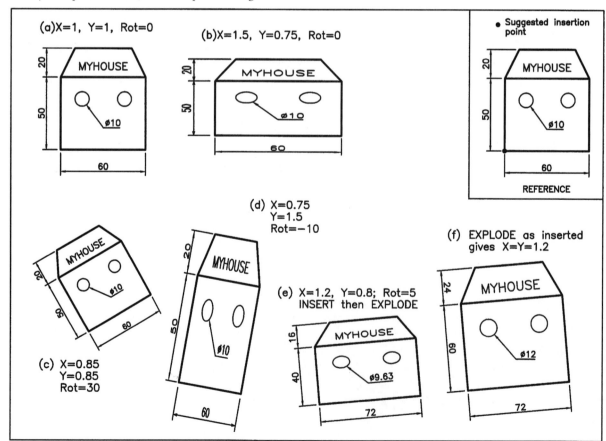

Figure 40.1   First block creation and insertion exercise.

Creating a block

Blocks can be created from both the command line and via a dialogue box. This first exercise will consider the keyboard entry method.

1 At the command line enter **-BLOCK <R>** and:

prompt	`Enter block name or [?]`
enter	**HOUSE <R>**
prompt	`Specify insertion base point`
respond	**Intersection icon and pick lower left corner**
prompt	`Select objects`
respond	**window the house and dimensions**
prompt	`14 found then Select objects`
respond	**right-click**.

2 The house shape will disappear from the screen – do not panic!

3 *Note:*
   a) the house shape has been 'stored' as a block within the current drawing
   b) this drawing has not yet been saved
   c) the -BLOCK keyboard entry will 'bypass' the dialogue box entry method.

Inserting a block

Created blocks can be inserted into the current drawing by either direct keyboard entry or via a dialogue box. We will investigate both methods.

Keyboard insertion

1 At the command line enter **-INSERT <R>** and:

prompt	`Enter block name or [?]`
enter	**HOUSE <R>**
prompt	`Specify insertion point or [Scale/X/Y/Z/Rotate/PScale..`
and	`'ghost' image of block attached to cursor`
enter	**35,200 <R>**
prompt	`Enter X scale factor, specify opposite corner..`
enter	**1 <R>** – an X scale factor of 1
prompt	`Enter Y scale factor <use X scale factor>`
enter	**1 <R>** – a Y scale factor of 1
prompt	*Specify rotation angle<0>*
enter	**0 <R>**.

2 The house block is inserted full-size as fig. (a).

3 Repeat the -INSERT command and:

prompt	`Block name` and enter: **HOUSE <R>**
prompt	`Insertion point` and enter: **145,210 <R>**
prompt	`X scale factor` and enter: **1.5 <R>**
prompt	`Y scale factor` and enter: **0.75 <R>**
prompt	`Rotation angle` and enter: **0 <R>** – fig. (b).

Dialogue box insertion

1 From the Draw toolbar select the INSERT BLOCK icon and:

prompt   `Insert dialogue box`

with   HOUSE as the Name. This is because we entered HOUSE at the command line INSERT command

respond   1) ensure Insertion point: Specify On-screen active – tick

        2) ensure Scale: Specify On-screen active – tick

        3) ensure Rotation: Specify On-screen active – tick

        4) pick OK

prompt   `Specify insertion point` and enter: **55,75 <R>**

prompt   `Enter X scale factor` and enter: **0.85 <R>**

prompt   `Enter Y scale factor` and enter: **0.85 <R>**

prompt   `Specify rotation angle` and enter: **30 <R>** – fig. (c).

2 Menu bar with **Insert-Block** and:

prompt   `Insert dialogue box`

with   HOUSE as block name

respond   1) deactivate the three On-screen prompts (no tick)

        2) alter Insertion Point to X: 120, Y: 40, Z: 0

        3) alter Scale to X: 0.75, Y: 1.5, Z: 1

        4) alter Rotation to Angle: −10

        5) dialogue box as Fig. 40.2

        6) pick OK – fig. (d).

Notes

1 An inserted block is a **single object**. Select the erase icon and pick any point on one of the inserted blocks then right-click. The complete block is erased. Undo the erase effect.

2 Blocks are inserted into a drawing with layers 'as used'. Freeze the DIMS layer and turn off the TEXT layer. The four inserted blocks will be displayed without dimensions or text. Now thaw the DIMS layer and turn on the TEXT layer.

3 Blocks can be inserted at varying X and Y scale factors and at any angle of rotation. The default scale is X=Y=1, i.e. the block is inserted full size. The default rotation angle is 0.

4 Dimensions which are attached to inserted blocks are not altered if the scale factors are changed.

5 A named block can be redefined and will be discussed later.

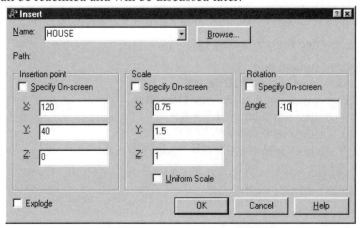

Figure 40.2 The Insert dialogue box.

Exploding a block

The fact that a block is a single object may not always be suitable to the user, i.e. you may want to copy parts of a block. AutoCAD uses the EXPLODE command to 'convert' an inserted block back to its individual objects.

The explode option can be used:
a) after a block has been inserted
b) during the insertion process.

1 At the command line enter -INSERT <R> and:
   prompt   Block name and enter: HOUSE
   prompt   Insertion point and enter: 220,25
   prompt   X scale factor and enter: 1.2
   prompt   Y scale factor and enter: 0.8
   prompt   Rotation angle and enter: 5.

2 Select the EXPLODE icon from the Modify toolbar and:
   prompt   Select objects
   respond   **pick the last inserted block then right-click**.

3 The exploded block is restored to its individual objects and the dimensions are **scaled to the factors entered** – fig. (e). The individual objects of this exploded block can now be modified if required.

4 Select the INSERT BLOCK icon and using the Insert dialogue box:
   a) deactivate the three Specify On-screen prompts, i.e. no tick
   b) Insertion Point X: 325; Y: 35; Z: 0
   c) Scale X: 1.2; Y: 0.8; Z: 1
   d) Rotation angle: 5
   e) Explode: ON, i.e. tick and *note the scale factor values*
   f) pick OK.

5 The block is exploded as it is inserted at a scale of X=Y=1.2 and the dimensions display this scale effect – fig. (e). Note the 'style' for the inserted/exploded dimensions!

6 *Note:*
   a) a block exploded after insertion will retain the original X and Y inserted scale factors
   b) a block exploded as it is inserted has X=Y scale factors.

Block exercise

1 Open the A:A3PAPER standard sheet with layer OUT current.

2 Refer to Fig. 40.3 and draw the four lines using the sizes given. Do not add the dimensions.

3 Menu bar with **Draw–Block–Make** and:

prompt	Block Definition dialogue box
respond	1) enter Name: SEAT
	2) at Base point: select Pick point
prompt	Specify insertion base point
respond	**midpoint icon and pick line indicated in Fig. 40.3**
prompt	Block Definition dialogue box
with	Base point: X and Y coordinates of selected point
respond	at Objects: select Select objects
prompt	Select objects
respond	**window the four lines then right-click**
prompt	Block Definition dialogue box
with	preview icon displayed
respond	1) at Description enter: **CHAIR block**
	2) pick OK.

Figure 40.3
Seat block.

4 Now erase the four lines as they have been made into a block.

5 Draw two 25 radius circles with centres at 100,150 and 250,150. These centre points are important.

6 Select the INSERT BLOCK icon from the Draw toolbar and use the Insert dialogue box to insert the block SEAT twice with:

a) Insertion point: X=130; Y=150; Z=0
   Scale: X=Y=Z=1
   Rotation: Angle=0

b) Insertion point: X=280; Y=150; Z=0
   Scale: X=Y=Z=1
   Rotation: Angle=0.

7 Now array the two inserted seat blocks with:

	first array	*second array*
objects:	pick left block and <R>	pick right block and <R>
type:	P <R>	P <R>
centre:	100,150 <R>	250,150 <R>
lens	5	7
angle:	360 <R>	360 <R>
rotate:	Y <R>	Y <R>.

8 Select the MAKE BLOCK icon from the Draw toolbar and:

prompt	Block Definition dialogue box
respond	1) enter Name: TABLE1
	2) enter Base point: X: 100; Y: 150; Z: 0
	3) at Objects: pick Select objects
prompt	Select objects
respond	**window the 5 seat arrangement then right-click**
prompt	Block Definition dialogue box with icon preview
respond	1) enter Description: 5 SEATER TABLE
	2) pick OK.

9 Repeat the Make Block icon selection and:
   a) name: enter TABLE2
   b) base point: enter X: 250; Y: 150; Z: 0
   c) pick select objects
   d) window the seven seat arrangement then right-click
   e) description: enter 7 SEAT TABLE
   f) dialogue box as Fig. 40.4
   g) pick OK.

10 Now erase any objects from the screen.

11 Menu bar with **Insert–Block** and:
   prompt   Insert dialogue box
   respond   1) scroll at Name and pick TABLE1
             2) Insertion point: X 60; Y 240; Z 0
             3) Scale: X 0.75; Y 0.75; Z 1
             4) Rotation: Angle 0
             5) pick OK.

12 Repeat the Insert–Block sequence with:
   a) name: TABLE2
   b) insertion point: X 110; Y 150; Z 0
   c) scale: X 0.75; Y 0.75; Z 1
   d) rotation: 0
   e) pick OK.

13 Menu bar with **Modify–Array** and:
   a) objects: pick any point on the 7 table block and right-click
   b) type: enter R <R> – rectangular array
   c) number of rows: enter 1 <R>
   d) number of columns: enter 3 <R>
   e) column distance: enter 100 <R>.

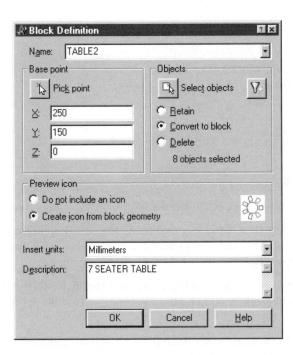

Figure 40.4 Block Definition dialogue box.

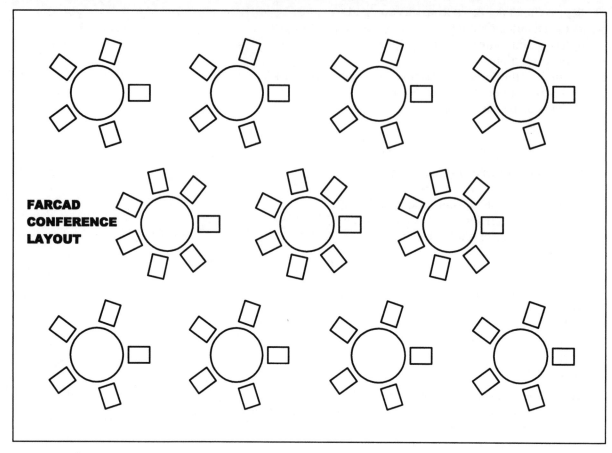

FARCAD
CONFERENCE
LAYOUT

Figure 40.5 Block exercise.

14 Rectangular array the 5 table block:
  a) for 2 rows and 4 columns:
  b) row distance: −180
  c) column distance: 100.

15 The final layout should be as Fig. 40.5 and can be saved.

Notes on blocks

Several points are worth discussing about blocks:

1 *The insertion point.* When a block is being inserted using the Insert dialogue box, the user has the option to decide whether the parameters are entered via the dialogue box or at the command line. The Specify On-screen selection allows this option.

2 *Exploding a block.* I would recommend that blocks are inserted before they are exploded. This maintains the original X and Y scale factors. Remember that blocks do not need to be exploded.

3 *Command line.* Entering -BLOCK and -INSERT will 'bypass' the dialogue boxes and allow all parameters to be entered from the keyboard.

4 *The ? option*. Both the command line -BLOCK and -INSERT commands have a query (?)
option which will list all the blocks in the current drawing. At the command line enter
-BLOCK <R> and:

prompt   Enter block name (or ?) and enter: **? <R>**
prompt   Enter block(s) to list<*> and enter: *** <R>**
prompt   AutoCAD Text Window
with   Defined blocks
           "SEAT"
           "TABLE1"
           "TABLE2"
           User
           Blocks
           3.

5 *Making a block*. Blocks can be created by command line entry or by a dialogue box and
the following is interesting:
   a) command line: the original shape disappears from the screen
   b) dialogue box: the original shape 'stays' on the screen.

6 *Nested blocks*.
   a) with the menu bar selection **Tools–Inquiry–List** pick any 7 seat table and:
      prompt   AutoCAD text Window
      with   details about the selected object
   b) this information tells the user that the selected object is a block with name TABLE2,
       created on layer OUT – Fig. 40.6(a)
   c) with the EXPLODE icon, pick the previous selected 7 seat table
   d) with the LIST command, pick ant seat of the exploded block and the text window
       will display details about the object, i.e. it is a block with name SEAT, created on layer
       OUT – Fig. 40.6(b)
   e) this is an example of a nested block, i.e. block SEAT is contained within block TABLE2
   f) if you exploded one of the seats of the exploded table, what would be displayed with
       the LIST command?

```
          BLOCK REFERENCE  Layer: "OUT"
                    Space: Model space
              Handle = 39A
              "TABLE2"
           at point, X=     60.00  Y=     60.00  Z=     0.00
              X scale factor        0.75
              Y scale factor        0.75
        rotation angle    0.0
              Z scale factor        1.00
         (a) First list selection

          BLOCK REFERENCE  Layer: "OUT"
                    Space: Model space
              Handle = 3B7
              "SEAT"
           at point, X=     54.99  Y=     38.06  Z=     0.00
              X scale factor        0.75
              Y scale factor        0.75
        rotation angle  257.1
              Z scale factor        1.00
         (b) Second list selection
```

Figure 40.6   Listing inserted blocks.

Using blocks

1 Open your A:A3PAPER standard sheet with layer OUT current.

2 Refer to Fig. 40.7 and draw a 20 sided square with diagonals and make a block:
name: BL1
insertion point: diagonal intersection
objects: window the shape – no dimensions

3 Draw an inclined line, a circle, an arc and a polyline shape of line and arc segments – discretion for sizes, but use Fig. 40.7 as a guide.

4 *Divide.* Menu bar with **Draw–Point–Divide** and:
prompt   Select object to divide
respond   **pick the line**
prompt   Enter the number of segments or [Block] and enter: **B <R>**
prompt   Enter name of block to insert and enter: **BL1 <R>**
prompt   Align block with object and enter: N <R>
prompt   Enter the number of segments and enter: **4 <R>** – fig. (a).

5 *Measure.* Menu bar with **Draw–Point–Measure** and:
prompt   Select object to measure and: **pick the circle**
prompt   Specify length of segment or [Block] and enter: **B <R>**
prompt   Enter name of block to insert and enter: **BL1 <R>**
prompt   Align block with object and enter: **Y <R>**
prompt   Specify length of segment and enter: **35 <R>** – fig. (b).

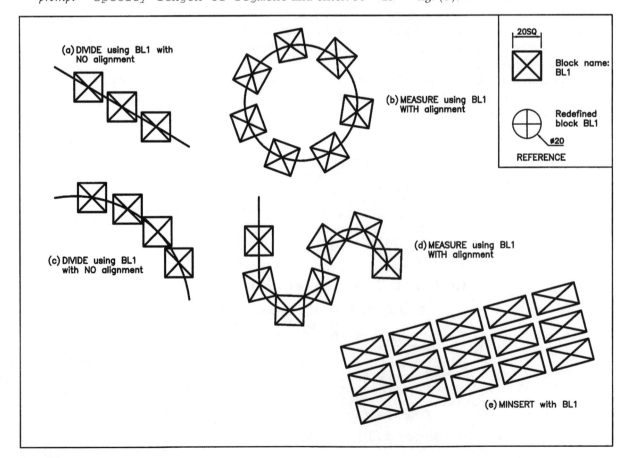

Figure 40.7   Using blocks exercise.

6 Using the DIVIDE and MEASURE commands:
   a) divide the arc: with block BL1, no alignment and with five segments – fig. (c)
   b) measure the polyline: with block BL1, with alignment and with a segment length of 35.

7 *MINSERT* (multiple insert). At the command line enter **MINSERT <R>** and:
   prompt Enter block name and enter: **BL1 <R>**
   prompt Specify insertion point and pick a suitable point on screen
   prompt Enter X scale factor and enter: **1.5 <R>**
   prompt Enter Y scale factor and enter: **0.75 <R>**
   prompt Specify rotation angle and enter: **15 <R>**
   prompt Enter number of rows and enter: **3 <R>**
   prompt Enter number of columns and enter: **5 <R>**
   prompt Enter distance between rows and enter: **20 <R>**
   prompt Specify distance between columns and enter: **35 <R>**
   The block BL1 is arrayed in a 3 × 5 rectangular matrix – fig. (e).

8 Using the EXPLODE icon, pick any of the minsert blocks and:
   prompt 1 was minserted, i.e. you cannot explode minserted blocks

9 *Redefining a block*
   a) draw a circle of radius 10 and add the vertical and horizontal diagonals
   b) change the colour of the circle and lines to blue
   c) at the command line enter **-BLOCK <R>** and:
       prompt Enter block name and enter: **BL1 <R>**
       prompt Block "BL1" already exist. Redefine it? [Yes/No]<N>
       enter   **Y <R>**
       prompt Specify insertion base point
       respond pick the centre of the circle
       prompt Select objects
       respond window the circle and lines then right-click
   d) interesting result? – all the red squares should be replaced by blue circles with the same alignment, scales, etc.

10 *Oops.* The OOPS command can be used to re-display a block which has been defined with the command line -BLOCK command. Entering **OOPS <R>** at the command line will 'restore' the block to the screen, but will not affect the 'saved block'.

Layer 0 and blocks

Blocks have been created with the objects drawn on their 'correct' layers. Layer 0 is the AutoCAD default layer and can be used for block creation with interesting results. We will use the command line entry with this example.

1 Erase all objects from the screen and draw:
   a) a 50 unit square on layer 0 – black
   b) a 20 radius circle inside the square on layer OUT – red
   c) two centre lines on layer CL – green.

2 With the command line entry -BLOCK, make a block of the complete shape with block name TRY, using the circle centre as the insertion point.

3 Make layer OUT current and with the command line -INSERT, insert block TRY at 55,210, full size with no rotation. The square is inserted with red continuous lines.

4 Make layer CL current and -INSERT the block at 135,210, full size and with no rotation. The square has green centre lines.

5 With layer HID current, -INSERT the block at 215,210 and the square will be displayed with coloured hidden lines.

6 Make layer 0 current and -INSERT at 295,210 – square is black.

7 With layer 0 still current, freeze layer OUT and:
a) no red circles
b) no red square from first insertion – when layer OUT was current.

8 Thaw layer OUT and insert block TRY using the Insert dialogue box with:
a) explode option active, i.e. tick in box
b) insertion point: 175,115
c) full size with 0 rotation
d) square is black – it is on layer 0.

9 Explode the first three inserted blocks and the square should be black, i.e. it has been 'transferred' to layer 0 with the explode command.

10 Finally freeze layer 0 and:
a) no black squares
b) no objects from fourth insertion – why?

11 This completes the block exercises.

Summary

1 A block is a single object 'stored' for recall in the drawing in which it was created.

2 Blocks are used for the insertion of frequently used 'shapes'.

3 An inserted block is a single object.

4 Blocks can be inserted full size (X=Y) or with differing X and Y scale factors and varying rotation angles.

5 The explode command 'restores' an inserted block to its original objects.

6 The explode command can be used after insertion (command line) or during insertion (dialogue box).

7 Blocks are inserted with 'layers intact'.

8 Blocks can be used with the divide and measure commands.

9 Multiple block inserts are permissible with the MINSERT command. The insertion gives a rectangular array pattern.

10 Existing blocks can be redefined. The current drawing will be 'updated' to display the new block definition.

11 Unused blocks can be purged from a drawing.

Assignment

One activity requiring blocks to be created has been included for you to attempt.

Activity 34: in line cam and roller follower.

1 Draw the two shapes using the reference sizes given, using your discretion for any omitted size.

2 Make a block of each shape with the block names CAM and FOL. Use the insertion point given.

3 Insert each block using the information given.

Chapter **41**

Wblocks

Blocks are useful when shapes/objects are required for repetitive insertion in a drawing, but they are **drawing specific**, i.e. they can only be used within the drawing in which they were created. There are however, blocks which can be created and accessed by all AutoCAD users, i.e. they are **global**. These are called WBLOCKS (write blocks) and they are created in a similar manner to 'ordinary' blocks. Wblocks are stored and recalled from a 'named folder/directory' which we will assume to be the A floppy drive – you may have an existing named folder/directory for your AutoCAD work.

Creating Wblocks

1 Open your A:A3PAPER standard sheet with layer OUT current.

2 Refer to Fig. 41.1 and draw a rectangular polyline shape – fig. (a). The start point is to be 5,5 and the polyline has to have a constant width of 5. Close the shape with the close option. The rectangle sizes will become apparent during the insertion process.

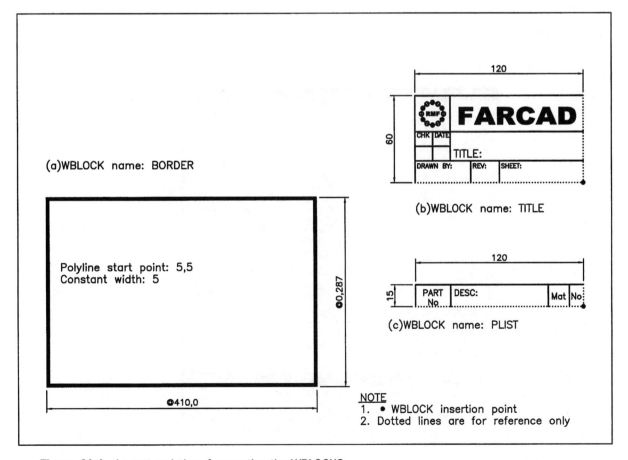

Figure 41.1 Layout and sizes for creating the WBLOCKS.

3 At the command line enter **WBLOCK <R>** and:

    prompt   `Write Block dialogue box` – similar to Block dialogue box

    with   Source: Entire drawing or Objects (active)

    respond   1) Base point: alter X: 2.5; Y:2.5; Z: 0

                2) Objects: pick Select objects

    prompt   `Select objects`

    respond   **pick any point on the polyline then right-click**

    prompt   `Write Block dialogue box`

    respond   At description, alter:

                1) File name: BORDER

                2) Location: A:\ or named folder

                3) Insert units: millimeters – Fig. 41.2

                4) pick OK

    prompt   `as the file is created, the WBLOCK preview is displayed.`

4 Construct the title box from the information in fig. (b), the actual detail being to your own design, e.g. text style, company name and logo, etc. The only requirement is to use the given sizes – the donut and dotted lines are for 'guidance' only and should not be drawn. Use layers correctly for lines, text, etc.

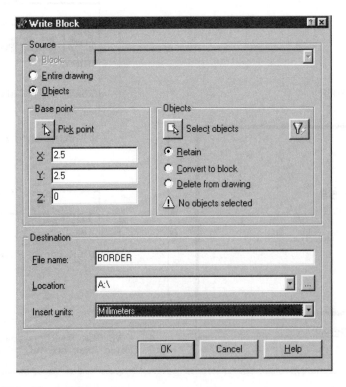

Figure 41.2 Write Block dialogue box.

5 Command line with **WBLOCK <R>** and:

prompt	Write Block dialogue box
respond	1) ensure Source: Objects
	2) Base point: select Pick points
prompt	Specify insertion base point
respond	pick point indicated by donut then right-click
prompt	Write Block dialogue box
respond	Objects: pick Select objects
prompt	Select objects
respond	**window the title box then right-click**
prompt	Write Block dialogue box
respond	at Description alter:
	1) File name: TITLE
	2) Location: A: drive or your named folder
	3) Insert units: millimeters
	4) pick OK
and	WBLOCK preview of saved file.

7 Create the parts list table headings using the basic layout in fig. (c). Again use your own design for text, etc.

8 With the WBLOCK command:

   a) Source: Objects
   b) Base point: Pick points and pick point indicated
   c) Objects: Select objects and window the shape
   d) File name: PLIST
   e) Location: A: drive or your named folder
   f) Insert units: millimeters
   g) pick OK.

9 Now proceed to the next part of the exercise.

Inserting Wblocks

1 Open A:A3PAPER – no to any save changes prompt?

2 Refer to Fig. 41.3 and draw the sectional pulley assembly. No sizes have been given, but you should be able to complete the drawing – use the snap to help. Add the hatching and the 'balloon' effect using donut–line–circle–middled text.

3 Select the INSERT icon from the Draw toolbar and:
  prompt   Insert dialogue box
  respond **pick Browse**
  prompt   Select Drawing File dialogue box
  respond 1) scroll and pick A: drive or your named folder
         2) scroll and pick BORDER
         3) pick Open
  prompt   Insert dialogue box with BORDER listed
  respond 1) ensure Insertion point, Scale and Rotation are specific to On-screen, i.e. tick in three boxes
         2) pick OK
  prompt   Specify insertion point and enter: **5,5 <R>**
  prompt   Enter X scale and enter: **1 <R>**
  prompt   Enter Y scale and enter: **1 <R>**
  prompt   Specify rotation angle and enter: **0 <R>**.

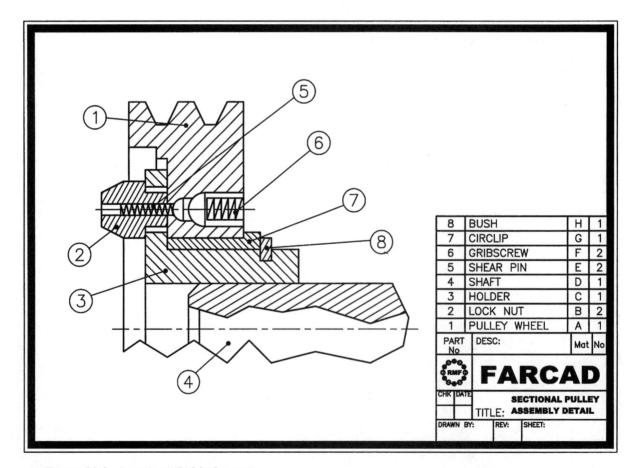

Figure 41.3 Inserting WBLOCKS exercise.

4 The polyline border should be inserted within the 'drawing frame' of the A3PAPER standard sheet.

5 Menu bar with **Insert–Block** and:

prompt   Insert dialogue box
respond **pick Browse**
prompt   Select Drawing File dialogue box
respond 1) scroll and pick A: drive or named folder
           2) scroll and pick TITLE
           3) pick Open
prompt   Insert dialogue box
respond 1) cancel the three on-screen prompts- no tick
           2) insertion point: X: 412.5; Y: 7.5; Z: 0
           3) scale: X: 1; Y: 1; Z: 1
           4) rotation: angle: 0
           5) pick OK.

6 The wblock TITLE will be inserted into the lower right corner of the BORDER wblock.

7 At the command line enter **-INSERT <R>**

prompt   Enter block name and enter: **PLIST <R>**
prompt   Specify insertion point and enter: **412.5,67.5 <R>**
prompt   Enter X scale and enter: **1 <R>**
prompt   Enter Y scale and enter: **1 <R>**
prompt   Specify rotation angle and enter: **0 <R>**.

8 The parts list wblock will be added 'on top' of the title box
9 Now complete the drawing by:
   a) adding a parts list similar to that shown
   b) complete the title box.

10 When these additions have been completed, save the drawing.

11 *Notes:*
   a) tree saved wblocks (BORDER, TITLE and PLIST) have been inserted into the drawing A:A3PAPER, these wblocks having been 'stored' in the A floppy disk (or a named folder). If the computer is networked, then all CAD users could access the three wblocks
   b) the border and title box could be permanently added to the A:A3PAPER standard sheet – you decide on this
   c) the three wblocks could be used in every exercise and activity from this point onwards – again you decide on this.

About Wblocks

Every drawing is a WBLOCK and every WBLOCK is a drawing

The above statement is true – think about it!

1 Open your A:A3PAPER standard sheet and refer to Fig. 41.4 which displays five saved activity drawings, inserted at varying scales and rotation angles. The drawings are:

Drawing File	IP	Xscale	Yscale	Rot
ACT_8	5,5	0.5	0.5	0
ACT_19	25,155	0.4	0.3	5
ACT_25	220,5	0.25	0.5	0
ACT_29	330,5	0.15	0.75	0
ACT_31	200,190	0.2	0.3	−5.

2 Insert some other previously saved drawings.

3 When creating a wblock, if the file name entered has already been used, AutoCAD will display the Message box with: *???.dwg already exists Do you want to replace it?*

4 *WBLOCK options*. When a wblock is being created, the user has three options for selecting the source. These are:
   a) Block: allows a previously created block to be 'converted' to a wblock
   b) entire drawing: the user can enter a new file name for the existing drawing
   c) Objects: allows parts of a drawing to be saved as a wblock, i.e. as a drawing file. This is probably the most common source selection method.

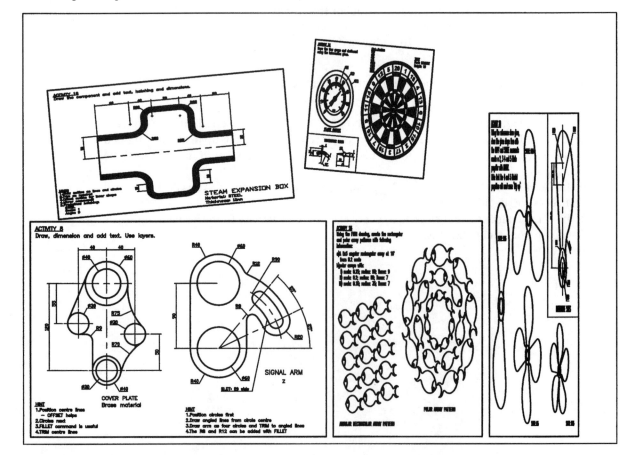

Figure 41.4 Inserting five activity drawings into the A:A3PAPER standard sheet.

Exploding Wblocks

1 Open A3PAPER and draw anywhere on the screen a circle of radius 25 and a square of side 50 – do not use the rectangle command.

2 Make WBLOCKS of the circle and square with the following:
   a) circle: Base point at the circle centre
      File name: CIR
   b) square: Base point at any corner of the square
      File name: SQ.

3 Now close the drawing (no save) and re-open A3PAPER.

4 Menu bar with Insert–Block and:
   a) browse and select CIR from your A: drive or named folder
   b) insert at a suitable point, full size with 0 rotation.

5 Menu bar with Insert–Block and:
   a) browse and pick SQ from your A: drive or named folder
   b) pick Explode from the dialogue box and note the scale
   c) insert at any suitable point – no rotation.

6 At the command line enter -BLOCK <R> and:
prompt	`Enter block name or [?]`
enter	**? <R>** – the query option
prompt	`Enter block(s) to list <*>`
enter	*** <R>**
prompt	`AutoCAD Text Window`
with	Defined blocks: "CIR"
	User blocks: 1
respond	cancel the text window.

7 With **LIST <R>** at the command line:
   a) pick the circle: BLOCK
   b) pick any line of square: LINE.

8 This exercise has demonstrated that:
   a) unexploded wblocks become blocks within the current drawing
   b) exploded wblocks do not become blocks.

9 This exercise is complete. Do not save.

Summary

1 Wblocks are global and could be accessed by all AutoCAD users.

2 Wblocks are usually saved to a named folder.

3 Wblocks are created with the command line entry WBLOCK <R> which results in the Write Block dialogue box.

4 Wblocks are inserted into a drawing in a manner similar to ordinary blocks, the user selecting:
   a) the named folder
   b) the drawing file name.

5 Wblocks can be exploded after/during insertion.

6 Unexploded wblocks become blocks in the current drawing.

7 All saved drawings are WBLOCKS.

Assignment

A single activity for you to attempt.

Activity 35: coupling arrangement.

1 Complete the drawing using your discretion for sizes not given. I have deliberately not given all sizes in this drawing.

2 Insert the wblock BORDER at 2.5,2.5 – full size with no rotation.

3 Insert the wblock TITLE at 412.5,7.5 and customize to suit.

4 Add all text and dimensions.

5 Save?

Chapter 42

Attributes

An attribute is an item of text attached to a block or a wblock and allows the user to add repetitive type text to frequently used blocks when they are inserted into a drawing. The text could be:

a) weld symbols containing appropriate information
b) electrical components with values
c) parts lists containing coded, number off, material, etc.

Attributes used as text items are useful, but their main advantage is that attribute data can be **extracted** from a drawing and stored in an attribute extraction file. This data could then be used as input to other computer packages, e.g. databases, spreadsheets, wordprocessors, etc.

This chapter is only a 'taster' as the topic will not be investigated fully. The editing and extraction features of attributes are beyond the scope of this book. The purpose of this chapter is to introduce the user to:

a) attaching attributes to a block
b) inserting an attribute block into a drawing.

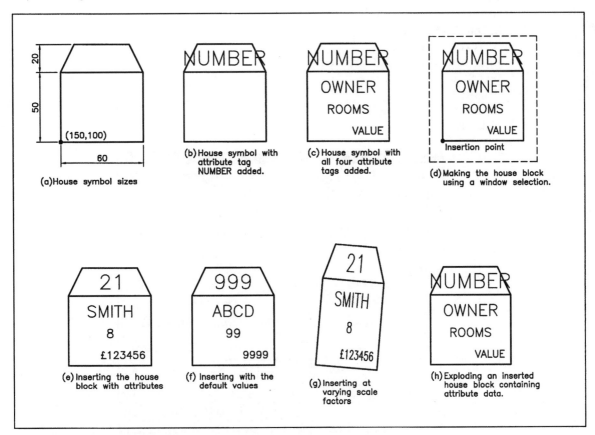

Figure 42.1 Making and using attributes the block: HOUSE.

Getting started

The attribute example for discussion is a small select housing complex, each house being represented by a symbol – a block. On each symbol the street number, house owner, number of rooms and the current market value is to be displayed, and this will be achieved using attributes.

1 Open your A:A3PAPER standard sheet with layer OUT current. Refer to Fig. 42.1.

2 Create the house symbol using the sizes in fig. (a) – discretion for sizes not given. Ensure that the lower left corner is positioned at the point 150,100 – this is important for the text which is to be added to the symbol.

Defining the attributes

Before a block containing attributes can be inserted into a drawing, the attributes must be defined, so:

1 Make layer TEXT current.

2 At the command line enter **ATTDEF <R>** and:

prompt   Attribute Definition dialogue box

with   selections for Modes, Attribute, Insertion point and Text options

respond 1) At Attribute enter:

          Tag: NUMBER

          Prompt: House number?

          Value: 999

      2) At Insertion point enter:

          X: 180 Y: 155 Z: 0

      3) At Text options alter:

          Justification: scroll and pick Center

          Text Style: ST1

          Height: 10

          Rotation: 0 – dialogue box as Fig. 42.2

      4) pick OK.

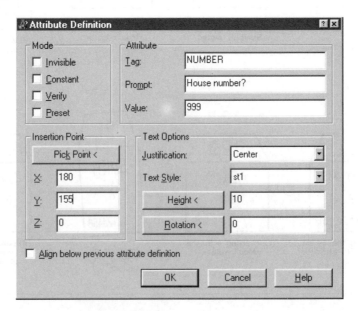

Figure 42.2 Attribute Definition dialogue box.

3 The attribute tag NUMBER will be displayed in the roof area of the house symbol as fig. (b).

4 Use the ATTDEF command three more times and enter the following attribute information in the Attribute Definition dialogue box using the same procedure as step 2.

	First entry	*Second entry*	*Third entry*
Attribute modes	blank	blank	blank
Attribute tag	OWNER	ROOMS	VALUE
Attribute prompt	House owner?	Number of rooms?	Current value?
Default value	ABCD	99	9999
Insertion Pt X	180	180	205
Insertion Pt Y	135	120	105
Insertion Pt Z	0	0	0
Justification	Centred	Centred	Right
Height	8	6	5
Rotation	0	0	0.

5 When all the attribute information has been entered, the house symbol will display the four tags – fig. (c).

6 *Note:*

   a) when attributes are used for the first time, the words Tag, Prompt and Value can cause confusion. The following description may help to overcome this confusion:

   tag: is the actual attribute 'label' which is attached to the drawing at the specified text start point. This tag item can have any text style, height and rotation.

   prompt: is an aid to the user when the attribute data is being entered with the inserted block

   value: is an artificial name/number for the attribute being entered. It can have any alpha-numeric value

   b) the Insertion point in the Attribute Definition dialogue box refers to the attribute text tag and not to a block.

7 In our first attribute definition sequence, we created the house number with the following attribute information:

   a) Tag: NUMBER

   b) Prompt: House number?

   c) Default value: 999

   d) Text insertion point for NUMBER, centred on 180,155.

Creating the attribute block

We will use the command line entry to make the block with the attributes, so:

1 At the command line enter **-BLOCK <R>** and:

   prompt   Enter block name and enter: **HOUSE <R>**

   prompt   Specify insertion base point

   respond **pick lower left corner of house symbol**

   prompt   Select objects

   respond **window the house and tags then right-click** – fig. (d).

2 The block will disappear as it has been made into a block with the command line BLOCK entry.

3 Remember OOPS, although it is not really necessary for us.

Testing the created block with attributes

Now that the block with attributes has been created, we want to 'test' the attribute information it contains. This requires the block to be inserted into the drawing, and this will be achieved with both command line and dialogue box entries.

1 Make layer OUT current.

2 At the command line enter **ATTDIA <R>** and:
   prompt   Enter new value for ATTDIA <?>
   enter   **0 <R>**.

   Note: this variable only allows attribute entry from the keyboard.

3 At the command line enter **-INSERT <R>** and:
   prompt   Enter block name and enter: **HOUSE <R>**
   prompt   Specify insertion point and pick a point to suit
   prompt   Enter X scale and enter: 1 <R>
   prompt   Enter Y scale and enter: **1 <R>**
   prompt   Specify rotation angle and enter: **0 <R>**
   prompt   Current value?<9999> and enter: **£123456 <R>**
   prompt   House number?<999> and enter: **21 <R>**
   prompt   House owner?<ABCD> and enter: **SMITH <R>**
   prompt   Number of rooms?<99> and enter: **8 <R>**.

4 The house will be displayed with the attribute information as fig. (e).

5 *Note:*
   a) the prompt and defaults values are displayed as entered
   b) the order of the last four prompt lines (i.e. house number–current value) may not be in the same order as mine. This is not your fault.

6 Now insert the house block twice more:
   a) at any suitable point, full size with 0 rotation and accept the default values, i.e. right-click at the prompt – fig. (f)
   b) at another point on the screen with the X scale factor as 0.75, the Y scale factor as 1.25 and the rotation angle as –5. Use the same attribute entries as step 2, i.e. 21, SMITH, 8, £123456. The result should be as fig. (g).

7 Explode any inserted block which contains attribute information and the tags will be displayed – fig. (h).

8 We are now ready to insert the 'real' attribute data.

Attribute information

1 The housing estate is to consist of eight houses, each house being represented by the house symbol with the appropriate attribute information displayed. The attribute information is listed in Table 42.1.

2 Attribute information can be added to an inserted block:
   a) from the keyboard – as previous example
   b) via a dialogue box which will now be discussed.

3 Erase all objects from the screen and make layer OUT current.

Table 42.1 Attribute data

Tag	Number	Owner	Rooms	Value
Data	1	BROWN	6	£85000
	2	BLUE	6	£90000
	3	CHERRY	8	£105000
	4	DONALD	10	£150000
	5	EAST	7	£95000
	6	FRENCH	9	£120000
	7	GRAY	5	£80000
	8	HORACE	3	£50000

4 At the command line enter **ATTDIA <R>** and:

prompt   Enter new value for ATTDIA<0>
enter   **1 <R>**.

5 Menu bar with **Insert–Block** and:

prompt   Insert dialogue box
with   Block name: HOUSE – from previous insertion
respond 1) ensure all on-screen prompts not active, i.e. no tick

2) insertion point:- X: 30; Y: 195; Z: 0

3) scale: X: 1; Y: 1; Z: 1

4) rotation: angle 0

5) pick OK

prompt   Edit Attributes dialogue box as Fig. 42.3(a)
with   Entered prompts and default values
respond 1) alter Current value 99999 to: £85000

2) alter House number 999 to: 1

3) alter House owner ABCD to: BROWN

4) alter Number of rooms 99 to: 6

5) dialogue box as Fig. 42.3(b)

6) pick OK.

6 The house block will be inserted with the attribute information displayed.

(a)   (b)

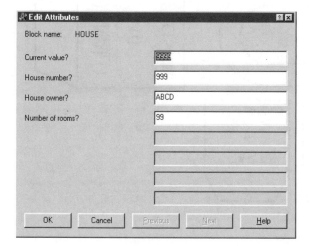
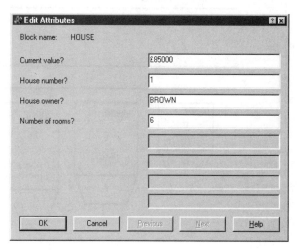

Figure 42.3 Edit Attribute dialogue box: (a) original and (b) modified.

7 Using step 5 as a guide with the attribute data from Table 42.1, refer to Fig. 42.4 and insert the HOUSE block to complete the housing estate – use your imagination with the scales and rotation angles.

8 Complete the estate layout and save?

9 This completes our brief 'taster' into attributes.

Point of interest?

In the previous chapter we created a title box as a wblock. This title box had text items attached to it, e.g. drawing name, date, revision, etc. These text items could have been made as attributes. When the title box was inserted into a drawing, the various text items (attributes) could have been entered to the drawing requirements. Think about this application of attributes!

Summary

1 Attributes are text items added to BLOCKS or WBLOCKS.

2 Attribute must be defined by the user.

3 Attribute data is added to a block when it is inserted into a drawing.

4 Attributes can be edited and extracted from a drawing, but these topics are beyond the scope of this book.

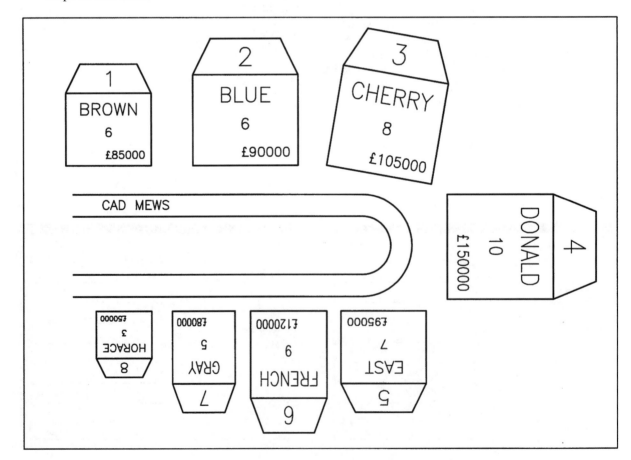

Figure 42.4 Estate layout with inserted block HOUSE and attribute data.

Assignment

A single activity which involves using a previously saved drawing and adding attribute data to a created block

Activity 36: fisherman's trophy room. A keen fisherman (not me) has a trophy room in which he displays his catches with labels of the type of fish, where it was caught and the year. It is these trophies which have to be created from a block with attributes.

1 Open the A:FISH drawing from activity 25 – hopefully saved?

2 Erase all objects to leave the fish outline, and scale the outline by a factor of 0.6 about the 'nose'.

3 Add the following three attributes to the fish outline:

Tag:	TYPE	RIVER	YEAR
Prompt:	What type?	Where caught?	Enter year caught
Default:	ABCD	WXYZ	9999

4 The attribute tags should be centre justified with text style ST1 and you should select a suitable point. The heights are at your discretion as is the rotation angle.

5 When the three attributes have been added to the outline, make a block of the complete shape, the block name being TROPHY.

6 Insert the TROPHY block at 0.8 full size, at suitable points and add the following attribute data:

Type	River	Year
SALMON	SPEY	1995
TROUT	TAY	1996
PIKE	DART	1997
CARP	NENE	1998
EELS	DERWENT	1999

7 Optimize your layout then save.

Chapter 43

External references

Wblocks contain information about objects, colour, layers, linetypes, dimension styles, etc. and all this information is inserted into the drawing with the wblock. All this inserted information may not be required, and it also takes time and uses memory space. Drawings which contain several wblocks are not automatically updated if one of the original wblocks is altered.

External references (**xrefs**) are similar to wblocks in that they are created by the user and can be inserted into a drawing, but they have one major advantage over the wblock. Drawings which contain external references are automatically updated if the original external reference 'wblock' is modified.

A worked example will be used to demonstrate external references. The procedure may seem rather involved as it requires the user to save and open several drawings, but the final result is well worth the effort. For the demonstration we will:

a) create a wblock
b) use the wblock as an xref to create two drawing layouts
c) modify the original wblock
d) view the two drawing layouts.
e) use your named directory/folder or the A drive.

Getting started

1 Open your A:A3PAPER standard sheet and refer to Fig. 43.1.

2 Make a new current layer named: XREF, colour: red with continuous linetype.

3 Draw *a*) a circle of radius 18 and *b*) a item of text, centred on the circle centre with height 5 and rotation angle 0. The item of text is: AutoCAD – fig. (a).

Creating the xref – a wblock

1 At the command line enter **WBLOCK <R>** and:
   prompt　　Write Block dialogue box
   respond　 1) Source: objects
   　　　　　　 2) Base point: pick circle centre point
   　　　　　　 3) Objects: window the circle and text then right-click
   　　　　　　 4) File name: XREFEX
   　　　　　　 5) Location: A drive or named folder
   　　　　　　 6) Insert units: millimeters
   　　　　　　 7) pick OK.

2 Now erase the circle and text item.

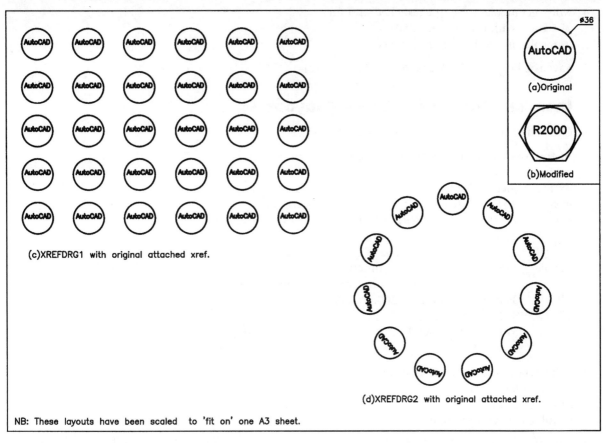

(c)XREFDRG1 with original attached xref.

(d)XREFDRG2 with original attached xref.

(a)Original

(b)Modified

NB: These layouts have been scaled to 'fit on' one A3 sheet.

Figure 43.1 External reference example.

Inserting the xref – drawing layout 1

1 Menu bar with **File–Close** (no to save changes) then menu bar with **File–Open** and select your A3PAPER standard sheet.

2 Menu bar with **Insert–External Reference** and:

prompt Select Reference File dialogue box
respond 1) scroll and pick A: drive or named folder
     2) scroll and pick XREFEX
     3) pick Open
prompt External Reference dialogue box
with Name: XREFEX and Path: A: drive or named folder
respond 1) ensure Reference Type: Attachment (black dot)
     2) all on-screen options active, i.e. tick
     3) pick Open
prompt Attach Xref "XREFEX": path name
and "XREFEX" loaded
then Specify insertion point and enter: **50,50 <R>**
prompt Enter X scale and enter: **1 <R>**
prompt Enter Y scale and enter: **1 <R>**
prompt Specify rotation angle and enter: **0 <R>**.

3 The named external reference (XREFEX) will be displayed at the insertion point entered. Similar to inserted a wblock?

4 Now rectangular array the attached xref for:
a) 5 rows with row distance: 50
b) 6 columns with column distance: 60.

5 Save the layout as **A:XREFDRG1** – Fig. 43.1(c).

Inserting the xref – drawing layout 2

1 Close the existing drawing then re-open A3PAPER.

2 At the command line enter **XREF <R>** and:
prompt   Xref Manager dialogue box
respond **pick Attach**
prompt   Select Reference File dialogue box
respond   1) scroll and pick XREFEX from your A drive or folder
       2) pick Open
prompt   External Reference dialogue box
respond   1) Reference Type: Attachment
       2) De-activate the three on-screen prompts (no tick)
       3) Insertion point: X: 200; Y: 250; Z: 0
       4) X,Y,Z scales: 1
       5) Rotation angle: 0
       6) pick OK.

3 Polar array the attached xref with:
a) centre point: 200,150
b) number of items: 11
c) full circle with rotation.

4 Save the layout as **A:XREFDRG2** – Fig. 43.1(d).

Modifying the original xref

1 Close the current drawing then open the drawing XREFEX from your A drive or named folder. This is the original wblock

2 *a*) Change the text item to R2000 and colour blue
  b) draw a hexagon, centred on the circle and circumscribed in a 19 radius circle. Change the colour of this hexagon to green. The modifications are shown in Fig. 43.1(b).

3 Menu bar with **File–Save** to automatically update A:XREFEX.

Viewing the original layouts

1 Close the existing drawing.

2 Menu bar with **File–Open** and:
a) pick XREFDRG1
b) note the Preview then pick Open
c) interesting result?

3 Menu bar with **File–Open** and:
a) pick XREFDRG2
b) note the Preview then pick Open
c) again an interesting result?

4 The layout drawings should display the modified XREFEX without any 'help' from us. This is the power of external references. Surely this is a very useful (and dangerous concept)?

5 Menu bar with **Format–Layer** and note the layer: **xrefex|xref**. This indicates that an external reference (xrefex) has been attached to layer xref. The (|) is a pipe symbol indicating as attached external reference.

6 This completes our simple investigation into xrefs.

Summary

1 External references are wblocks which can be attached to drawings.

2 When the original xref wblock is altered, all drawing files which have the external reference attached are automatically updated to include the modifications to the original wblock.

Chapter 44

Isometric drawings

An isometric is a 2D representation of a 3D drawing and is useful as it can convey additional information about a component which is not always apparent with the traditional orthogonal views. Although an isometric appears as a 3D drawing, the user should never forget that it is a 'flat 2D' drawing without any 'depth'.

Isometric drawings are created by the user with polar coordinates and AutoCAD has the facility to display an isometric grid as a drawing aid.

Setting the isometric grid

There are two methods for setting the isometric grid.

Dialogue box

1 From the menu bar select **Tools–Drafting Settings** and:

prompt Drafting Settings dialogue box

respond 1) Snap Type & Style:

      a) Grid snap on – black dot

      b) Isometric snap on

    2) set Grid Y Spacing: 10

    3) set Snap Y Spacing: 5

    4) dialogue box as Fig. 44.1

    5) pick OK.

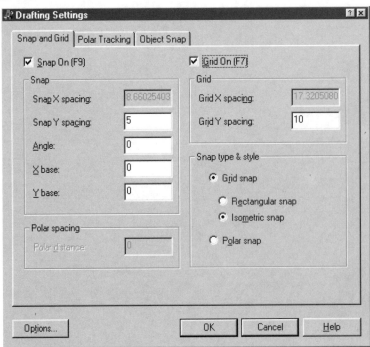

Figure 44.1   Drafting Settings dialogue box.

2 The screen will display an isometric grid of 10 spacing, with the on-screen cursor 'aligned' to this grid with a snap of 5.

3 Use the Drafting Settings dialogue box to 'turn the isometric grid off', i.e. pick the Rectangular snap.

4 The screen will display the standard grid pattern.

Keyboard

1 At the command line enter **SNAP <R>** and:

prompt	Specify snap spacing or [ON/OFF/Aspect/Rotate/Style/Type]
enter	**S <R>** – the style option
prompt	Enter snap grid style [Standard/Isometric]
enter	**I <R>** – the isometric option
prompt	Specify vertical spacing<5.00>
enter	**10 <R>**.

2 The screen will again display the isometric grid pattern with the cursor 'snapped to the grid points'.

3 Leave this isometric grid on the screen.

Isoplanes

1 AutoCAD uses three 'planes' called isoplanes when creating an isometric drawing, these being named top, right and left. The three planes are designated by two of the X, Y and Z axes as shown in Fig. 44.2(a) and are:
a) isoplane top: XZ axes
b) isoplane right: YX axes
c) isoplane left: YZ axes.

2 When an isoplane is 'set' or 'current', the on-screen cursor is aligned to that isoplane axis – Fig. 44.2(b).

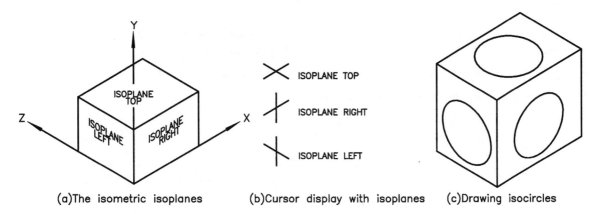

(a)The isometric isoplanes   (b)Cursor display with isoplanes   (c)Drawing isocircles

Figure 42.2 Three isometric concepts.

3 The isoplane can be set by one of three methods:
 a) at the command line enter **ISOPLANE <R>** and:
   prompt Enter isometric plane setting[Left/Top/Right]
   enter   **R <R>** – right plane
 b) using a 'toggle' effect by:
   1) holding down the Ctrl key (control)
   2) pressing the **E** key
   3) toggles to isoplane left
   4) Ctrl E again – toggles to isoplane top
 c) using the F5 function key:
   1) press F5 – toggles isoplane right
   2) press F5 – toggles isoplane left, etc.

4 *Note:* it is the users preference as to what method is used to set the isometric grid and isoplane, but my recommendation is:
 a) set the isometric grid ON from the Drafting Settings dialogue box with a grid spacing of 10 and a snap spacing of 5
 b) toggle to the required isoplane with Ctrl E or F5
 c) isoplanes are necessary when creating 'circles' in an isometric 'view'.

Isocircles

Circles in isometric are called isocircles and are created using the ellipse command and the correct isoplane **must** be set. Try the following exercise:

1 Set the isometric grid on with spacing of 10 and toggle to isoplane top.

2 Using the isometric grid as a guide and with the snap on, draw a cuboid shape as Fig. 44.2(c). The size of the shape is not important at this stage – only the basic shape.

3 Select the ELLIPSE icon from the Draw toolbar and:
   prompt Specify axis endpoint or [Arc/Center/Isocircle]
   enter   **I <R>** – the isocircle option
   prompt Specify center of isocircle
   respond **pick any point on top 'surface'**
   prompt Specify radius of isocircle
   respond **drag and pick as required**.

4 Toggle to isoplane right – Ctrl E.

5 At the command line enter **ELLIPSE <R>** and:
   prompt Specify axis endpoint or [Arc/Center/Isocircle]
   enter   **I <R>**
   prompt Specify center of isocircle and pick a point on 'right side'
   prompt Specify radius of isocircle and drag/pick to suit.

6 Toggle to isoplane left, and draw an isocircle on the left side of the cuboid.

7 The cuboid now has an isocircle on the three 'sides'.

8 Now continue with the example which follows.

Isometric example

1 Open your A:A3PAPER standard sheet and refer to Fig. 44.3.

2 Set the isometric grid on, with a grid spacing of 10 and a snap spacing of 5.

3 With the LINE icon draw:
First point: pick towards lower centre of the screen
Next point and enter: @80<30 <R>
Next point and enter: @100<150 <R>
Next point and enter: @80<–150 <R>
Next point and enter: @100<–30 <R>
Next point and enter: @50<90 <R>
Next point and enter: @80<30 <R>
Next point and enter: @50<–90 <R><R> – fig. (a).

4 With the COPY icon:
   a) objects: pick lines D1, D2 and D3 then right-click
   b) base point: pick intersection of pt 1
   c) displacement: pick intersection of pt 2.

5 Draw the two lines (endpoint–endpoint) to complete the base, sides and top and draw a top diagonal line – fig. (b).

6 Toggle to isoplane top.

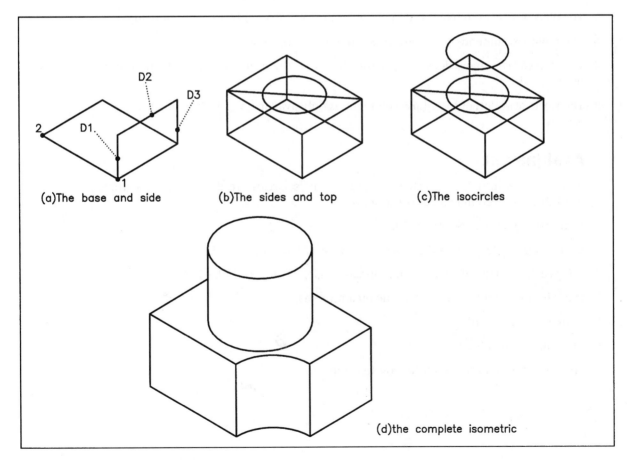

(a)The base and side   (b)The sides and top   (c)The isocircles

(d)the complete isometric

Figure 44.3   Isometric exercise.

7 With the ELLIPSE–Isocircle command:
   a) pick midpoint of diagonal as the centre
   b) enter a radius of 30.

9 Copy the isocircle:
   a) from the diagonal midpoint
   b) by: @50<90 – fig. (c).

10 Erase the diagonal.

11 Draw in the two 'cylinder' sides using the quadrant snap and picking the isocircles.

12 Trim objects to these lines and erase unwanted objects to give the complete isometric.

13 *Task:* draw two additional 30 radius isocircles and modify to give the completed isometric as fig. (d).

14 Save if required.

Summary

1 An isometric is a 'flat' 2D drawing having 3D visualization.

2 An isometric grid is available as a drafting setting.

3 Isometrics are constructed with polar coordinates.

4 Circles are drawn with the ellipse–isocircle option and the correct isoplane must be set.

5 The objects snaps (endpoint, midpoint, etc.) are available with isometric drawings.

6 The modify commands (e.g. copy, trim, etc.) are available with isometrics.

7 The OFFSET command does not give the effect that the user would expect, and should not be used.

8 The isocircle option of the ellipse command is only available when the isometric grid is 'set on'.

Assignment

Activity 37: 6 into 1. This activity requires that isocircles are drawn with the three isoplanes. The recommended procedure is:

1 Draw an isometric cube of side 50.

2 Draw six isocircles, one at the centre of each face. The radius is 25.

3 Copy each isocircle by 50 at the appropriate angle, i.e. 30, 90, 150, –150,–90 and –30.

4 Draw in the 'cylinder sides' using the quadrant snap.

5 Trim as required with care.

6 Erase unwanted objects.

7 The sectional isometric is left for you to complete.

Chapter 45

Model space and paper space

AutoCAD has two drawing environments these being model space and paper space with:

- model space: used to draw the component
- paper space: used to layout the drawing paper for plotting.

The two drawing environments are independent of each other and while the concept is particularly applicable to 3D modelling we will demonstrate its use with a previously saved 2D drawing. Up until now, all our work has been in model space.

Note

1 The user must realize that this chapter is an introduction to the model/paper space concept. Paper space with R2000 is particularly targeted for plotting and as I have no idea what type of plotter you have access to, I have assumed that no plotter is available. This does not affect the exercise.

2 When the paper space environment is entered, a new icon will be displayed. The model space and paper space icons are shown in Fig. 45.1.

3 Before paper space can be used, the paper space environment must be 'entered'. This can be achieved by:
   a) picking MODEL from the status bar
   b) picking one of the layout tabs from the drawing screen
   c) entering TILMODE then 1 at the command line.

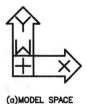
(a)MODEL SPACE

(b)PAPER SPACE

Figure 45.1 The model space and paper space icons.

Getting started

1 Open your A3PAPER standard sheet and
   a) erase the rectangular border
   b) make two new layers, VP and SHEET both with your own colour selection and with
      continuous linetype.
   c) make layer VP current.

2 Menu bar with **Tools–Wizards–Create Layout** and:

prompt	Create Layout - Begin dialogue box
respond	**alter Layout name to FACTORY then pick Next** – Fig. 45.2
prompt	Create Layout - Printer dialogue box
respond	**pick None then Next**
prompt	Create Layout - Paper Size dialogue box
respond	1) Drawing units: Millimeters
	2) scroll at paper size and pick **ISOA3 (420.00 × 297.00)**
	3) pick Next
prompt	Create Layout - Orientation dialogue box
respond	**pick Landscape then Next**
prompt	Create Layout - Title Block dialogue box
respond	**pick None then Next**
prompt	Create Layout - Define Viewports dialogue box
respond	1) Viewport setup: Single
	2) View scale: Scaled to Fit
	3) pick Next
prompt	Create Layout - Pick Location dialogue box
respond	**pick Select location**
prompt	Drawing screen returned
and	Specify first corner
enter	**10,10 <R>**
prompt	Specify opposite corner
enter	**210,145 <R>**
prompt	Create Layout - Finish dialogue box
respond	**pick Finish**.

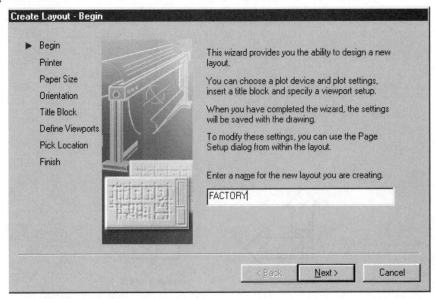

Figure 45.2   Create Layout (Begin) dialogue box.

3 The drawing screen will be returned in Paper Space (note icon) with:
   a) a white area – the A3 drawing paper
   b) a dotted line area – the plottable area
   c) a coloured rectangle – the created viewport
   d) a new tab – FACTORY.

The sheet layout

Our A3 drawing paper has a paper space viewport and we now want to create another three viewports. Refer to Fig. 45.3 and:

1 With layer VP current, menu bar with **View–Viewports–1 Viewport** and:
   prompt   Specify corner of viewport and enter: **230,75 <R>**
   prompt   Specify opposite corner and enter: **380,170 <R>**.

2 Repeat the menu bar View–Viewports–1 Viewport selection and create another viewport from **190,180** to **280,250**.

3 Menu bar with **View–Viewports–Polygon Viewport** and:
   prompt   Specify start point and enter: **50,160 <R>**
   prompt   Specify next point and enter: **@50<0 <R>**
   prompt   Specify next point and enter: **@50<72 <R>**
   prompt   Specify next point and enter: **@50<144 <R>**
   prompt   Specify next point and enter: **@50<–144 <R>**
   prompt   Specify next point and enter: **C <R>**.

4 We have now created three rectangular paper space viewports and one pentagonal paper space viewport.

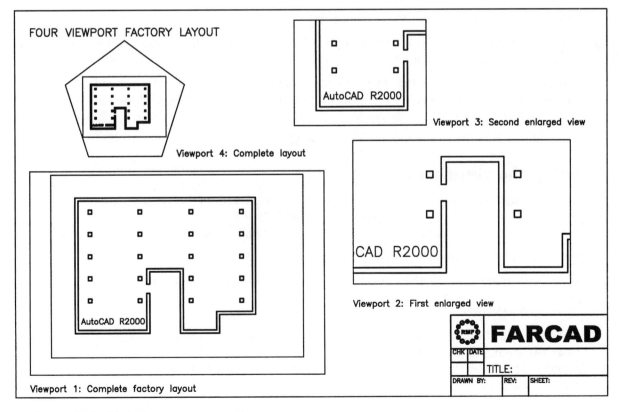

Figure 45.3 Model/paper space exercise.

The model

Rather than draw a new component we will insert an already completed and saved (I hope) drawing into our created viewports. This drawing is the large–scale factory layout (LARGESC) from Chapter 38.

1 Enter model space with a left-click on PAPER in the Status bar.

2 The model space environment will be entered and the traditional model space icon will be displayed in the rectangular viewports.

3 Make the first created viewport (lower left) active by:
  a) moving the pointer into the rectangular area
  b) left-click
  c) cursor cross-hairs displayed and the viewport border appears highlighted.

4 Menu bar with **Insert–Block** and:
  prompt   Insert dialogue box
  respond   1) pick Browse
             2) scroll and pick the A: drive or your named folder
             3) scroll and pick LARGESC (or your entered name)
             4) pick Open
  prompt   Insert dialogue box with Name: LARGESC
  respond   1) ensure Specify On-screen active, i.e. ticks
             2) ensure Explode active, i.e. tick
             3) pick OK
  prompt   Specify insertion point for block and enter: **0,0 <R>**
  prompt   Specify scale factor for XYZ axes and enter: **1 <R>**
  prompt   Specify rotation angle and enter: **0 <R>**.

5 Now select from the menu bar **View–Zoom-All**

6 The active viewport will display the complete factory layout while the other three viewports may display some lines.

7 Make each viewport active in turn by moving the pointing arrow into the viewport and left-click, then View–Zoom-All from the menu bar and the layout will be displayed in each viewport.

8 Erase all text from the layout and freeze layer DIMS.

Using the viewports

1 With the lower right viewport active select View–Zoom–Window from the menu bar and:
  prompt   Specify first corner and enter: **5000,1500 <R>**
  prompt   Specify opposite corner and enter: **13000,8000 <R>**.

2 With the top right viewport active, zoom a window from 1000,1000 to 9000,8000

3 With the pentagonal viewport active, menu bar with **View–Zoom–Scale** and:
  prompt   Enter a scale factor
  enter   **0.015 <R>**.

4 Make layer TEXT current and the lower left viewport active and select from menu bar **Draw–Text–Single Line Text** and:
  prompt   Specify start point of text and enter: **2500,2750 <R>**
  prompt   Specify height and enter: **450 <R>**
  prompt   Specify rotation angle and enter: **0 <R>**
  prompt   Enter text and enter: **AutoCAD R2000 <R>**.

5 The entered item of text will be displayed in all viewports.

6 Make layer OUT current with the lower right viewport active.

7 Draw two lines:
   a) first point: 7250,5250   next point: 8750,5250
   b) first point: 7250,6000   next point: 8750,6000.

8 Use the TRIM command to trim these lines to give an opening into the factory – displayed in all viewports. You may have to zoom in on the wall area to complete the trim, but remember to zoom previous.

Using the paper space environment

1 Enter paper space with a left-click on MODEL in the status bar and try and erase any object from a viewport – you cannot as they were created in model space.

2 Make layer TEXT current and add the following text items to the layout:

	Start	Ht	Rot	Text item
a)	10,4	4	0	Viewport 1: Complete factory layout
b)	230,60	4	0	Viewport 2: First enlarged view
c)	285,180	4	0	Viewport 3: Second enlarged view
d)	110,160	4	0	Viewport 4: Complete layout
e)	10,240	5	0	FOUR VIEWPORT FACTORY LAYOUT.

4 Now enter model space with a left-click on PAPER in the status bar and try to erase any of the added text items – you cannot as they were created in paper space.

Completing the layout

1 Enter paper pace and make layer SHEET current.

2 With the LINE command draw:

   first point: 0,   next point: @405,0   next point: @0,257
   next point: @–405,0   next point: close.

3 Menu bar with **Insert–Block** and:
   a) select Browse
   b) pick your A: drive or named folder
   c) scroll and pick TITLE then Open
   d) insertion point: X 405; Y 0; Z 0
   e) scale: uniform at 0.9
   f) activate Explode then pick OK.

4 The factory layout – created in paper space is now complete.

Task

1 If you have access to a printer/plotter:
   a) plot from model space with any viewport active
   b) plot from paper space.

2 In model space, investigate the coordinates of the top right corner of the left viewport
   – about 22000,15000?

3 In paper space investigate the coordinates of:
   a) top right corner of our sheet: 405,257?
   b) top right corner of white area: 410,275?

4 *Question:* how can a drawing area on 22000,15000 be displayed on an A3 sheet of paper?
   This is the 'power' of model/paper space.

   This completes the brief introduction to model/paper space.

Chapter 46

Toolbar customization

The toolbars supplied with R2000 are more than adequate for the user's draughting requirements. It is possible however, to create a new toolbar and customise it with your own icons.

We will demonstrate how a new toolbar can be customized to include six icons from four existing toolbars.

1   Open your A:A3PAPER standard sheet.

2   Menu bar with **View–Toolbars** and:
    prompt   Toolbars dialogue box
    respond **pick New**
    prompt   New Toolbar dialogue box
    with   Menu Group: ACAD
    respond 1) Toolbar Name: enter **MYOWN**
               2) dialogue box as Fig. 46.1
               3) pick OK
    prompt   Toolbars dialogue box
    with   MYOWN added to the list
    respond 1) ensure MYOWN is active, i.e. X in box
               2) pick Close – for now.

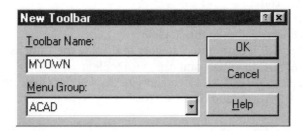

Figure 46.1   New Toolbar dialogue box.

(a)New toolbar created

(b)LINE and CIRCLE icons
added

(c)Other icons added

Figure 46.2 Toolbar customization exercise.

3 The new toolbar will be displayed on the screen – probably at the top. This toolbar is quite small – Fig. 46.2(a), and does not yet contain any icons.

4 Move the new toolbar to the left-side of the drawing screen by
  a) left click in the blue title bar
  b) hold down the left button
  c) move to required position and release left button.

5 Menu bar with **View–Toolbars** and:
prompt	Toolbar dialogue box
respond	**pick Customize**
prompt	Customize Toolbars dialogue box
respond	1) pick scroll arrow at Categories
	2) scroll and pick Draw
prompt	Draw icons
respond	1) left-click on the LINE icon and hold down the button
	2) drag the LINE icon 'into' the new toolbar
	3) left-click on the CIRCLE icon and hold down the button
	4) drag the CIRCLE icon onto the new toolbar
	5) the new toolbar extends
	6) pick Close
prompt	Toolbars dialogue box
respond	pick Close – for now.

6 The toolbar MYOWN is displayed with the LINE and CIRCLE icons as fig. (b).

7 Select **View–Toolbars** again and:
prompt	Toolbars dialogue box
respond	pick Customize
prompt	Customize Toolbar dialogue box
respond	scroll and pick Modify Category
prompt	Modify icons
respond	1) pick ERASE icon
	2) hold down left button and drag icon into toolbar
	3) pick MOVE icon and drag into toolbar
	4) scroll and pick Dimensioning Category to display the Dimensioning icons
	5) pick LINEAR DIMENSION and drag into toolbar
	6) scroll and pick OBJECT SNAP category to display the Object Snap icons
	7) pick ENDPOINT icon and drag into toolbar
	8) pick Close
prompt	Toolbars dialogue box
respond	pick Close.

8 The new toolbar will display the six icons as fig. (c).

9 It is as easy (or as hard) as that! You can now add other icons to your toolbar or create new toolbars as required.

Note

1 The new toolbar will always be displayed unless it has been cancelled with the close icon in the top-left corner.

2 The new toolbar MYOWN is permanently included in the list of named icons in the toolbar dialogue box and can be activated from this dialogue box.

3 If required the new toolbar can be deleted from the list.

4 I have not investigated 'fly-out' icons in this brief introduction.

Chapter 47

Templates

This topic has been left to the end, when it should probably have been included nearer the beginning. There were two reasons for this, these being to allow the user to:
a) become proficient at draughting with AutoCAD
b) understand the concepts of paper space and attributes.

What is a template?

A template is a prototype drawing, i.e. it is equivalent to our A:A3PAPER standard sheet which has been used when every new exercise/activity has been started. The terms prototype/standard drawing are used whenever a drawing requires to be used with various default settings, e.g. layers, text styles, dimension styles, etc.

With AutoCAD, all drawings are saved with the file extension .dwg while template files have the extension .dwt. Any drawing can be saved as a template.

Template drawings (files) are used to 'safeguard' the prototype drawing being mistakenly overwritten – have you ever saved work on your A:A3PAPER standard sheet by mistake? Templates overcome this problem.

AutoCAD has several templates which conform to the following drawing standards:
a) ansi: a0 to a4
b) din: a0 to a4
c) iso: a0 to a4
d) jis: a0 to a4.

Other templates are also available.

Using an AutoCAD template file

1 Open your A:A3PAPER standard sheet.

2 Menu bar with **File–New** and:
   prompt   Create New Drawing dialogue box
   respond **pick Use a Template**
   prompt   Use a Template dialogue box
   respond 1) scroll at Select a Template
            2) pick **Iso a3-named plot styles.dwt**
            3) pick OK.

3 The screen will display:
   a) a layout with a title box
   b) the paper space icon
   c) a new tab – ISO A3 TITLE BLOCK.

4 *Investigate.*
   a) Format–Layers and note the Frame names
   b) Dimension–Style and note the style names and the current style.

5 Enter model space and select from the menu bar **Insert–Block** and:

prompt Insert dialogue box
respond **pick Browse**
prompt Select Drawing File dialogue box
respond 1) scroll and pick the A: drive or your named folder
2) scroll and pick a saved activity, e.g. act19
3) pick Open
prompt Insert dialogue box
with Name: act19
respond 1) activate Explode
2) activate the On-screen prompts
3) pick OK
prompt Specify insertion point for block and enter: **10,40**
prompt Specify scale factor for XYZ axes and enter: **1 <R>**
prompt Specify rotation angle and enter: **0 <R>**.

6 The selected drawing file (a wblock) will be inserted into the ISO A3 template file/drawing.

7 *a*) Erase unwanted objects (e.g. the border) which have been inserted
b) move the drawing to a suitable area of the screen
c) optimize your drawing layout.

8 Enter paper space.

9 From the menu bar select **Modify–Attribute–Single** and:

prompt Select block reference
respond **pick any item of the 'title block'**
prompt Edit Attributes dialogue box
with information that can be altered by the user
respond alter the following:
1) File name: R2000/1/2
2) Drawing number: 456
3) Owner: FARCAD
4) Checked by: RMF
5) Designed by: HTC
6) Approved by – Date: PQR: 22/11/99
7) Date: 11/11/99 – Fig. 47.1
then pick Next
prompt Edit Attributes dialogue box
with further information for the user to alter
respond alter as follows:
1) Scale: 1:1
2) Edition: 1
3) Sheet: 1/1
4) pick OK.

10 In paper space zoom in on the title box to 'see' the edited attribute information, then zoom previous.

11 The screen layout will be similar to Fig. 47.2 and can be saved as a drawing file (.dwg) with the name A:MYTEST or similar.

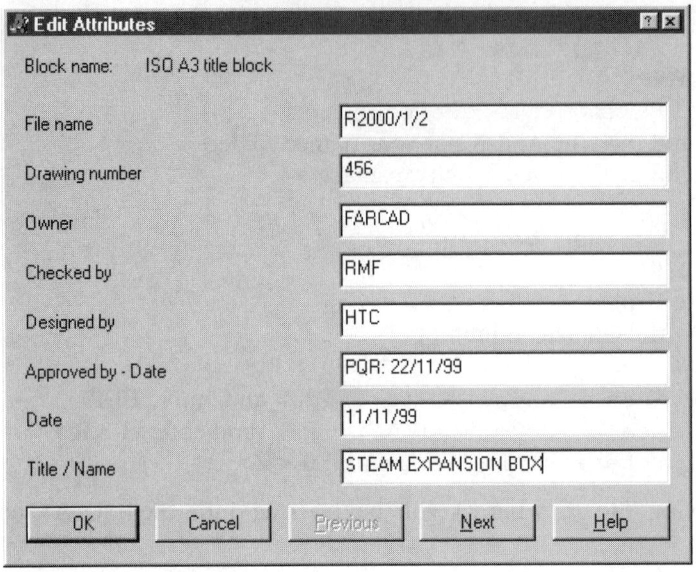

Figure 47.1 Edit Attributes dialogue box.

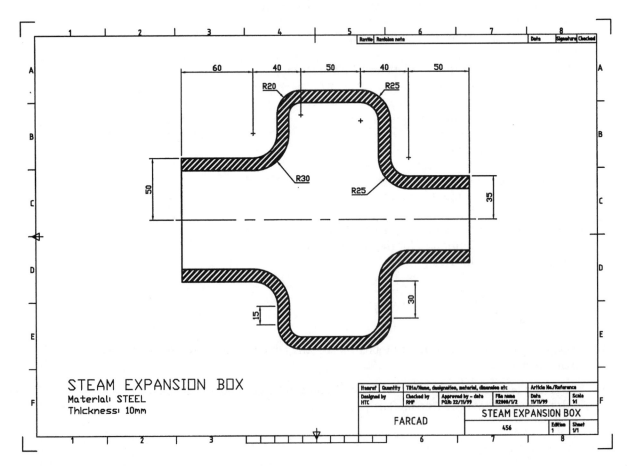

Figure 47.2 Using AutoCAD's ISO A3 template.

Creating our own A3 template file

1 Open your A3PAPER standard sheet and erase the black border.

2 Make a new layer named VP, continuous linetype and colour to suit. Make this new layer current.

3 Menu bar with **Tools–Wizards–Create Layout** and:
prompt   Create Layout - Begin dialogue box
respond   alter the various dialogue boxes as follows:
　　　　　　 1) Begin Layout name: MY A3 LAYOUT
　　　　　　 2) Printer: None
　　　　　　 3) Paper size: Millimeters ISO A3 (420 × 297)
　　　　　　 4) Orientation: Landscape
　　　　　　 5) Title Block: none for now
　　　　　　 6) Define viewports: none for now
　　　　　　 7) Finish: pick Finish.

4 Still with layer VP current, select **View–Viewports–Polygonal Viewport** from the menu bar and:
prompt   From point and enter: 10,10 <R>
prompt   Next point
respond   enter the following coordinates:
　　　　　　 275,10   275,70   395,70
　　　　　　 395,250   10,250   close.

5 Menu bar with **Insert–Block** and:
a) pick Browse
b) scroll and pick BORDER from your A drive/folder then Open
c) activate the three on-screen prompts then OK
d) insertion point: 0,0
e) X scale: 0.976; Y scale: 0.895; rotation: 0.

6 Menu bar with Insert-Block and select TITLE from your A drive or folder and insert with:
a) insertion point: 400,5
b) X scale: 1; Y scale: 1; rotation: 0.

7 Menu bar with **File–Save** and:
prompt   Save Drawing As dialogue box
respond   1) scroll at Save as type
　　　　　　 2) pick **Drawing Template File (*.dwt)**
prompt   Save Drawing As dialogue box
with   R2000 Template file opened
respond   1) decide whether you want your template file in the R2000 folder, your A: drive or your named folder
　　　　　　 2) scroll and pick destination
　　　　　　 3) File name: enter **A3LAYOUT**
　　　　　　 4) pick Save
prompt   Template Description dialogue box
enter   This is my modified A3PAPER standard sheet layout created in paper space. My wblocks BORDER and TITLE have been inserted. The layout sheet has layers, text style, units and dimension styles customized to my own requirements
and   dialogue box as Fig. 47.3
respond   pick OK.

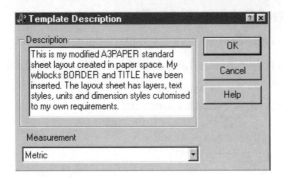

Figure 47.3 Template Description dialogue box.

4 Your A3PAPER standard sheet will be saved as a template file and:
   a) added to the list of existing templates
   b) be able to be 'opened' as a template
   c) will not be 'over-written' when a drawing is saved.

Exercise

1 Menu bar with **File–New** and:
   prompt   Create New Drawing dialogue box
   respond **pick Use a Template**
   prompt   Use a Template dialogue box
   respond 1) scroll and pick the source of your template files
              2) pick **A3LAYOUT**
              3) pick Open.

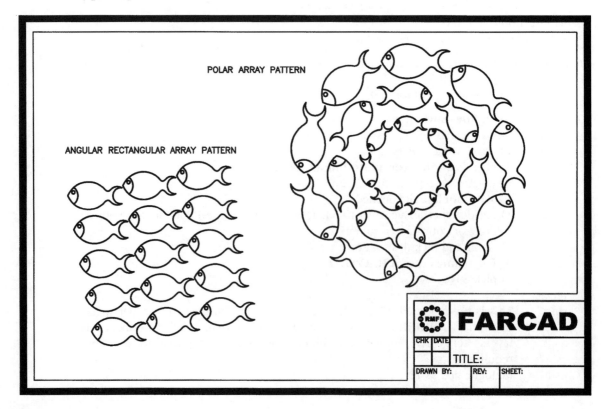

Figure 47.4 Using your A3LAYOUT template file.

2 The screen will display your A3 layout template file

3 *a*) Insert any drawing (e.g. ACT25) full size with 0 rotation
 b) modify and reposition the inserted drawing
 c) layout similar to Fig. 47.4.

4 Save the layout as A:WHATEVER.dwg.

5 File–New and re-select your template file which should be displayed 'as new'.

Summary

1 A template file is a prototype drawing with various defaults set to user requirements.

2 AutoCAD has several drawing standard prototypes.

3 Template files can be created by the user.

4 Template files 'safeguard' the prototype drawing being 'overwritten'.

Chapter 48

The AutoCAD Design Centre

The AutoCAD Design Centre is new to R2000. It is basically a drawing management system with several powerful advantages to the user including:

- the ability to browse different drawing sources
- viewing object definitions prior to opening
- shortcuts to commonly used drawings and folders
- searching for specific drawing content
- opening drawings by drag mode
- viewing and attaching raster image files into the drawing area
- palette control.

In this chapter we will investigate several of these topics.

Accessing the Design Centre

1 Open your A3PAPER standard sheet and cancel any floating toolbars.

2 Menu bar with **Tools–AutoCAD Design Centre** and:
   prompt   DesignCenter dialogue box.

3 The first time that the design center is activated, it is usually docked at the left of the drawing screen area. Move and resize by:
   a) left-click in the design center title bar and hold down the button
   b) drag into the drawing area
   c) resize to suit.

4 The Design Center dialogue box consists of two distinct areas:
   a) the tree view and hierarchy area on the left
   b) the palette with icons on the right.

5 Figure 48.1 displays the basic Design Center dialogue box.

Using the tree view and hierarchy

The tree view side of the design center dialogue box consists of a list of names with a (+) or a (−) beside them. If a name in the tree view side is selected (left-click) then the palette side of the dialogue box will reveal the contents of the selected item. If the (+) beside an item is selected then that item is 'expanded' and the tree view side of the dialogue box will reveal the 'contents' of the selected item. The selected item's (+) will be replaced with a (−) indicated that it has been expanded. If the (−) is then selected, the expanded effect is removed and the (+) is returned. The selection of the (−) is termed 'collapsing'.

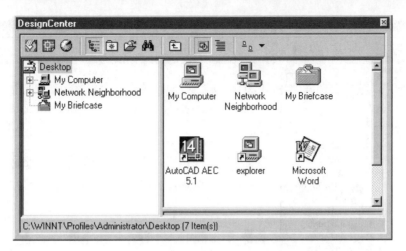

(a) Tree view with   (b) Palette with icons
    hierarchies.

Figure 48.1   The Design Center dialogue box.

Refer to Fig. 48.2 and:

1   Note the Design Center layout as opened – fig. (a). Your display may differ from mine, but this is not important.

2   Expand My Computer (if available) by picking the (+) to give a tree expansion similar to fig. (b).

3   Expand the C: drive by selecting the (+) to give fig. (c).

4   Expand your named folder from the C: drive (or expand your A: drive) and then right-click the named folder and:

  prompt   Shortcut pop-up menu
  respond   **pick Explore**
  and   palette side of the Design Center dialogue box will display icons of the contents
              of the named folder.

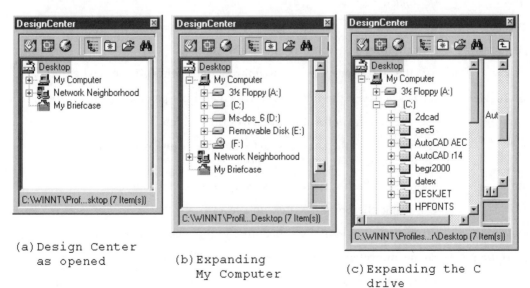

(a) Design Center   (b) Expanding   (c) Expanding the C
    as opened   My Computer   drive

Figure 48.2   Tree expansions.

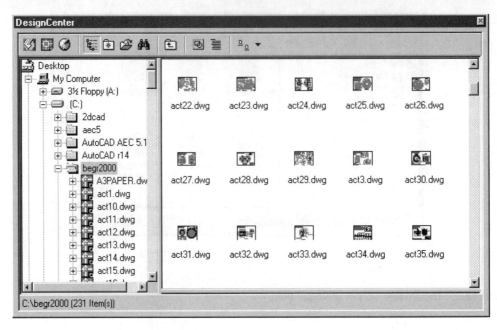

Figure 48.3 Expansion of a named folder.

5 Figure 48.3 displays part of my named folder selection.

6 *a*) Collapse your named folder by picking the (–) at its name
   b) collapse the C: drive
   c) collapse My Computer and the Design Center should be displayed 'as opened'.

The Design Center menu bar

The menu bar of the Design Center allows the user access to the following icons. These are (from left to right):

	Icon	Description
1	Desktop	list local/network drives
2	Open Drawing	lists all drawings currently opened in AutoCAD
3	History	lists the last 20 locations accessed through the AutoCAD Design Center
4	Tree Toggle	toggles between the tree/palette screen and the palette screen
5	Favourites	lists the contents of AutoCAD's favourites folder
6	Load	allows access to the Load Design Center palette and will display details about a selected item in the palette area
7	Find	allows searches for named files using user entered names
8	Up	will toggle the Design Center 'up a level'
9	Preview	displays a preview of a selected item in the palette area
10	Description	details information about a selected item if applicable
11	Views	allows the user to access large/small icons as well as lists and details.

Design Center exercise 1

1 Ensure AutoCAD has been started and the Design Center activated.

2 Position the Design Center dialogue box in centre of screen.

3 Expand the following:
a) My Computer
b) the C: drive
c) your named folder – begr2000 is my named folder.

4 Right-click on the folder name and pick Explore.

5 The palette area will display information about the selected folder. This may not be in the 'form' we want.

6 From the Design Center menu bar:
a) scroll at Views
b) pick Large icons.

7 The palette area will display icons for the selected folder.

8 From the Design Center menu bar select Preview and Description and the palette area will display two additional areas.

9 Scroll at right of palette and pick any drawing icon, e.g. act19.dwg and a preview and description (if applicable) will be displayed as Fig. 48.4.

10 Scroll and pick another item. If possible try and pick another type of file format. Fig. 48.5 displays a BMP file of Fig. 40.4 which was the Block Definition dialogue box. This display is a screen dump pasted and saved in the Paint application package.

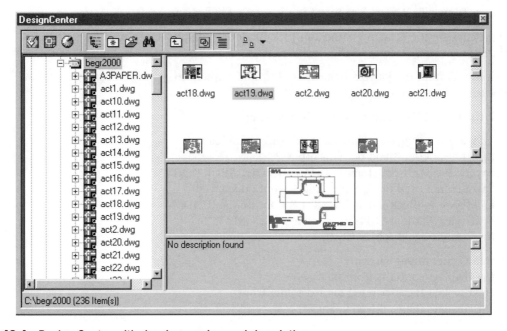

Figure 48.4 Design Center with drawing preview and description.

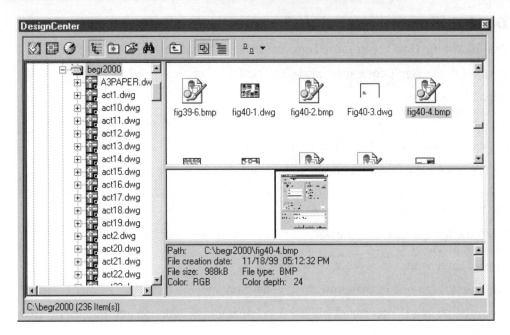

Figure 48.5 Design Center with BMP preview and description.

Design Center exercise 2

1 Still with the Design Center displayed?

2 Scroll in the tree area until the saved drawing from Chapter 41 is displayed. This is Fig. 41.3.

3 Expand this named drawing (in my case Fig. 41.3) by picking the (+) at its name. The expansion will display the following names:

Blocks, Dimstyles, Layers, Layouts, Linetypes, Text styles and Xrefs

4 Right-click on the drawing name and pick Explore to display icons in the palette area of the seven named items in the tree.

5 Pick Blocks from the palette area, right-click and Explore to display information about blocks in the named drawing.

6 Pick the block TITLE and note the display – Fig. 48.6.

7 Investigate selecting the following from the expanded tree:
   a) Dimstyles: A3DIM and perhaps others?
   b) Layers: 0 CL CONS Defpoints DIMS HID OUT SECT TEXT
   c) Layouts: not used but Layout1 and Layout2 displayed
   d) Linetypes: ByBlock ByLayer CENTER Continuous HIDDEN
   e) Textstyles: Standard ST1 and perhaps ST2 – ST4?
   f) Xrefs: none listed (obviously?).

8 Design Center menu bar with:
   a) Up: displays contents from Blocks
   b) Up: displays the expanded named folder icons
   c) Up: displays the C: drive expansion.

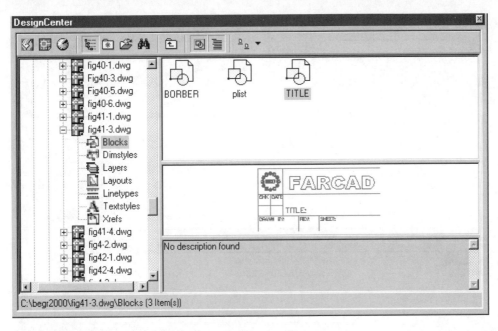

Figure 48.6 Design Center with block preview.

Design Center exercise 3

1 Still have the Design Center displayed from example 2?

2 Design Center menu bar and pick the **Find** icon and:

prompt	`Find dialogue box`
respond	1) scroll at **Look for** and pick Xrefs
	2) pick Browse
prompt	`Browse for Folders dialogue box`
respond	1) scroll and pick your named folder, e.g. C:\begr2000
	2) pick OK
prompt	`Find dialogue box`
with	named folder display at **In**
respond	1) scroll at Search for the name and pick *
	2) pick Find Now
and	the search will begin.

3 When the search is complete, all drawings with xrefs will be listed as Fig. 48.7 (overleaf). In my case (and yours?) two drawings used external references.

4 Now cancel the Find dialogue box and cancel the Design Center.

This chapter has introduced the user to the AutoCAD R2000 Design Center. Hopefully having tried the three exercises, you will be able to navigate your way through it. It is fairly easy, but takes some patience and practice.

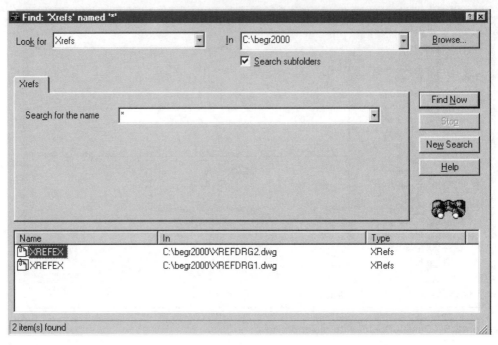

Figure 48.7   Design Center find option.

Activities

ACTIVITY 1
Draw the simple shapes using the LINE and CIRCLE commands.
Set the grid and snap spacing to suit.

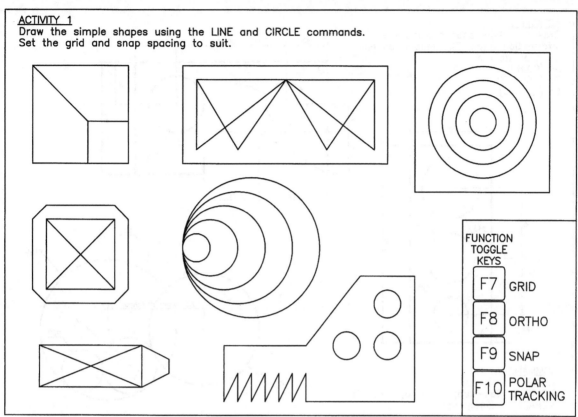

FUNCTION
TOGGLE
KEYS

F7	GRID
F8	ORTHO
F9	SNAP
F10	POLAR TRACKING

ACTIVITY 2
Draw the three templates using the sizes
given. Suggested start points are:
A(80,110), B(260,200) and C(380,40).

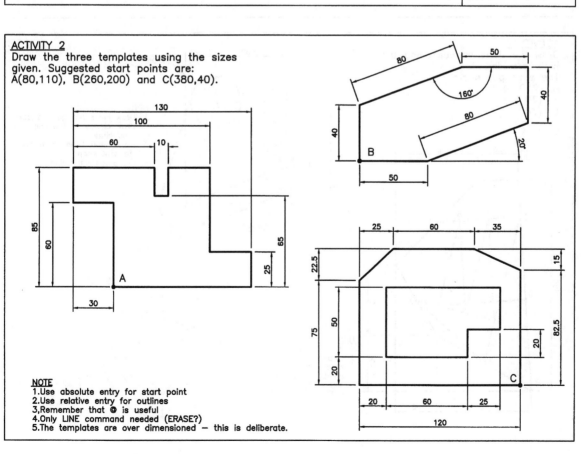

NOTE
1. Use absolute entry for start point
2. Use relative entry for outlines
3. Remember that @ is useful
4. Only LINE command needed (ERASE?)
5. The templates are over dimensioned – this is deliberate.

ACTIVITY 3
Draw the three shapes using the information given. The recommended start points are:
A: (60,60)
B: (180,260)
C: (270,70)

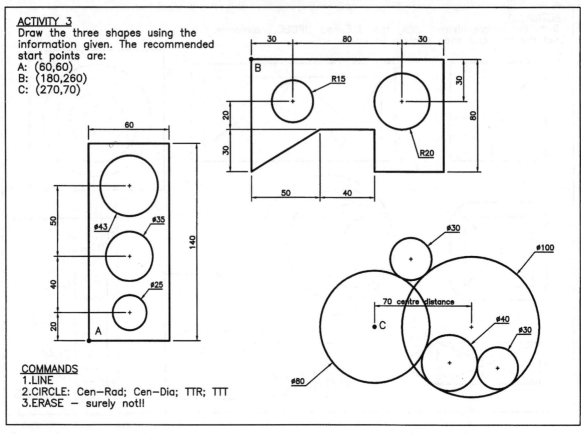

COMMANDS
1. LINE
2. CIRCLE: Cen–Rad; Cen–Dia; TTR; TTT
3. ERASE – surely not!!

ACTIVITY 4
Draw the three shapes using the hints provided.
The start points are:
A: (210,195)
B: (30,35)
C: (300,60)

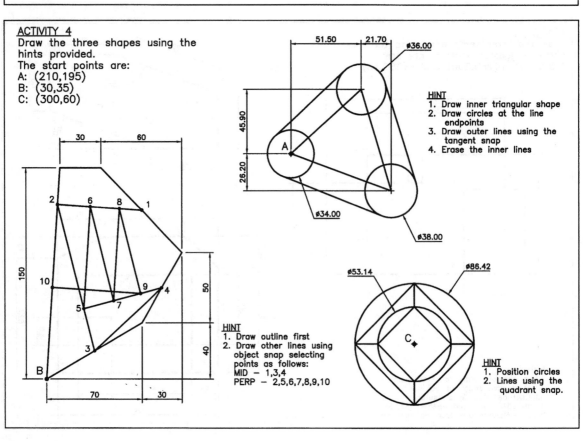

HINT
1. Draw inner triangular shape
2. Draw circles at the line endpoints
3. Draw outer lines using the tangent snap
4. Erase the inner lines

HINT
1. Draw outline first
2. Draw other lines using object snap selecting points as follows:
MID – 1,3,4
PERP – 2,5,6,7,8,9,10

HINT
1. Position circles
2. Lines using the quadrant snap.

ACTIVITY 5
Draw full size the two templates.
Suggested start points are:
A: (80,160)
B: (370,90)

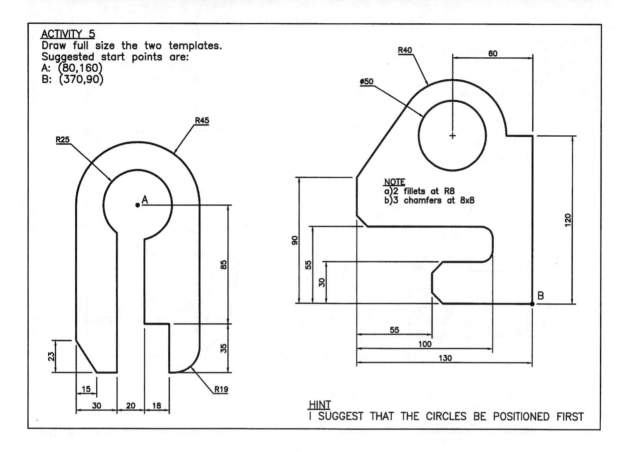

NOTE
a) 2 fillets at R8
b) 3 chamfers at 8x8

HINT
I SUGGEST THAT THE CIRCLES BE POSITIONED FIRST

ACTIVITY 6
Draw the four shapes to the sizes given.
Make use of OFFSET and TRIM where possible.
Add all text, but DO NOT dimension
Discretion for start points and dimensions not given.

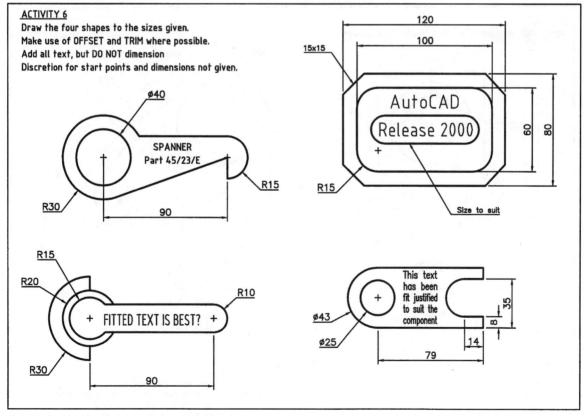

SPANNER
Part 45/23/E

AutoCAD
Release 2000

Size to suit

FITTED TEXT IS BEST?

This text
has been
fit justified
to suit the
component

ACTIVITY 7
1. Draw the two components full size
2. Add all text
3. Add all dimensions
4. Use layers correctly
5. Suggested start points are A: (50,70)
   and B: (380,220)

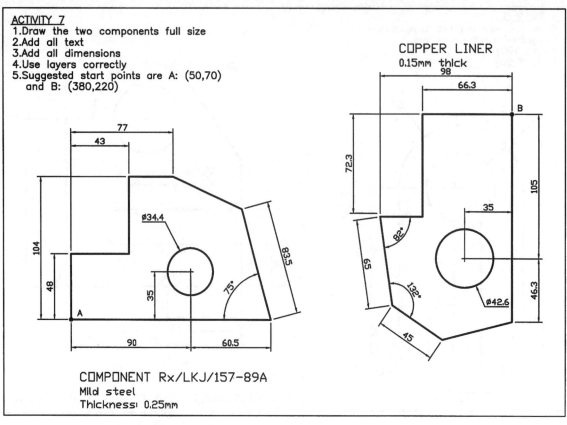

COMPONENT Rx/LKJ/157-89A
Mild steel
Thickness: 0.25mm

COPPER LINER
0.15mm thick

ACTIVITY 8
Draw, dimension and add text. Use layers.

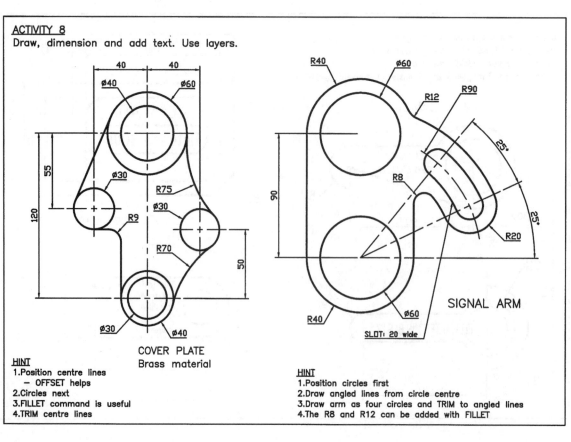

COVER PLATE
Brass material

SIGNAL ARM

HINT
1. Position centre lines
   – OFFSET helps
2. Circles next
3. FILLET command is useful
4. TRIM centre lines

HINT
1. Position circles first
2. Draw angled lines from circle centre
3. Draw arm as four circles and TRIM to angled lines
4. The R8 and R12 can be added with FILLET

ACTIVITY 9
Draw, fully dimension and add text
Easier than you think!!!

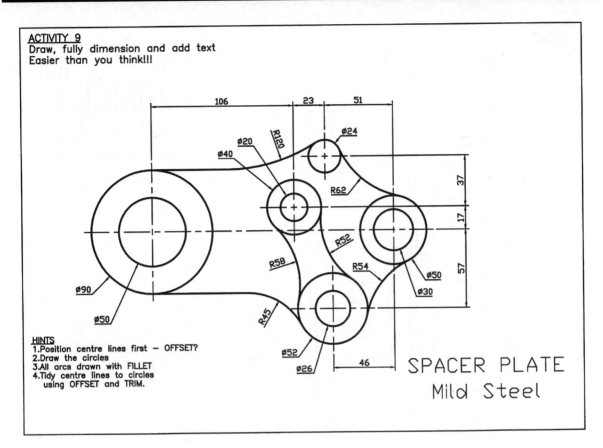

HINTS
1.Position centre lines first — OFFSET?
2.Draw the circles
3.All arcs drawn with FILLET
4.Tidy centre lines to circles
  using OFFSET and TRIM.

SPACER PLATE
Mild Steel

ACTIVITY 10
Draw the three components to the
sizes given and add all text and
dimensions.
Use your discretion for sizes which
are not specified.

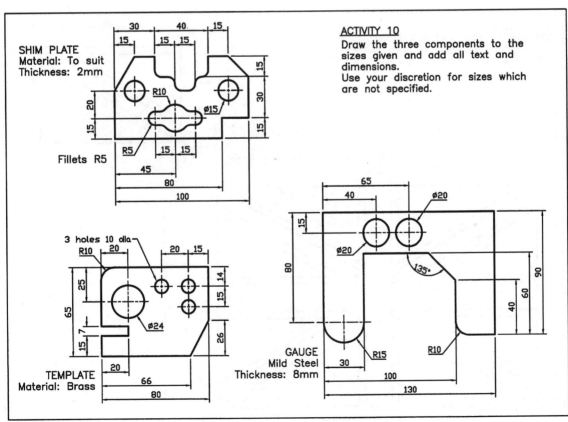

SHIM PLATE
Material: To suit
Thickness: 2mm

Fillets R5

TEMPLATE
Material: Brass

GAUGE
Mild Steel
Thickness: 8mm

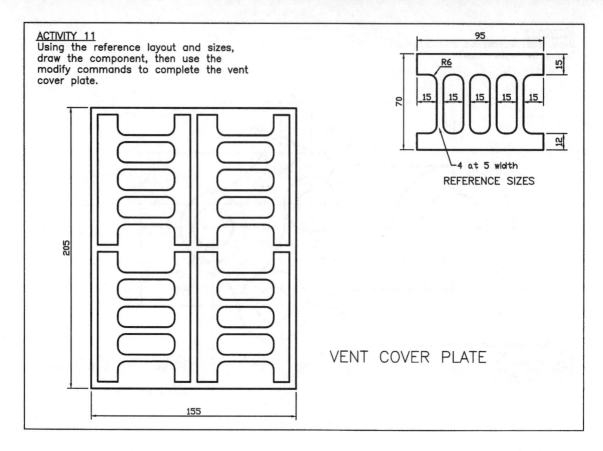

ACTIVITY 11
Using the reference layout and sizes,
draw the component, then use the
modify commands to complete the vent
cover plate.

REFERENCE SIZES

VENT COVER PLATE

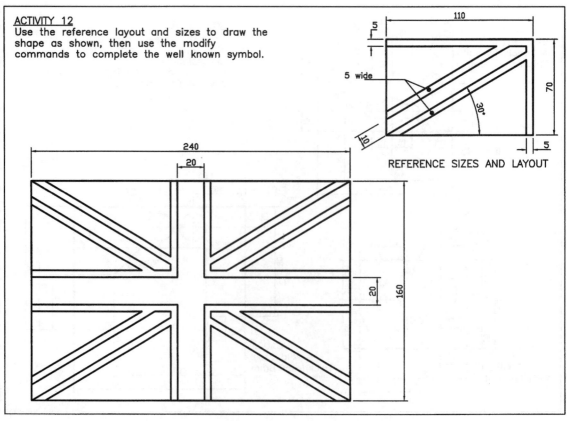

ACTIVITY 12
Use the reference layout and sizes to draw the
shape as shown, then use the modify
commands to complete the well known symbol.

REFERENCE SIZES AND LAYOUT

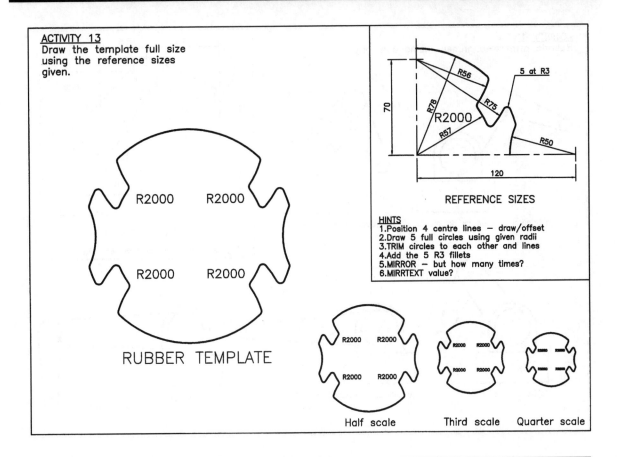

ACTIVITY 13
Draw the template full size using the reference sizes given.

REFERENCE SIZES

HINTS
1. Position 4 centre lines — draw/offset
2. Draw 5 full circles using given radii
3. TRIM circles to each other and lines
4. Add the 5 R3 fillets
5. MIRROR — but how many times?
6. MIRRTEXT value?

RUBBER TEMPLATE

Half scale   Third scale   Quarter scale

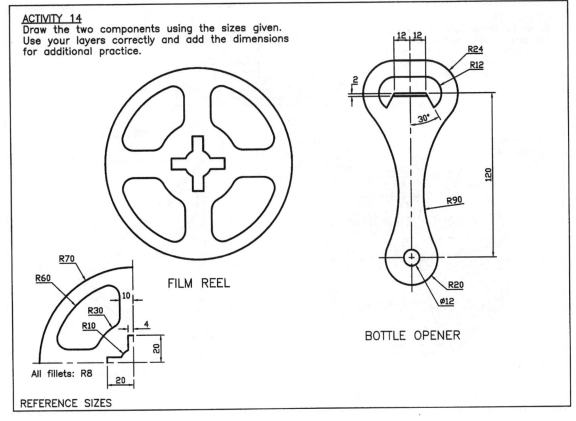

ACTIVITY 14
Draw the two components using the sizes given.
Use your layers correctly and add the dimensions for additional practice.

FILM REEL

BOTTLE OPENER

All fillets: R8

REFERENCE SIZES

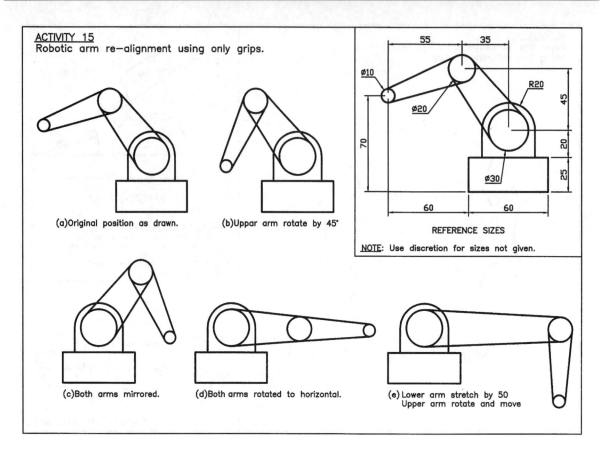

ACTIVITY 15
Robotic arm re-alignment using only grips.

(a)Original position as drawn.

(b)Uppar arm rotate by 45°

REFERENCE SIZES

NOTE: Use discretion for sizes not given.

(c)Both arms mirrored.

(d)Both arms rotated to horizontal.

(e) Lower arm stretch by 50
Upper arm rotate and move

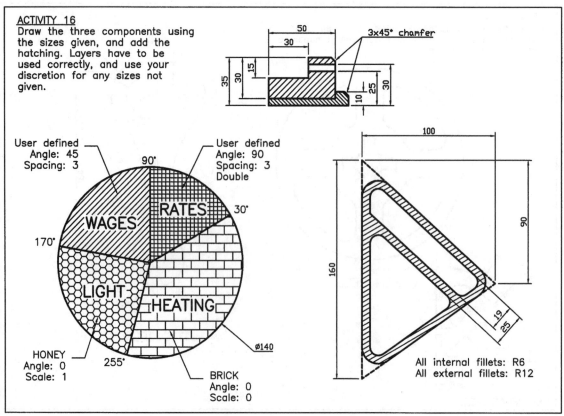

ACTIVITY 16
Draw the three components using the sizes given, and add the hatching. Layers have to be used correctly, and use your discretion for any sizes not given.

3x45° chamfer

User defined
Angle: 45
Spacing: 3

User defined
Angle: 90
Spacing: 3
Double

WAGES

RATES

LIGHT

HEATING

HONEY
Angle: 0
Scale: 1

BRICK
Angle: 0
Scale: 0

Ø140

All internal fillets: R6
All external fillets: R12

ACTIVITY 17
Draw the three views of the component
and add hatching, text and dimensions.
Use layers correctly.

COVER PLATE
Materiali Mild Steel

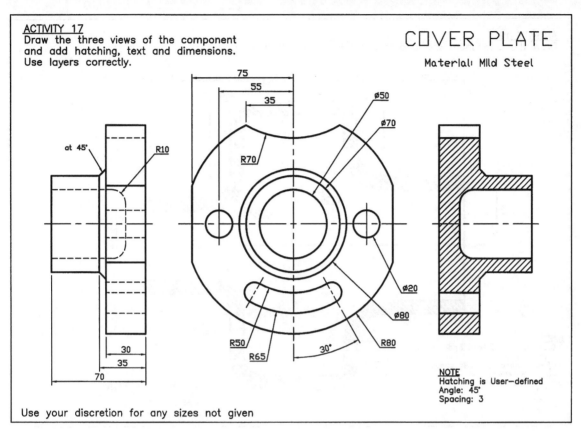

NOTE
Hatching is User—defined
Angle: 45°
Spacing: 3

Use your discretion for any sizes not given

ACTIVITY 18
Draw the four views and add the hatching, text and diimensions.

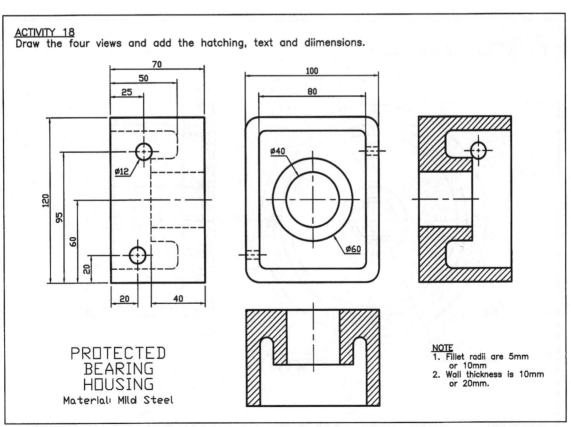

PROTECTED
BEARING
HOUSING
Materiali Mild Steel

NOTE
1. Fillet radii are 5mm
   or 10mm
2. Wall thickness is 10mm
   or 20mm.

ACTIVITY 19
Draw the component and add text, hatching and dimensions.

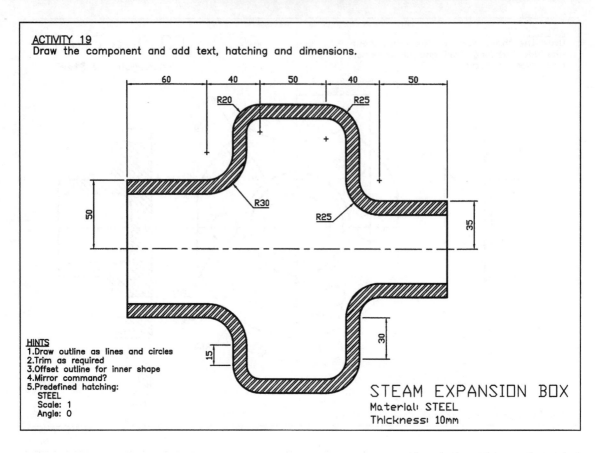

| 60 | 40 | 50 | 40 | 50 |

R20   R25

R30

R25

50

35

HINTS
1. Draw outline as lines and circles
2. Trim as required
3. Offset outline for inner shape
4. Mirror command?
5. Predefined hatching:
   STEEL
   Scale: 1
   Angle: 0

15   30

STEAM EXPANSION BOX

Materiali STEEL
Thickness: 10mm

ACTIVITY 20
Draw full size, adding the hatching.

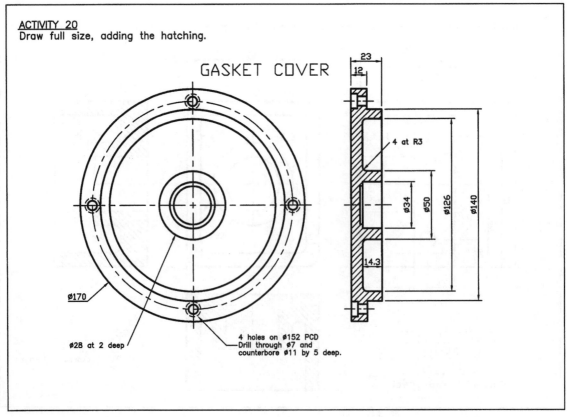

GASKET COVER

23
12

4 at R3

ø34   ø50   ø126   ø140

14.3

ø170

ø28 at 2 deep

4 holes on ø152 PCD
Drill through ø7 and
counterbore ø11 by 5 deep.

ACTIVITY 21
Draw the games board using the information given.

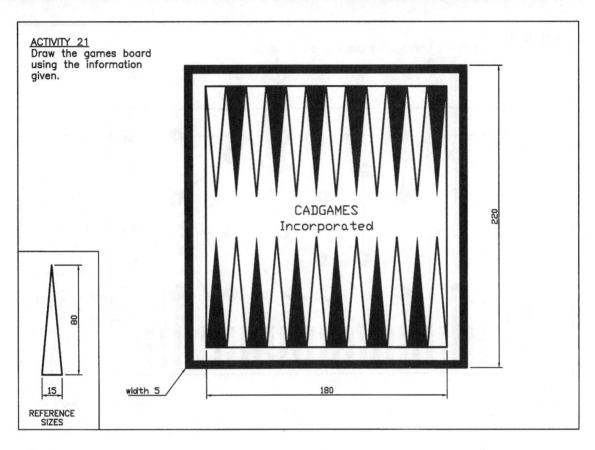

CADGAMES
Incorporated

REFERENCE SIZES

80

15

width 5

180

220

ACTIVITY 22
Draw the polyline shapes using the sizes given.

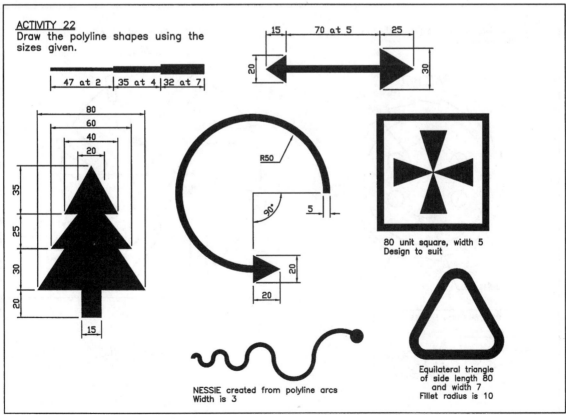

47 at 2 | 35 at 4 | 32 at 7

15   70 at 5   25

20   30

80
60
40
20

35
25
30
20

15

R50

90°

5

20

20

80 unit square, width 5
Design to suit

Equilateral triangle
of side length 80
and width 7
Fillet radius is 10

NESSIE created from polyline arcs
Width is 3

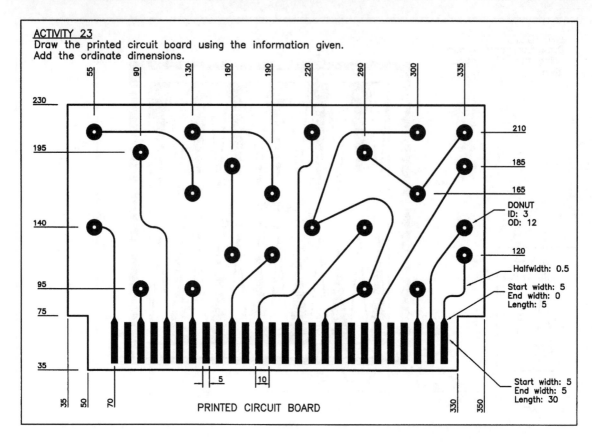

ACTIVITY 23
Draw the printed circuit board using the information given.
Add the ordinate dimensions.

DONUT
ID: 3
OD: 12

Halfwidth: 0.5

Start width: 5
End width: 0
Length: 5

Start width: 5
End width: 5
Length: 30

PRINTED CIRCUIT BOARD

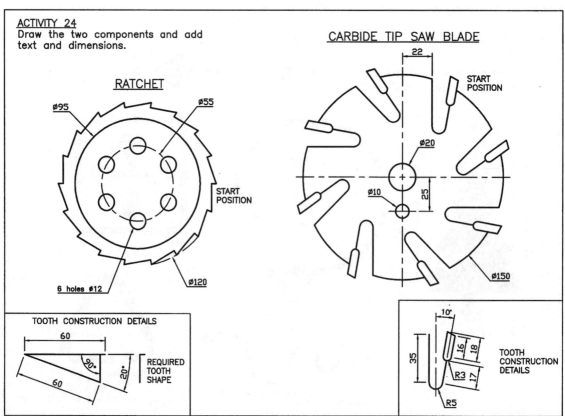

ACTIVITY 24
Draw the two components and add
text and dimensions.

CARBIDE TIP SAW BLADE

RATCHET

Ø95   Ø55

START
POSITION

6 holes Ø12   Ø120

Ø20

Ø10   25

Ø150

START
POSITION

TOOTH CONSTRUCTION DETAILS

60   90°   20°
60
REQUIRED
TOOTH
SHAPE

TOOTH
CONSTRUCTION
DETAILS

10°
16 18
35
R3 17
R5

ACTIVITY 25

Using the FISH drawing, create the rectangular and polar array patterns with following information:

a) A 5x3 angular rectangular array at 10°
  from 0.2 scale

b) polar arrays with:
  i) scale: 0.25; radius: 90; items: 9
  ii) scale: 0.2; radius: 60; items: 7
  iii) scale: 0.15; radius: 35; items: 7

ANGULAR RECTANGULAR ARRAY PATTERN

POLAR ARRAY PATTERN

ACTIVITY 26

Draw the basic bulb using the dimensions given then produce the array design.

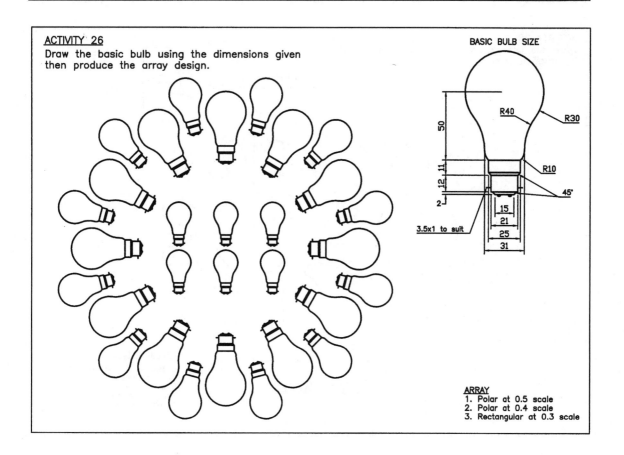

BASIC BULB SIZE

R40
R30
R10
45°
50
11
12
2
3.5x1 to suit
15
21
25
31

ARRAY
1. Polar at 0.5 scale
2. Polar at 0.4 scale
3. Rectangular at 0.3 scale

ACTIVITY 27
Draw the two components using the information given. Use your discretion for any sizes which are not given.

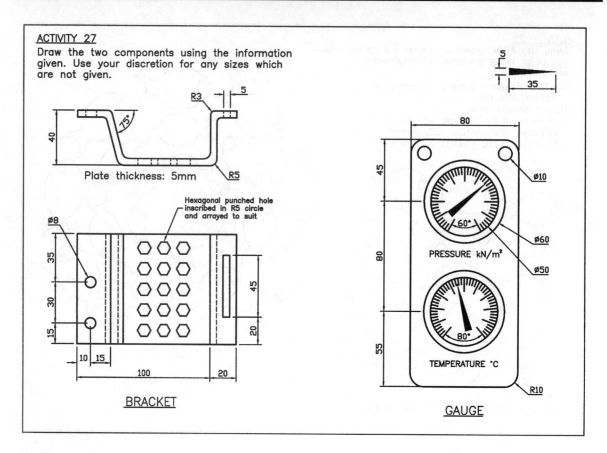

Plate thickness: 5mm

Hexagonal punched hole inscribed in R5 circle and arrayed to suit

BRACKET

GAUGE

PRESSURE kN/m²

TEMPERATURE °C

ACTIVITY 28
Draw the gear wheel arrangement using the information given.

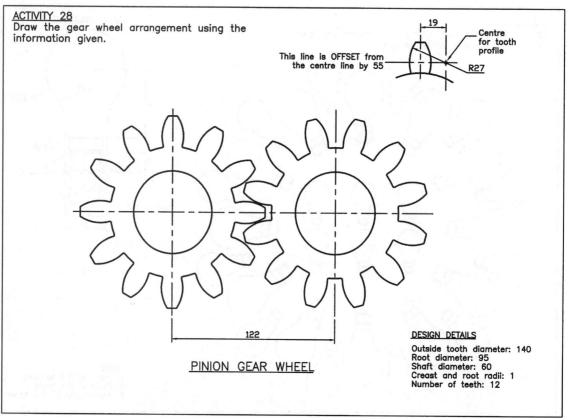

This line is OFFSET from the centre line by 55

Centre for tooth profile

PINION GEAR WHEEL

DESIGN DETAILS
Outside tooth diameter: 140
Root diameter: 95
Shaft diameter: 60
Creast and root radii: 1
Number of teeth: 12

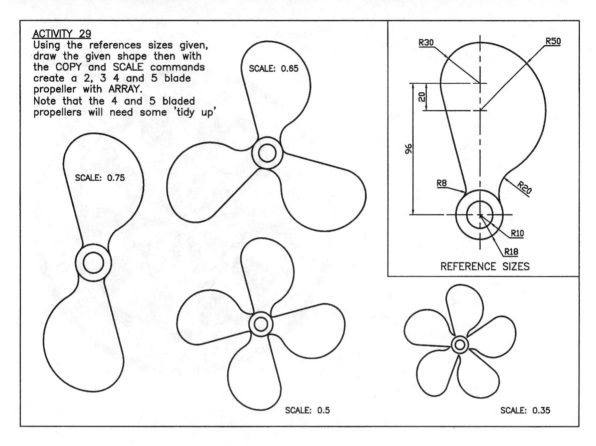

ACTIVITY 29
Using the references sizes given, draw the given shape then with the COPY and SCALE commands create a 2, 3 4 and 5 blade propeller with ARRAY.
Note that the 4 and 5 bladed propellers will need some 'tidy up'

SCALE: 0.65

SCALE: 0.75

SCALE: 0.5

SCALE: 0.35

REFERENCE SIZES

R30 R50 20 96 R8 R20 R10 R18

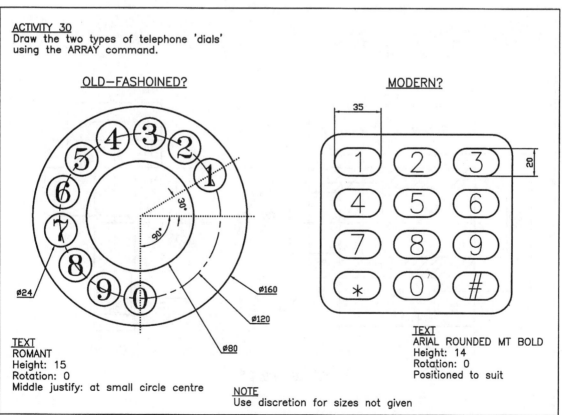

ACTIVITY 30
Draw the two types of telephone 'dials' using the ARRAY command.

OLD—FASHOINED?

MODERN?

Ø24 Ø160 Ø120 Ø80

TEXT
ROMANT
Height: 15
Rotation: 0
Middle justify: at small circle centre

35 20

TEXT
ARIAL ROUNDED MT BOLD
Height: 14
Rotation: 0
Positioned to suit

NOTE
Use discretion for sizes not given

ACTIVITY 31

Draw the flow gauge and dartboard using the information given.

Circle diameters
Ø10
Ø20
Ø80
Ø95
Ø160
Ø175
Ø215
Ø225

TEXT
Font: ROMANT
Height: 10

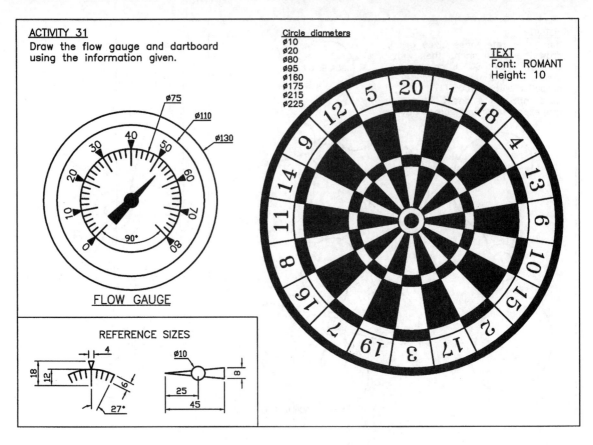

FLOW GAUGE

REFERENCE SIZES

ACTIVITY 32

Draw the given components and add all dimensions, creating appropriate dimension styles for the tolerance dimensions.

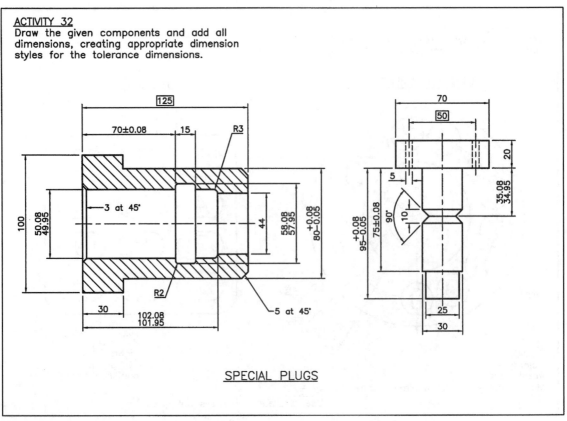

SPECIAL PLUGS

ACTIVITY 33
Draw the component shown and add the dimensions and geometric tolerance.

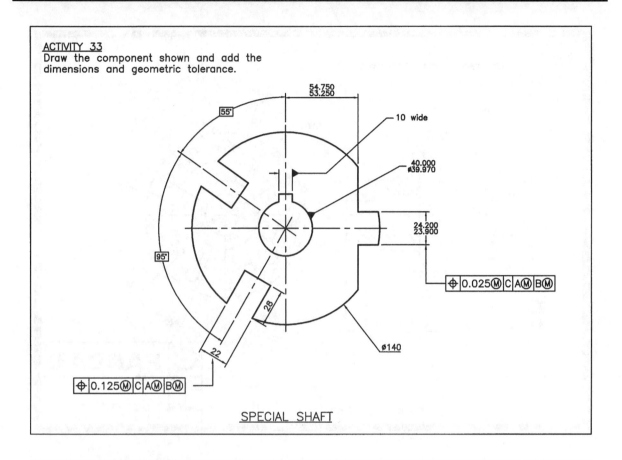

SPECIAL SHAFT

ACTIVITY 34
1. Draw the two shapes with sizes given
2. Make blocks of the shapes with the suggested block names and insertion points
3. Insert the two blocks using the information given below
4. Draw a 1 wide polyline through the roller centres then edit the polyline to a spline fit
5. With the DISTANCE command, find the vertical distance between the leftmost and rightmost roller centre points. MY distance was 14.98

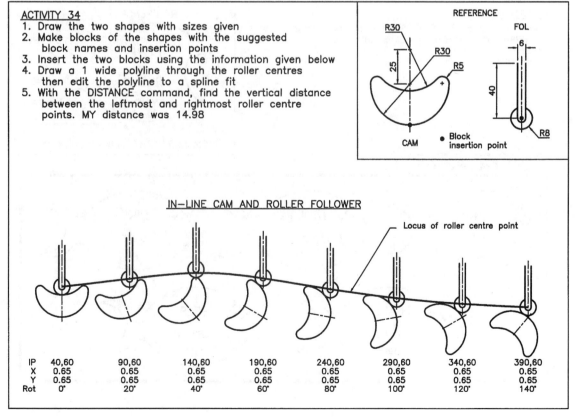

IN–LINE CAM AND ROLLER FOLLOWER

IP	40,60	90,60	140,60	190,60	240,60	290,60	340,60	390,60
X	0.65	0.65	0.65	0.65	0.65	0.65	0.65	0.65
Y	0.65	0.65	0.65	0.65	0.65	0.65	0.65	0.65
Rot	0°	20°	40°	60°	80°	100°	120°	140°

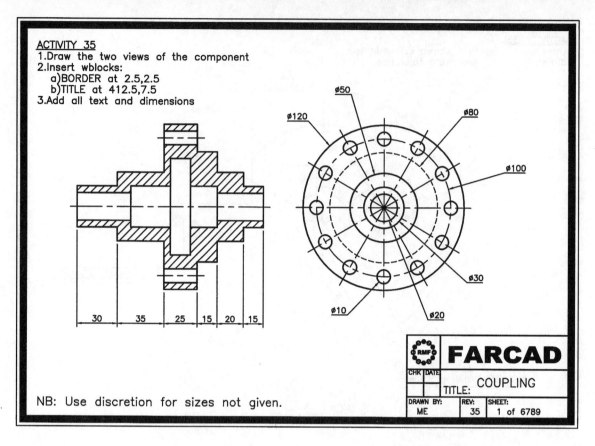

ACTIVITY 35
1. Draw the two views of the component
2. Insert wblocks:
   a) BORDER at 2.5,2.5
   b) TITLE at 412.5,7.5
3. Add all text and dimensions

Ø50
Ø120
Ø80
Ø100
Ø30
Ø10
Ø20

30 35 25 15 20 15

NB: Use discretion for sizes not given.

FARCAD
CHK | DATE
TITLE: COUPLING
DRAWN BY: ME | REV: 35 | SHEET: 1 of 6789

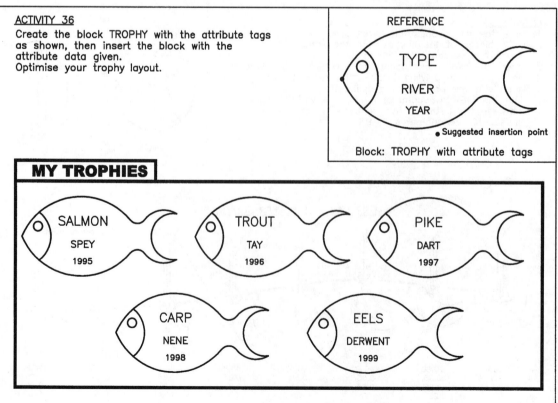

ACTIVITY 36
Create the block TROPHY with the attribute tags
as shown, then insert the block with the
attribute data given.
Optimise your trophy layout.

REFERENCE
TYPE
RIVER
YEAR
● Suggested insertion point

Block: TROPHY with attribute tags

MY TROPHIES

SALMON
SPEY
1995

TROUT
TAY
1996

PIKE
DART
1997

CARP
NENE
1998

EELS
DERWENT
1999

ACTIVITY 37
Create the isometric then produce
the section as given.

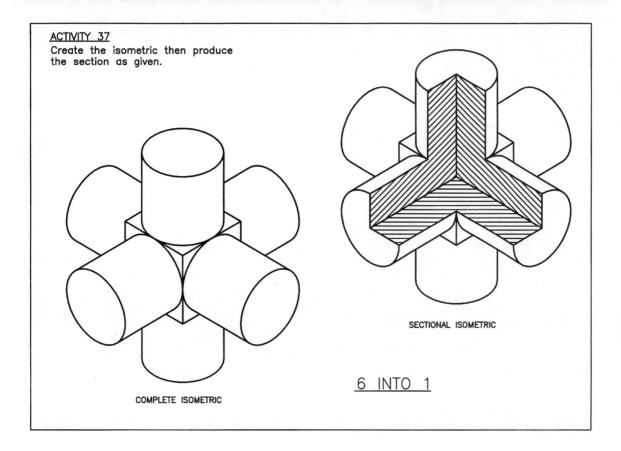

SECTIONAL ISOMETRIC

COMPLETE ISOMETRIC

6 INTO 1

Index